Praise for *AI and Machine Learning for On-Device Development*

AI and Machine Learning for On-Device Development by Laurence Moroney is exactly what's needed to inspire the next generation of ML development. ML for industry software engineers has never been more accessible than through ML Kit, and this book is an excellent intro to those methods and algorithms.

—*Dominic Monn, Machine Learning Engineer at Doist*

This book is a must-read for mobile developers interested in learning how to implement ML models on-device. It has excellent explanations with code examples to help you choose from the various options.

—*Margaret Maynard-Reid, ML Google Developer Expert*

If you want to get started building apps using ML and AI, I highly recommend this book. It simplifies the complexity of the world of ML/AI and provides practical approaches on common AI scenarios.

—*Su Fu, Lead Software Engineer, Tableau*

The book starts an amazing learning journey in the world of TensorFlow. Laurence Moroney did a fantastic job on introducing TensorFlow applications for on-device development through practical use cases and detailed examples.

—*Jialin Huang Ph.D., Sr. Quantitative User Experience Researcher at Facebook*

On-device development is the last mile for AI and machine learning technology. This book shows you how.

—*Pin-Yu Chen, Research Staff Member, IBM Research*

Once again Laurence is sharing with his charisma, insights, and knowledge of Tensorflow ecosystem a view on how to get started on the development of ML models in the mobile world. I was able to grasp the main concepts and techniques quite quickly and without difficulties. If you have an idea for an ML application and you want to put it into action, then this book is for you.

—*Laura Uzcategui, Software Engineer, Microsoft*

Highly recommended for AI/ML engineers working on end-to-end pipelines and projects. Laurence has covered all the necessary concepts in great detail and with enough hands-on projects to keep you engaged throughout.

—*Vishwesh Ravi Shrimali*

This is a great book to learn about machine learning on mobile devices becauses it covers both Android and iOS—showing how to implement the same type of application in both using ML Kit. The code examples are very clear and easy to follow even if you have never developed for mobile devices before. The later chapters also dive deeper into TensorFlow lite, and the book includes a chapter on how to think responsibly about applied machine learning.

—*Martin Kemka, Analyst, Northraine*

AI and Machine Learning for On-Device Development

A Programmer's Guide

Laurence Moroney

Beijing · Boston · Farnham · Sebastopol · Tokyo

AI and Machine Learning for On-Device Development

by Laurence Moroney

Published by O'Reilly Media, Inc., 1005 Gravenstein Highway North, Sebastopol, CA 95472.

O'Reilly books may be purchased for educational, business, or sales promotional use. Online editions are also available for most titles (*http://oreilly.com*). For more information, contact our corporate/institutional sales department: 800-998-9938 or *corporate@oreilly.com*.

Acquisitions Editor: Rebecca Novack	**Indexer:** Potomac Indexing, LLC
Development Editor: Jill Leonard	**Interior Designer:** David Futato
Production Editor: Daniel Elfanbaum	**Cover Designer:** Karen Montgomery
Copyeditor: Charles Roumeliotis	**Illustrator:** Kate Dullea
Proofreader: nSight, Inc.	

August 2021:   First Edition

Revision History for the First Edition
2021-08-11:   First Release

See *http://oreilly.com/catalog/errata.csp?isbn=9781098101749* for release details.

978-1-098-10174-9

[LSI]

Table of Contents

Preface

Welcome to *AI and Machine Learning for On-Device Development*. Successful authors have always told me that the best book you can write is the book you want to read. So I wrote this book because I feel it's essential for all mobile developers to add machine learning to their toolbox. I hope that you find it helpful on your learning journey.

Who Should Read This Book?

If you're a mobile developer who loves to write code that executes on Android or iOS and who enjoys delighting users through apps or sites, but you always were curious about how machine learning fits into your workflow, then this book is for you! This book aims to show you how the various frameworks to get you up and running quickly are a helpful first step. It also guides you when you want to go further, customizing models and looking deeper into machine learning.

Why I Wrote This Book

My goal at Google is to make AI easy for all developers, demystify the seemingly arcane mathematics, and put AI literally into everybody's hands. One key to this is to empower mobile developers, be they Android or iOS, to open new mobile paradigms using machine learning.

There's an old joke that in the early days of the internet, common wisdom and advice was to not talk to strangers, and you most certainly should never get into an unfamiliar car. However, nowadays, thanks to the change in paradigm, we happily summon strangers from the internet and get into their cars! This behavior was made possible by mobile internet-connected computing devices. Thus, how we do things has changed forever.

The next wave of new things that we can do with our computing devices will be powered by machine learning. I can only guess what they might be! So I wrote this book to help you, dear reader, navigate the plethora of choices available to you. And you will be the person who could write the app that could change everything. I can't wait to see what you do with it!

Navigating This Book

It's really up to you how you want to read it. If you are a mobile developer who wants to understand machine learning, you can simply start at the beginning and work your way through. If you want to sample particular "getting started" technologies such as ML Kit or Create ML, there are dedicated chapters for them. Towards the end of the book, I discuss technologies and techniques you need to consider when you're further along in your journey, such as multiple model hosting with Firebase and tools you need to consider for fairness in AI.

Technology You Need to Understand

This book will give you a straightforward introduction to machine learning (ML) before going deeper into using models on mobile devices. Should you want to go deeper into ML, you can use my book *AI and Machine Learning for Coders,* also from O'Reilly.

The book will take you through some sample scenarios for mobile development but isn't designed to teach you Android development with Kotlin or iOS with Swift. We'll guide you to learning resources for these at the appropriate time.

Conventions Used in This Book

The following typographical conventions are used in this book:

Italic
> Indicates new terms, URLs, email addresses, filenames, and file extensions.

`Constant width`
> Used for program listings, as well as within paragraphs to refer to program elements such as variable or function names, databases, datatypes, environment variables, statements, and keywords.

`Constant width bold`
> Shows commands or other text that should be typed literally by the user.

`Constant width italic`
> Shows text that should be replaced with user-supplied values or by values determined by context.

This element signifies a tip or suggestion.

This element signifies a general note.

This element indicates a warning or caution.

Using Code Examples

Supplemental material (code examples, exercises, etc.) is available for download at *https://github.com/lmoroney/odmlbook*.

If you have a technical question or a problem using the code examples, please send email to *bookquestions@oreilly.com*.

This book is here to help you get your job done. In general, if example code is offered with this book, you may use it in your programs and documentation. You do not need to contact us for permission unless you're reproducing a significant portion of the code. For example, writing a program that uses several chunks of code from this book does not require permission. Selling or distributing examples from O'Reilly books does require permission. Answering a question by citing this book and quoting example code does not require permission. Incorporating a significant amount of example code from this book into your product's documentation does require permission.

We appreciate, but generally do not require, attribution. An attribution usually includes the title, author, publisher, and ISBN. For example: "*AI and Machine Learning for On-Device Development* by Laurence Moroney (O'Reilly). Copyright 2021 Laurence Moroney, 978-1-098-10174-9."

If you feel your use of code examples falls outside fair use or the permission given above, feel free to contact us at *permissions@oreilly.com*.

O'Reilly Online Learning

O'REILLY® For more than 40 years, *O'Reilly Media* has provided technology and business training, knowledge, and insight to help companies succeed.

Our unique network of experts and innovators share their knowledge and expertise through books, articles, and our online learning platform. O'Reilly's online learning platform gives you on-demand access to live training courses, in-depth learning paths, interactive coding environments, and a vast collection of text and video from O'Reilly and 200+ other publishers. For more information, visit *http://oreilly.com*.

How to Contact Us

Please address comments and questions concerning this book to the publisher:

O'Reilly Media, Inc.
1005 Gravenstein Highway North
Sebastopol, CA 95472
800-998-9938 (in the United States or Canada)
707-829-0515 (international or local)
707-829-0104 (fax)

We have a web page for this book, where we list errata, examples, and any additional information. You can access this page at *https://oreil.ly/ai-and-ml-on-devices*.

Email *bookquestions@oreilly.com* to comment or ask technical questions about this book.

For news and information about our books and courses, visit *http://oreilly.com*.

Find us on Facebook: *http://facebook.com/oreilly*.

Follow us on Twitter: *http://twitter.com/oreillymedia*.

Watch us on YouTube: *http://www.youtube.com/oreillymedia*.

Acknowledgements

There are so many people that were involved in the creation of this book and I'd like to thank each of them.

To the team at O'Reilly, starting with Rebecca Novack, who believed enough in me to let me write two books, I really appreciate you!

Jill Leonard guided the manuscript from the first pixels on the screen to the last, with the constant good cheer that not only made my job easy but fun!

Kristen Brown managed the production team; Danny Elfanbaum, was the production editor who guided the final manuscript from my rough words to the polished one that you have in your hands right now; and Charles Roumeliotis, copy editor extraordinaire!

To the fantastic team of tech reviewers who challenged me constantly to write a better book, create better code, and build better apps: Martin Kemka, Laura Uzcátegui, Vishwesh Ravi Shrimali, Jialin Huang, Margaret Maynard-Reid, Su Fu, Darren Richardson, Dominic Monn, and Pin-Yu Chen. Thank you so much for everything you have all done!

I've been very blessed to work alongside some of the greats of AI, including (but not limited to) Andrew Ng, Eddy Shu, Ryan Keenan, and Ortal Arel at Deeplearning.AI; Jeff Dean, Kemal El Moujahid, Magnus Hyttsten, Francois Chollet, Sarah Sirajuddin and Wolff Dobson at Google; and many more!

But most of all, I'd like to thank my family who make all of this worthwhile. My wife, Rebecca Moroney, a woman of infinite patience; my daughter, Claudia, who is changing the world through her caring medical work; and my son, Christopher, a future AI star in his own right!

## CHAPTER 1

Introduction to AI and Machine Learning

You've likely picked this book up because you're curious about artificial intelligence (AI), machine learning (ML), deep learning, and all of the new technologies that promise the latest and greatest breakthroughs. Welcome! In this book, my goal is to explain a little about how AI and ML work, and a lot about how you can put them to work for you in your mobile apps using technologies such as TensorFlow Lite, ML Kit, and Core ML. We'll start light, in this chapter, by establishing what we actually *mean* when we describe artificial intelligence, machine learning, deep learning, and more.

What Is Artificial Intelligence?

In my experience, artificial intelligence, or AI, has become one of the most fundamentally misunderstood technologies of all time. Perhaps the reason for this is in its name—artificial intelligence evokes the *artificial* creation of an *intelligence*. Perhaps it's in the use of the term widely in science fiction and pop culture, where AI is generally used to describe a robot that looks and sounds like a human. I remember the character Data from *Star Trek: The Next Generation* as the epitome of an artificial intelligence, and his story led him in a quest to be human, because he was intelligent and self-aware but lacked emotions. Stories and characters like this have likely framed the discussion of artificial intelligence. Others, such as nefarious AIs in various movies and books, have led to a fear of what AI can be.

Given how often AI is seen in these ways, it's easy to come to the conclusion that they define AI. However, none of these are actual definitions or examples of what artificial intelligence is, at least in today's terms. It's not the artificial creation of intelligence— it's the artificial *appearance* of intelligence. When you become an AI developer, you're not building a new lifeform—you're writing code that acts in a different way to traditional code, and that can very loosely emulate the way an intelligence reacts to something. A common example of this is to use deep learning for *computer vision* where, instead of writing code that tries to understand the contents of an image with a lot of if...then rules that parse the pixels, you can instead have a computer *learn* what the contents are by "looking" at lots of samples.

So, for example, say you want to write code to tell the difference between a T-shirt and a shoe (Figure 1-1).

Figure 1-1. A T-shirt and a shoe

How would you do this? Well, you'd probably want to look for particular shapes. The distinct vertical lines in parallel on the T-shirt, with the body outline, are a good signal that it's a T-shirt. The thick horizontal lines towards the bottom, the sole, are a good indication that it's a shoe. But there's a lot of code you would have to write to detect that. And that's just for the general case—of course there would be many exceptions for nontraditional designs, such as a cutout T-shirt.

If you were to ask an intelligent being to pick between a shoe and a T-shirt, how would you do it? Assuming it had never seen them before, you'd show the being lots of examples of shoes and lots of examples of T-shirts, and it would just figure out what made a shoe a shoe, and what made a T-shirt a T-shirt. You wouldn't need to give it lots of *rules* saying which one is which. *Artificial* Intelligence acts in the same way. Instead of figuring out all those rules and inputting them into a computer in order to tell that difference, you give the computer lots of examples of T-shirts and lots of examples of shoes, and it just figures out how to distinguish them.

But the computer doesn't do this by itself. It does it with code that you write. That code will look and feel *very* different from your typical code, and the framework by which the computer will learn to distinguish isn't something that you'll need to figure out how to write for yourself. There are several frameworks that already exist for this purpose. In this book you'll learn how to use one of them, *TensorFlow,* to create applications like the one I just mentioned!

TensorFlow is an end-to-end open source platform for ML. You'll use many parts of it extensively in this book, from creating models that use ML and deep learning, to converting them to mobile-friendly formats with TensorFlow Lite and executing them on mobile devices, to serving them with TensorFlow-Serving. It also underpins technology such as ML Kit, which provides many common models as *turnkey scenarios* with a high-level API that's designed around mobile scenarios.

As you'll see when reading this book, the techniques of AI aren't particularly new or exciting. What *is* relatively new, and what made the current explosion in AI technologies possible, is increased, low-cost computing power, along with the availability of mass amounts of data. Having both is key to building a system using machine learning. But to demonstrate the concept, let's start small, so it's easier to grasp.

What Is Machine Learning?

You might have noticed in the preceding scenario that I mentioned that an intelligent being would look at lots of examples of T-shirts and shoes and just figure out what the difference between them was, and in so doing, would *learn* how to differentiate between them. It had never previously been exposed to either, so it gains new knowledge about them by being *told* that these are T-shirts, and these are shoes. From that information, it then was able to move forward by learning something new.

When programming a computer in the same way, the term m*achine learning* is used. Similar to artificial intelligence, the terminology can create the false impression that the computer is an intelligent entity that learns the way a human does, by studying, evaluating, theorizing, testing, and then remembering. And on a very surface level it does, but how it does it is far more mundane than how the human brain does it.

To wit, machine learning can be simply described as having code functions figure out their own parameters, instead of the human programmer supplying those parameters. They figure them out through trial and error, with a smart optimization process to reduce the overall error and drive the model towards better accuracy and performance.

Now that's a bit of a mouthful, so let's explore what that looks like in practice.

Moving from Traditional Programming to Machine Learning

To understand, in detail, the core difference between coding for machine learning and traditional coding, let's go through an example.

Consider the function that describes a line. You might remember this from high school geometry:

```
y = Wx + B
```

This describes that for something to be a line, every point y on the line can be derived by multiplying x by a value W (for weight) and adding a value B (for bias).

(Note: AI literature tends to be very math heavy. Unnecessarily so, if you're just getting started. This is one of a very few math examples I'll use in this book!)

Now, say you're given two points on this line, let's say they are at x = 2, y = 3 and x = 3, y = 5. How would we write code that figures out the values of W and B that describe the line joining these two points?

Let's start with W, which we call the weight, but in geometry, it's also called the slope (sometimes gradient). See Figure 1-2.

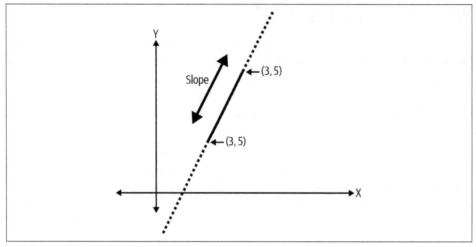

Figure 1-2. Visualizing a line segment with slope

Calculating it is easy:

```
W = (y2-y1)/(x2-x1)
```

So if we fill in, we can see that the slope is:

```
W = (5-3)/(3-2) = (2)/(1) = 2
```

Or, in code, in this case using Python:

```
def get_slope(p1, p2):
  W = (p2.y - p1.y) / (p2.x - p1.x)
  return W
```

This function sort of works. It's naive because it ignores a divide by zero when the two x values are the same, but let's just go with it for now.

OK, so we've now figured out the W value. In order to get a function for the line, we also need to figure out the B. Back to high school geometry, we can use one of our points as an example.

So, assume we have:

```
y = Wx + B
```

We can also say:

```
B = y - Wx
```

And we know that when x = 2, y = 3, and W = 2 we can backfill this function:

```
B = 3 - (2*2)
```

This leads us to derive that B is −1.

Again, in code, we would write:

```
def get_bias(p1, W):
    B = p1.y - (W * p1.x)
    return B
```

So, now, to determine any point on the line, given an x, we can easily say:

```
def get_y(x, W, B):
  y = (W*x) + B
  return y
```

Or, for the complete listing:

```
def get_slope(p1, p2):
    W = (p2.y - p1.y) / (p2.x - p1.x)
    return W

def get_bias(p1, W):
    B = p1.y - (W * p1.x)
    return B

def get_y(x, W, B):
    y = W*x + B

p1 = Point(2, 3)
p2 = Point(3, 5)

W = get_slope(p1, p2)
B = get_bias(p1, W)

# Now you can get any y for any x by saying:
x = 10
y = get_y(x, W, B)
```

From these, we could see that when x is 10, y will be 19.

You've just gone through a typical programming task. You had a problem to solve, and you could solve the problem by figuring out the *rules* and then expressing them in code. There was a *rule* to calculate W when given two points, and you created that code. You could then, once you've figured out W, derive another rule when using W and a single point to figure out B. Then, once you had W and B, you could write yet another rule to calculate y in terms of W, B, and a given x.

That's traditional programming, which is now often referred to as rules-based programming. I like to summarize this with the diagram in Figure 1-3.

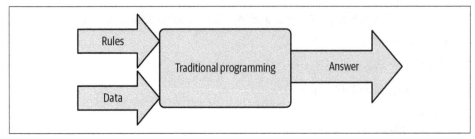

Figure 1-3. Traditional programming

At its highest level, traditional programming involves creating *rules* that act on *data* and which give us *answers*. In the preceding scenario, we had data—two points on a line. We then figured out the rules that would act on this data to figure out the equation of that line. Then, given those rules, we could get answers for new items of data, so that we could, for example, plot that line.

The core job of the programmer in this scenario is to *figure out the rules*. That's the value you bring to any problem—breaking it down into the rules that define it, and then expressing those rules in terms that a computer can understand using a coding language.

But you may not always be able to express those rules easily. Consider the scenario from earlier when we wanted to differentiate between a T-shirt and a shoe. One could not always figure out the rules to determine between them, and then express those rules in code. Here's where machine learning can help, but before we go into it for a computer vision task like that, let's consider how machine learning might be used to figure out the equation of a line as we worked out earlier.

How Can a Machine Learn?

Given the preceding scenario, where you as a programmer figured out the rules that make up a line, and the computer implemented them, let's now see how a Machine Learning approach would be different.

Let's start by understanding how machine learning code is structured. While this is very much a "Hello World" problem, the overall structure of the code is very similar to what you'd see even in far more complex ones.

I like to draw a high-level architecture outlining the use of machine learning to solve a problem like this. Remember, in this case, we'll have x and y values, so we want to figure out the W and B so that we have a line equation; once we have that equation, we can then get new y values given x ones.

Step 1: Guess the answer

Yes, you read that right. To begin with, we have no idea what the answer might be, so a guess is as good as any other answer. In real terms this means we'll pick random values for W and B. We'll loop back to this step with more intelligence a little later, so subsequent values won't be random, but we'll start purely randomly. So, for example, let's assume that our first "guess" is that W = 10 and B = 5.

Step 2: Measure the accuracy of our guess

Now that we have values for W and B, we can use these against our known data to see just how good, or how bad, those guesses are. So, we can use y = 10x + 5 to figure out a y for each of our x values, compare that y against the "correct" value, and use that to derive how good or how bad our guess is. Obviously, for this situation our guess is really bad because our numbers would be way off. We'll go into detail on that shortly, but for now, we realize that our guess is really bad, *and* we have a measure of how bad. This is often called the *loss*.

Step 3: Optimize our guess

Now that we have a guess, and we have intelligence about the results of that guess (or the loss), we have information that can help us create a new and better guess. This process is called *optimization*. If you've looked at any AI coding or training in the past and it was heavy on mathematics, it's likely you were looking at optimization. Here's where fancy calculus, in a process called *gradient descent,* can be used to help make a better guess. Optimization techniques like this figure out ways to make small adjustments to your parameters that drive towards minimal error. I'm not going to go into detail on that here, and while it's a useful skill to understand how optimization works, the truth is that frameworks like TensorFlow implement them for you so you can just go ahead and use them. In time, it's worth digging into them for more sophisticated models, allowing you to tweak their learning behavior. But for now, you're safe just using a built-in optimizer. Once you've done this, you simply go to step 1. Repeating this process, by definition, helps us over time and many loops, to figure out the parameters W and B.

And that's why this process is called m*achine learning*. Over time, by making guesses, figuring out how good or how bad that guess might be, optimizing the next guess based on that intel, and then repeating it, the computer will "learn" the parameters for W and B (or indeed anything else), and from there, it will *figure out* the rules that make up our line. Visually, this might look like Figure 1-4.

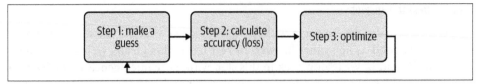

Figure 1-4. The machine learning algorithm

Implementing machine learning in code

That's a lot of description, and a lot of theory. Let's now take a look at what this would look like in code, so you can see it running for yourself. A lot of this code may look alien to you at first, but you'll get the hang of it over time. I like to call this the "Hello World" of machine learning, as you use a very basic neural network (which I'll explain a little later) to "learn" the parameters W and B for a line when given a few points on the line.

Here's the code (a full notebook with this code sample can be found in the GitHub for this book):

```
model = Sequential(Dense(units=1, input_shape=[1]))
model.compile(optimizer='sgd', loss='mean_squared_error')

xs = np.array([-1.0, 0.0, 1.0, 2.0, 3.0, 4.0], dtype=float)
ys = np.array([-3.0, -1.0, 1.0, 3.0, 5.0, 7.0], dtype=float)

model.fit(xs, ys, epochs=500)

print(model.predict([10.0]))
```

 This is written using the TensorFlow Keras APIs. Keras is an open source framework designed to make definition and training of models easier with a high level API. It became tightly integrated into TensorFlow in 2019 with the release of TensorFlow 2.0.

Let's explore this line by line.

First of all is the concept of a *model*. When creating code that learns details about data, we often use the term "model" to define the resultant object. A model, in this case, is roughly analogous to the get_y() function from the coded example earlier. What's different here is that the model doesn't *need* to be given the W and the B. It will figure them out for itself based on the given data, so you can just ask it for a y and give it an x, and it will give you its answer.

So our first line of code looks like this—it's defining the model:

```
model = Sequential(Dense(units=1, input_shape=[1]))
```

But what's the rest of the code? Well, let's start with the word `Dense`, which you can see within the first set of parentheses. You've probably seen pictures of neural networks that look a little like Figure 1-5.

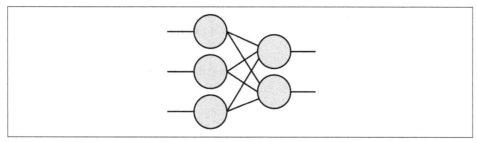

Figure 1-5. Basic neural network

You might notice that in Figure 1-5, each circle (or neuron) on the left is connected to each neuron on the right. Every neuron is connected to every other neuron in a dense manner. Hence the name `Dense`. Also, there are three stacked neurons on the left, and two stacked neurons on the right, and these form very distinct "layers" of neurons in sequence, where the first "layer" has three neurons, and the second has two neurons.

So let's go back to the code:

```
model = Sequential(Dense(units=1, input_shape=[1]))
```

This code is saying that we want a sequence of layers (`Sequential`), and within the parentheses, we will define those sequences of layers. The first in the sequence will be `Dense`, indicating a neural network like that in Figure 1-5. There are no other layers defined, so our `Sequential` just has one layer. This layer has only one unit, indicated by the `units=1` parameter, and the input shape to that unit is just a single value.

So our neural network will look like Figure 1-6.

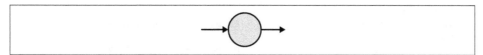

Figure 1-6. Simplest possible neural network

This is why I like to call this the "Hello World" of neural networks. It has one layer, and that layer has one neuron. That's it. So, with that line of code, we've now defined our model architecture. Let's move on to the next line:

```
model.compile(optimizer='sgd', loss='mean_squared_error')
```

Here we are specifying *built-in* functions to calculate the loss (remember step 2, where we wanted to see how good or how bad our guess was) and the optimizer (step 3, where we generate a new guess), so that we can improve on the parameters within the neuron for W and B.

In this case `'sgd'` stands for "stochastic gradient descent," which is beyond the scope of this book; in summary, it uses calculus alongside the mean squared error loss to figure out how to minimize loss, and once loss is minimized, we should have parameters that are accurate.

Next, let's define our data. Two points may not be enough, so I expanded it to six points for this example:

```
xs = np.array([-1.0, 0.0, 1.0, 2.0, 3.0, 4.0], dtype=float)
ys = np.array([-3.0, -1.0, 1.0, 3.0, 5.0, 7.0], dtype=float)
```

The `np` stands for "NumPy," a Python library commonly used in data science and machine learning that makes handling of data very straightforward. You can learn more about NumPy at *https://numpy.org*.

We'll create an array of x values and their corresponding y values, so that given x = −1, y will be −3, when x is 0, y is −1, and so on. A quick inspection shows that you can see the relationship of y = 2x − 1 holds for these values.

Next let's do the loop that we had spoken about earlier—make a guess, measure how good or how bad that loss is, optimize for a new guess, and repeat. In TensorFlow parlance this is often called *fitting*—namely we have x's and y's, and we want to fit the x's to the y's, or, in other words, figure out the rule that gives us the correct y for a given x using the examples we have. The `epochs=500` parameter simply indicates that we'll do the loop 500 times:

```
model.fit(xs, ys, epochs=500)
```

When you run code like this (you'll see how to do this later in this chapter if you aren't already familiar with it), you'll see output like the following:

```
Epoch 1/500
1/1 [==============================] - 0s 1ms/step - loss: 32.4543
Epoch 2/500
1/1 [==============================] - 0s 1ms/step - loss: 25.8570
Epoch 3/500
1/1 [==============================] - 0s 1ms/step - loss: 20.6599
Epoch 4/500
1/1 [==============================] - 0s 2ms/step - loss: 16.5646
Epoch 5/500
1/1 [==============================] - 0s 1ms/step - loss: 13.3362
```

Note the `loss` value. The unit doesn't really matter, but what does is that it is getting smaller. Remember the lower the loss, the better your model will perform, and the closer its answers will be to what you expect. So the first guess was measured to have a loss of 32.4543, but by the fifth guess this was reduced to 13.3362.

If we then look at the last 5 epochs of our 500, and explore the loss:

```
Epoch 496/500
1/1 [==============================] - 0s 916us/step - loss: 5.7985e-05
Epoch 497/500
1/1 [==============================] - 0s 1ms/step - loss: 5.6793e-05
Epoch 498/500
1/1 [==============================] - 0s 2ms/step - loss: 5.5626e-05
Epoch 499/500
1/1 [==============================] - 0s 1ms/step - loss: 5.4484e-05
Epoch 500/500
1/1 [==============================] - 0s 4ms/step - loss: 5.3364e-05
```

It's a *lot* smaller, on the order of 5.3 x 10^{-5}.

This is indicating that the values of W and B that the neuron has figured out are only off by a tiny amount. It's not zero, so we shouldn't expect the exact correct answer. For example, assume we give it x = 10, like this:

```
print(model.predict([10.0]))
```

The answer won't be 19, but a value *very close* to 19, and it's usually about 18.98. Why? Well, there are two main reasons. The first is that neural networks like this deal with probabilities, not certainties, so that the W and B that it figured out are ones that are *highly probable* to be correct but may not be 100% accurate. The second reason is that we only gave six points to the neural network. While those six points *are* linear, that's not proof that every other point that we could possibly predict is necessarily on that line. The data could skew away from that line...there's a very low probability that this is the case, but it's nonzero. We didn't *tell* the computer that this was a line, we just asked it to figure out the rule that matched the x's to the y's, and what it came up with looks like a line but isn't guaranteed to be one.

This is something to watch out for when dealing with neural networks and machine learning—you will be dealing with probabilities like this!

There's also the hint in the method name on our model—notice that we didn't ask it to *calculate* the y for x = 10.0, but instead to *predict* it. In this case a prediction (often called an inference) is reflective of the fact that the model will *try* to figure out what the value will be based on what it knows, but it may not always be correct.

Comparing Machine Learning with Traditional Programming

Referring back to Figure 1-3 for traditional programming, let's now update it to show the difference between machine learning and traditional programming given what you just saw. Earlier we described traditional programming as follows: you figure out the rules for a given scenario, express them in code, have that code act on data, and get answers out. Machine learning is very similar, except that some of the process is reversed. See Figure 1-7.

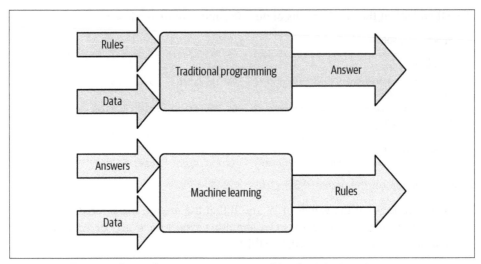

Figure 1-7. From traditional programming to machine learning

As you can see the key difference here is that with machine learning *you do not figure out the rules!* Instead you provide it answers and data, and the machine will figure out the rules for you. In the preceding example, we gave it the correct y values (aka the answers) for some given x values (aka the data), and the computer figured out the rules that fit the x to the y. We didn't do any geometry, slope calculation, interception, or anything like that. The machine figured out the patterns that matched the x's to the y's.

That's the *core* and *important* difference between machine learning and traditional programming, and it's the cause of all of the excitement around machine learning because it opens up whole new scenarios of application. One example of this is computer vision—as we discussed earlier, trying to write the *rules* to figure out the difference between a T-shirt and a shoe would be much too difficult to do. But having a computer figure out how one matches to another makes this scenario possible, and from there, scenarios that are more important—such as interpreting X-rays or other medical scans, detecting atmospheric pollution, and a whole lot more—become possible. Indeed, research has shown that in many cases using these types of algorithms along with adequate data has led to computers being as good as, and sometimes better than, humans at particular tasks. For a bit of fun, check out this blog post (*https://oreil.ly/D2Ssu*) about diabetic retinopathy—where researchers at Google trained a neural network on pre-diagnosed images of retinas and had the computer figure out what determines each diagnosis. The computer, over time, became as good as the best of the best at being able to diagnose the different types of diabetic retinopathy!

Building and Using Models on Mobile

Here you saw a very simple example of how you transition from rules-based programming to ML to solve a problem. But it's not much use solving a problem if you can't get it into your user's hands, and with ML models on mobile devices running Android or iOS, you'll do exactly that!

It's a complicated and varied landscape, and in this book we'll aim to make that easier for you, through a number of different methods.

For example, you might have a turnkey solution available to you, where an *existing* model will solve the problem for you, and you just want to learn how to do that. We'll cover that for scenarios like face detection, where a model will detect faces in pictures for you, and you want to integrate that into your app.

Additionally, there are many scenarios where you don't need to build a model from scratch, figuring out the architecture, and going through long and laborious training. A scenario called t*ransfer learning* can often be used, and this is where you are able to take parts of preexisting models and repurpose them. For example, Big Tech companies and researchers at top universities have access to data and computer power that you may not, and they have used that to build models. They've shared these models with the world so they can be reused and repurposed. You'll explore that a lot in this book, starting in Chapter 2.

Of course, you may also have a scenario where you need to build your own model from scratch. This can be done with TensorFlow, but we'll only touch on that lightly here, instead focusing on mobile scenarios. The partner book to this one, called *AI and Machine Learning for Coders,* focuses heavily on that scenario, teaching you from first principles how models for various scenarios can be built from the ground up.

Summary

In this chapter, you got an introduction to artificial intelligence and machine learning. Hopefully it helped cut through the hype so you can see, from a programmer's perspective, what this is really all about, and from there you can identify the scenarios where AI and ML can be extraordinarily useful and powerful. You saw, in detail, how machine learning works, and the overall "loop" that a computer uses to learn how to fit values to each other, matching patterns and "learning" the rules that put them together. From there, the computer could act somewhat intelligently, lending us the term "artificial" intelligence. You learned about the terminology related to being a machine learning or artificial intelligence programmer, including models, predictions, loss, optimization, inference, and more.

From Chapter 3 onwards you'll be using examples of these to implement machine learning models into mobile apps. But first, let's explore building some more models of our own to see how it all works. In Chapter 2 we'll look into building some more sophisticated models for computer vision!

Introduction to Computer Vision

While this book isn't designed to teach you all of the fundamentals of architecting and training machine learning models, I do want to cover some basic scenarios so that the book can still work as a standalone. If you want to learn more about the model creation process with TensorFlow, I recommend my book, *AI and Machine Learning for Coders,*, published by O'Reilly, and if you want to go deeper than that, Aurelien Geron's excellent book *Hands-on Machine Learning with Scikit-Learn, Keras, and TensorFlow* (O'Reilly) is a must!

In this chapter, we'll go beyond the very fundamental model you created in Chapter 1 and look at two more sophisticated ones, where you will deal with computer vision—namely how computers can "see" objects. Similar to the terms "artificial intelligence" and "machine learning," the phrases "computer vision" and "seeing" might lead one to misunderstand what is fundamentally going on in the model.

Computer vision is a huge field, and for the purposes of this book and this chapter, we'll focus narrowly on a couple of core scenarios, where we will use technology to parse the contents of images, either labeling the primary content of an image, or finding items within an image.

It's not really about "vision" or "seeing," but more having a structured algorithm that allows a computer to parse the pixels of an image. It doesn't "understand" the image any more than it understands the meaning of a sentence when it parses the words into individual strings!

If we were to try to do that task using the traditional rules-based approach, we would end up with many lines of code for even the simplest images. Machine learning is a key player here; as you'll see in this chapter, by using the same code pattern we had in Chapter 1, but getting a little deeper, we can create models that can parse the contents of images...with just a few lines of code. So let's get started.

Using Neurons for Vision

In the example you coded in Chapter 1, you saw how a neural network could "fit" itself to the desired parameters for a linear equation when given some examples of the points on a line in that equation. Represented visually, our neural network could look like Figure 2-1.

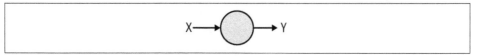

Figure 2-1. Fitting an X to a Y with a neural network

This was the simplest possible neural network, where there was only one layer, and that layer had only one neuron.

 In fact, I cheated a little bit when creating that example, because neurons in a dense layer are fundamentally linear in nature as they learn a weight and a bias, so a single one is enough for a linear equation!

But when we coded this, recall that we created a `Sequential`, and that `Sequential` contained a `Dense`, like this:

```
model = Sequential(Dense(units=1))
```

We can use the same pattern of code if we want to have more layers; for example, if we want to represent a neural network like that in Figure 2-2, it would be quite easy to do.

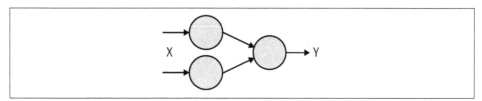

Figure 2-2. A slightly more advanced neural network

First, let's consider the elements within the diagram of Figure 2-2. Each vertical arrangement of neurons should be considered a *layer*. Figure 2-3 shows us the layers within this model.

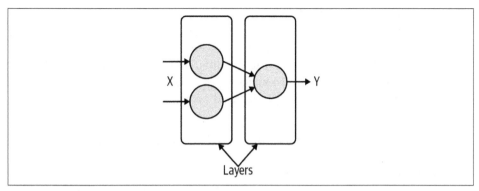

Figure 2-3. The layers within the neural network

To code these, we simply list them within the `Sequential` definition, updating our code to look like this:

```
model = Sequential(
          [Dense(units=2),
           Dense(units=1)])
```

We simply define our layers as a comma-separated list of definitions, and put that within the `Sequential`, so as you can see here, there's a `Dense` with two units, followed by a `Dense` with one unit, and we get the architecture shown in Figure 2-3.

But in each of these cases our *output* layer is just a single value. There's one neuron at the output, and given that the neuron can only learn a weight and a bias, it's not very useful for understanding the contents of an image, because even the simplest image has too much content to be represented by just a single value.

So what if we have *multiple* neurons on the output? Consider the model in Figure 2-4.

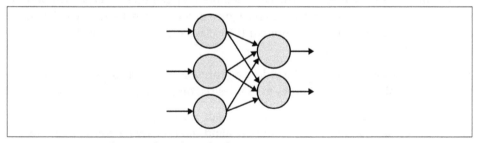

Figure 2-4. A neural network with multiple outputs

Now we have multiple inputs and multiple outputs. To design something to recognize and parse the contents in an image (as you'll recall, this is how we're defining computer vision), what if we then assign the output neurons to classes that we want to recognize?

What do we mean by that? Well, much like learning a language, you learn it word by word, so in learning how to parse an image, we have to limit the number of things that the computer can understand how to "see." So, for example, if we want to start simple and have the computer recognize the difference between a cat and a dog, we could create this "vocabulary" of two image types (cats or dogs) and assign an output neuron to each. The term *class* is typically used here, not to be confused with classes in object-oriented programming.

And because you have a fixed number of "classes" that you want your model to recognize, the term that is used is typically *classification* or *image classification*, and your model may also be called a *classifier*.

So, to recognize cats or dogs, we could update Figure 2-4 to look like Figure 2-5.

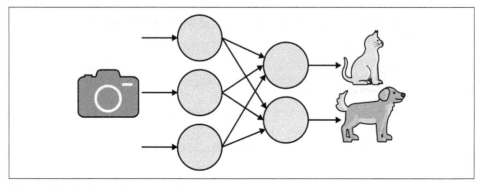

Figure 2-5. Updating for cats or dogs

So we feed a picture into the neural network, and at the end it has two neurons. These will each output a number, and we want that number to represent whether the network thinks it "sees" a dog or a cat. This methodology can then be expanded beyond this for other classes, so if you want to recognize different animals, then you just need additional output neurons that represent their classes. But let's stick with two for the time being, to keep it simple.

So now our problem becomes, how do we represent our data so that the computer will start matching our input images to our desired output neurons?

One method is to use something called *one-hot encoding*. This, at first, looks a bit onerous and wasteful, but when you understand the underlying concept and how it matches a neural network architecture, it begins to make sense. The idea behind this type of encoding is to have an array of values that is the size of our number of classes. Each entry in this array is zero, except for the one representing the class that you want. In that case you set it to 1.

So, for example, if you look at Figure 2-5, there are two output neurons—one for a cat, and one for a dog. Thus, if we want to represent "what a cat looks like," we can represent this as [1,0], and similarly if we want to represent "what a dog looks like," we can encode that to [0,1]. At this point you're probably thinking how wasteful this would look when you're recognizing more classes—say 1,000, where each label on your data will have 999 0s and a single 1.

It's definitely not efficient, but you'll only store data like this for your images while you are training the model, and you can effectively throw it away when you're done. The output layers of your model will have neurons that match this encoding, so when you read them, you'll know which ones represent which class.

So, if we update our diagram from Figure 2-5 with these encodings of what a cat looks like and what a dog looks like, then if we feed in an image of, say, a cat, we'd want the outputs to look like those encodings, as in Figure 2-6.

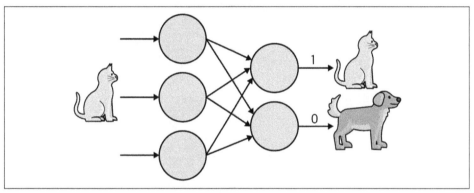

Figure 2-6. Using one-hot encodings to label a cat

Now the neural network is behaving the way that we'd want it to. We feed in the image of a cat, and the output neurons respond with the encoding [1,0] indicating that it "sees" a cat. This gives us the basis of the data representation that can be used to train a network. So, if we have a bunch of images of cats and dogs, for example, and we label these images accordingly, then, over time, it's possible that a neural network can "fit" itself to these input contents and these labels, so that future ones will give the same output.

In fact, what will happen is that the output neurons, instead of giving a 1 or a 0, will give a value between 0 and 1. This also just happens to be a *probability* value. So if you train a neural network on images using one-hot-encoded labels, and output one neuron per class, you'll end up having a model that parses an image and returns a list of probabilities of what it can see, something like Figure 2-7.

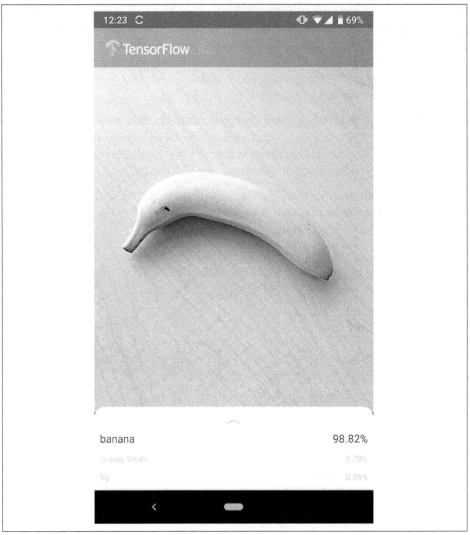

Figure 2-7. Parsing the contents of an image

Here, you can see that the model determined that there was a 98.82% chance it was looking at a banana, with smaller chances that it was looking at a Granny Smith apple or a fig. And while it's obvious that this is a banana, when this app looked at the image, it was extracting features from the image, and some of those features may be present in an apple—such as the skin texture, or maybe the color.

So, as you can imagine, if you want to train a model to see, you'll need lots of examples of images, and these need to be labelled according to their classes. Thankfully there are some basic datasets that limit the scope to make it easy to learn, and we'll look at building a classifier from scratch for these next.

Your First Classifier: Recognizing Clothing Items

For our first example, let's consider what it takes to recognize items of clothing in an image. Consider, for example, the items in Figure 2-8.

Figure 2-8. Examples of clothing

There are a number of different clothing items here, and you can recognize them. You understand what a shirt is, or a coat, or a dress. But how would you explain this to somebody who has never seen clothing? How about a shoe? There are two shoes in this image, but how would you describe that to somebody? This is another area where the rules-based programming we spoke about in Chapter 1 can fall down. Sometimes it's just infeasible to describe something with rules.

Of course, computer vision is no exception. But consider how you learned to recognize all these items—by seeing lots of different examples and gaining experience with how they're used. Can we do the same with a computer? The answer is yes, but with limitations. Let's take a look at a first example of how to teach a computer to recognize items of clothing, using a well-known dataset called Fashion MNIST.

The Data: Fashion MNIST

One of the foundational datasets for learning and benchmarking algorithms is the Modified National Institute of Standards and Technology (MNIST) database by Yann LeCun, Corinna Cortes, and Christopher Burges. This dataset is comprised of images of 70,000 handwritten digits from 0 to 9. The images are 28 × 28 grayscale.

Fashion MNIST (*https://oreil.ly/GmmUB*) is designed to be a drop-in replacement for MNIST that has the same number of records, the same image dimensions, and the same number of classes—so, instead of images of the digits 0 through 9, Fashion MNIST contains images of 10 different types of clothing.

You can see an example of the contents of the dataset in Figure 2-9. Here, three lines are dedicated to each clothing item type.

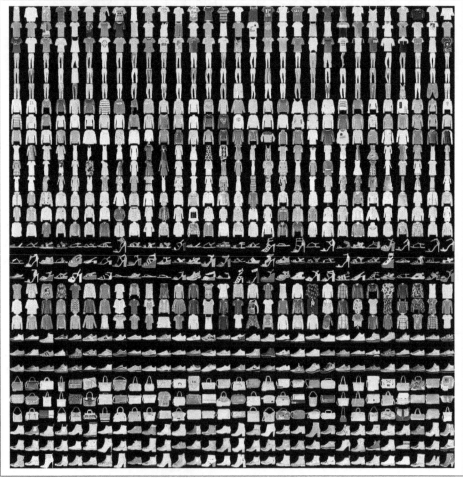

Figure 2-9. Exploring the Fashion MNIST dataset

It has a nice variety of clothing, including shirts, trousers, dresses, and lots of types of shoes! As you may notice, it's grayscale, so each picture consists of a certain number of pixels with values between 0 and 255. This makes the dataset simpler to manage.

You can see a close-up of a particular image from the dataset in Figure 2-10.

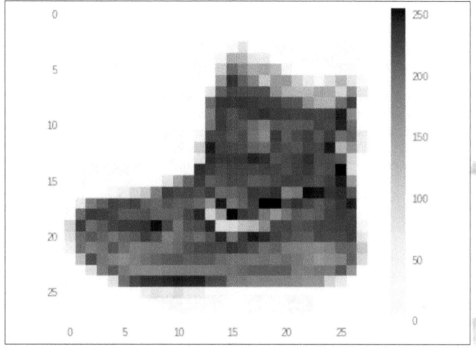

Figure 2-10. Close-up of an image in the Fashion MNIST dataset

Like any image, it's a rectangular grid of pixels. In this case the grid size is 28 × 28, and each pixel is simply a value between 0 and 255, as mentioned previously.

A Model Architecture to Parse Fashion MNIST

Let's now take a look at how you can use these pixel values with the architecture for computer vision that we saw previously.

You can see a representation of this in Figure 2-11. Note that there are 10 classes of fashion in Fashion MNIST, so we'll need an output layer of 10 neurons. Note that to make it easier to fit on the page, I've rotated the architecture so that the output layer of 10 neurons is at the bottom, instead of on the right.

The number of neurons "above" these, currently set to 20 to fit onto the page, may change as you write your code. But the idea is that we will feed the pixels of the image into these neurons.

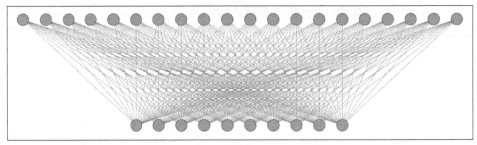

Figure 2-11. A neural network architecture to recognize fashion images

Given that our image is rectangular, and 28 × 28 pixels in size, we'll need to represent it in the same way the neurons in a layer are represented, i.e., a one-dimensional array, so we can follow a process called "flattening" the image, so that it becomes, instead of 28 × 28, a 784 × 1 array. It then has a similar "shape" to the input neurons, so we can begin to feed it in. See Figure 2-12. Note that because the ankle boot image from Figure 2-10 is class "9" in Fashion MNIST, we'll also train by saying that's the neuron that should light up in one-hot encoding. We start counting from 0, so the neuron for class 9 is the 10th, or rightmost one, in Figure 2-12. The reason for the term "Dense" being given to this layer type should now be more visually apparent!

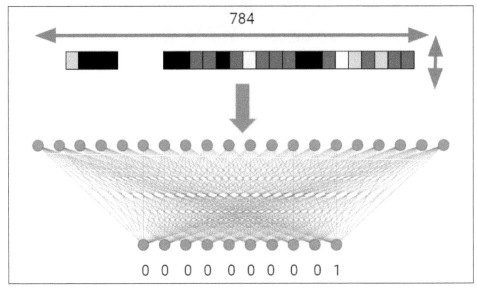

Figure 2-12. Training a neural network with Fashion MNIST

Given that there are 60,000 images in the training set, the training loop that we mentioned in Chapter 1 will take place. First, every neuron in the network will be randomly initialized. Then, for each of the 60,000 labeled images, a classification will be made. The accuracy and loss on this classification will help an optimizer tweak the values of the neurons, and we'll try again and so on. Over time, the internal weights and biases in the neurons will be tuned to match the training data. Let's now explore this in code.

Coding the Fashion MNIST Model

The model architecture described earlier is shown here:

```
model = Sequential(
    [Flatten(input_shape=(28,28)),
     Dense(20, activation=tf.nn.relu),
     Dense(10, activation=tf.nn.softmax)])
```

It's really that simple! There are a few new concepts here, so let's explore them.

First of all, we can see that we're using a Sequential. Recall that this allows us to define the layers in our network using a list. Each element in that list defines a layer type (in this case a Flatten followed by two Dense layers), as well as details about the layer, such as the number of neurons and the activation function.

The first layer is:

```
Flatten(input_shape=(28,28))
```

This demonstrates part of the power of layers—you don't just define the model architecture using them, you can also have functionality encapsulated within the layer. So here your input shape of 28 × 28 gets flattened into the 784 × 1 that you need to feed into the neural network.

After that you have the two layers that we showed in the diagram in Figure 2-12, a Dense layer with 20 neurons, and another Dense layer with 10 neurons.

But there's something new here too—the activation parameter. This defines an activation function, which executes on a layer at the end of the processing of that layer. Activation functions can help the network recognize more complex patterns and also change the behavior of information as it flows from layer to layer, helping the network to learn better and faster.

They're optional, but they're very useful and often recommended to use.

On the 20-neuron layer, the activation function is tf.nn.relu, where *relu* stands for "rectified linear unit." This is a pretty fancy term that effectively equates to—if the value is less than zero, set it to zero; otherwise, keep it as it is. Kind of like:

```
if val<0:
    return 0
else:
    return val
```

How this helps is that, if any of the neurons in the layer return a *negative* value, that could cancel out the *positive* value on another neuron, effectively ignoring what it learned. So, instead of doing lots of checking on every neuron at every iteration, we simply have an activation function on the layer do it for us.

Similarly the output layer has an activation called softmax. The idea here is that our output layer has 10 neurons in it. Ideally they would all contain zero, except for one of them, which would have the value 1. That one would be our class. In reality this rarely happens, and each neuron will have a value in it. The biggest one will be our best candidate for the classification of the input image. However, in order to report a *probability*, we would want the values of each of the neurons to add up to 1, and their values scaled appropriately. Instead of writing the code to handle this, we can simply apply a softmax activation function to the layer, and it will do that for us!

This is just the model architecture. Now let's explore the full code, including getting the data, compiling the model, and then performing the training:

```
import tensorflow as tf

data = tf.keras.datasets.mnist
(training_images, training_labels), (val_images, val_labels) = data.load_data()

training_images  = training_images / 255.0
val_images = val_images / 255.0

model = tf.keras.models.Sequential(
          [tf.keras.layers.Flatten(input_shape=(28,28)),
           tf.keras.layers.Dense(20, activation=tf.nn.relu),
           tf.keras.layers.Dense(10, activation=tf.nn.softmax)])

model.compile(optimizer='adam',
              loss='sparse_categorical_crossentropy',
              metrics=['accuracy'])

model.fit(training_images, training_labels, epochs=20)
```

Remember earlier when I mentioned that traditional coding to parse the contents of images, even simple ones like Fashion MNIST, could have many thousands of lines of code to handle it, but machine learning can do it in just a few lines? Well, here they are!

First is getting the data. The Fashion MNIST dataset is built into TensorFlow, so we can get it easily like this:

```
data = tf.keras.datasets.fashion_mnist
(training_images, training_labels), (val_images, val_labels) = data.load_data()
```

After executing this line of code, training_images will have our 60,000 training images and training_labels will have their associated labels. Additionally val_images and val_labels will have 10,000 images and their associated labels. We'll hold them back and not use them when training, so we can have a set of data that the neural network hasn't previously "seen" when we explore its efficacy.

Next are these lines:

```
training_images  = training_images / 255.0
val_images = val_images / 255.0
```

Using NumPy in Python is powerful in that if you divide an array by a value, you'll divide every item in that array by the value. But why are we dividing by 255?

This process is called *normalization*, which again is quite a fancy term that means to set a value to something between 0 and 1. Our pixels are between 0 and 255, so by dividing by 255, we'll normalize them. Why normalize? The math within a Dense works best when values are between 0 and 1, so that errors don't massively inflate when they are greater. You might remember for the y = 2x – 1 example in Chapter 1 we didn't normalize. That was a trivial example that didn't need it, but for the most part you will need to normalize your data prior to feeding it into a neural network!

Then, after defining the model architecture, you compile your model, specifying the loss function and the optimizer:

```
model.compile(optimizer='adam',
              loss='sparse_categorical_crossentropy',
              metrics=['accuracy'])
```

These are different from the sgd and mean_squared_error you used in Chapter 1. TensorFlow has a library of these functions and you can generally pick from these to experiment and see what works best for your model. There are some constraints here, most notably in the loss function. Given that this model is going to have more than one output neuron, and these neurons are giving us classes or *categories* of output, we will want to use a *categorical* loss function to measure them effectively, and for this I chose sparse_categorical_crossentropy. Understanding how each of these work is beyond the scope of this book, but it's good to experiment with the different loss functions and optimizers that you can find on TensorFlow.org. For the optimizer, I chose adam, which is an enhanced version of sgd that internally tunes itself for better performance.

Note also that I use another parameter—metrics=['accuracy']—which asks TensorFlow to report on accuracy while training. As we are doing categorical model training, where we want the classifier to tell us what it thinks it sees, we can use basic accuracy, i.e., how many of the training images it got "right" with its guess, and report on that along with the loss value. By specifying metrics at compile time, TensorFlow will report this back to us.

Finally we can fit the training values to the training data with:

```
model.fit(training_images, training_labels, epochs=20)
```

I set it to do the whole training loop (make a guess, evaluate and measure the loss, optimize, repeat) 20 times by setting epochs to 20, and asking it to fit the training images to the training labels.

As it trains, you'll see output like this:

```
Epoch 1/20
1875/1875 [=====================] - 2s 1ms/step - loss: 0.4214 - accuracy: 0.8844
Epoch 2/20
1875/1875 [=====================] - 2s 1ms/step - loss: 0.2237 - accuracy: 0.9356
Epoch 3/20
1875/1875 [=====================] - 2s 1ms/step - loss: 0.1897 - accuracy: 0.9450
```

Note the accuracy: after only three loops, it's already at 94.5% accuracy on the training set! I trained this using Google Colab, and we could see that each loop, despite processing 60,000 images, only took two seconds. Finally, you see the values 1875/1875, and you might be wondering what they are? When training you don't have to process one image at a time, and TensorFlow supports batching to make things faster. Fashion MNIST defaults to each batch having 32 images, so it trains with one batch of images at a time. This gives you 1875 batches of images to make up 60,000 images (i.e., 60,000 divided by 32 = 1875).

By the time you reach epoch 20, you'll see that the accuracy is now over 97%:

```
Epoch 19/20
1875/1875 [=====================] - 2s 1ms/step - loss: 0.0922 - accuracy: 0.9717
Epoch 20/20
1875/1875 [=====================] - 2s 1ms/step - loss: 0.0905 - accuracy: 0.9722
```

So, with just a few lines of code, and less than a minute of training, you now have a model that can recognize Fashion MNIST images with greater than 97% accuracy.

Remember earlier that you also held back 10,000 images as the validation dataset? You can pass them to the model now to see how the model parses them. Note that it has never seen these images before, so it's a great way to test if your model is really accurate—if it can classify images that it hasn't previously seen with a high level of accuracy. You can do this by calling model.evaluate, passing it the set of images and labels:

```
model.evaluate(val_images, val_labels)
313/313 [=====================] - 0s 872us/step - loss: 0.1320 - accuracy: 0.9623
```

From this you can see that your model is 96% accurate on data it hadn't previously seen, telling you that you have a really good model for predicting fashion data. A concept in machine learning called *overfitting* is what you are looking to avoid here. Overfitting is what happens when your model becomes really good at understanding its training data, but not so good at understanding other data. This would be indicated by a large difference between the training accuracy and the validation accuracy. Think of it as if you were teaching an intelligent being what shoes were, but only ever showed it high-heeled shoes. It would then "think" that all shoes are high-heeled, and if you subsequently showed it a pair of sneakers, it would be overfit to high-heeled shoes. You want to avoid this practice in neural networks too, but we can see that we're doing well here with only a small difference between training and validation accuracy!

This shows you how you can create a simple model to learn how to "see" contents of an image, but it relies on very simple, monochrome images where the data is the only thing in the picture, centered within the frame of the image. The models to recognize real-world images will need to be far more complicated than this one, but it's possible to build them using something called a "convolutional neural network." Going into how they work in detail is beyond the scope of this book, but check out the other books I mentioned at the top of this chapter for more in-depth coverage.

One thing you *can* do though, without going further in depth into model architecture types, is something called *transfer learning*, and we'll explore that next.

Transfer Learning for Computer Vision

Consider the architecture for Fashion MNIST discussed previously in Figure 2-12. It's already looking quite sophisticated and complicated despite the relative simplicity of the data it's designed to classify. Then, extend this to larger images, more classes, color, and other levels of sophistication. You'll end up with really complex architectures in order to handle them. For example, Table 2-1 is a chart describing the layers of an architecture called *MobileNet* which, as its name suggests, is designed to be mobile-friendly, low in battery consumption while high in performance.

Table 2-1. MobileNet description

Input	Operator	t	c	n	s
$224^2 \times 3$	conv2d	–	32	1	2
$112^2 \times 32$	bottleneck	1	16	1	1
$112^2 \times 16$	bottleneck	6	24	2	2
$56^2 \times 24$	bottleneck	6	32	3	2
$28^2 \times 32$	bottleneck	6	64	4	2
$14^2 \times 64$	bottleneck	6	96	3	1
$14^2 \times 96$	bottleneck	6	160	3	2
$7^2 \times 160$	bottleneck	6	320	1	1
$7^2 \times 320$	conv2d 1x1	–	1280	1	1
$7^2 \times 1280$	avgpool 7x7	–	–	1	–
$1 \times 1 \times 1280$	conv2d 1x1	–	k		–

Here you can see that there are many layers, mostly of type "bottleneck" (which use convolutions), that take a color image of size 224 × 224 × 3 (where the image is 224 × 224 pixels, and three bytes are required for color), and break it down into 1,280 values that are called "feature vectors." These vectors can then be fed into a classifier for the 1,000 images that make up the MobileNet model. It's designed to work with a version of the ImageNet database (*https://oreil.ly/qnBpY*) that was created for the Image-Net Large Scale Visual Recognition Challenge (ILSVRC), which used 1,000 classes of image.

Designing and training a model like this is a very complex undertaking.

But *reusing* the model and what it learned is possible, even if you want to use it to recognize images *other* than the 1,000 it was trained to recognize.

The logic goes like this: if a model like MobileNet, trained on hundreds of thousands of images to recognize thousands of classes, works very well, then it has become very effective at *generally* spotting what's in an image. If we take the values that it learned in its internal parameters and apply them to a *different* set of images, they will likely work very well given their general nature.

So, for example, if we go back to Table 2-1 and say that we want to create a model that recognizes only three different classes of image, instead of the 1,000 that it already recognizes, then we could use everything that was learned by MobileNet to get the 1,280 feature vectors and feed them into our own output of only three neurons for our three classes.

Fortunately, this is very simple to do because of the existence of *TensorFlow Hub*, a repository for models and model architectures that are pretrained.

You can include TensorFlow Hub in your code by importing it:

```
import tensorflow_hub as hub
```

So, for example, if I want to use MobileNet v2, I can use code like this:

```
model_handle =
    "https://tfhub.dev/google/imagenet/mobilenet_v2_035_224/feature_vector/4"
```

Here I define that I want to use MobileNet and take its feature vectors. There's lots of different types of architectures for MobileNet tuned in different ways in TensorFlow Hub, leading to numbers like 035_224 in the URL. I won't go into detail on them here, but the 224 represents the image dimensions that we want to use. Look back to Table 2-1 and you'll see that the MobileNet image was 224 × 224.

The important thing is that I want to load a model that is already trained from Hub. It outputs feature vectors that I can classify, so my model will look like this:

```
feature_vector = hub.KerasLayer(model_handle, trainable=False,
                                input_shape=(224, 224, 3))

model = tf.keras.models.Sequential([
  feature_vector,
  tf.keras.layers.Dense(3, activation = 'softmax'),
])
```

Note the `trainable=False` setting in the first line. This means that we will reuse the model but will not edit it in any way—just use what it already learned.

So my model is really only two lines of code. It's a `Sequential` with the feature vector followed by a `Dense` containing three neurons. Everything that was learned in the many hours training MobileNet with ImageNet data is available to me; I don't need to retrain!

Using this and the Beans dataset, which classifies three types of bean disease in plants, I can now create a classifier with this very simple code that recognizes even very complex images. Figure 2-13 shows the output of this, and the code to get it is available in the download for this book.

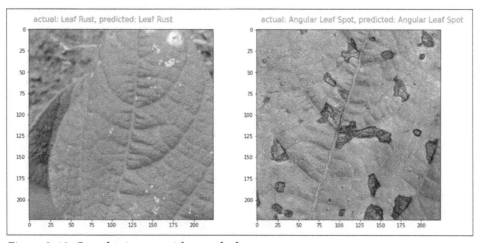

Figure 2-13. Complex images with transfer learning

Given the power that you get from transfer learning to quickly build very complex models, the main focus of model creation in this book will be to use transfer learning. As such, I hope this was a useful introduction!

Summary

In this chapter you got an introduction to computer vision and saw what it really means—writing code to help a computer parse the contents of images. You learned how a neural network can be architected to recognize multiple classes, before building one from scratch that could recognize 10 fashion items. After that you got introduced to the concept of transfer learning, where you can take existing models that have been pretrained on millions of images to recognize many classes and use their internal variables to apply them to your scenario. From this, you saw how models can be downloaded from TensorFlow Hub and reused to give you very complex models in very few lines of code. As an example, you saw a classifier for bean disease in plants that was written using a model that was defined with just two layers! This will form the methodology that you'll primarily use in this book, because the focus from here on out will be *using* models in mobile apps. We'll start that journey in Chapter 3 with an introduction to ML Kit, a framework that helps you rapidly prototype or use turnkey ML scenarios across Android and iOS.

Introduction to ML Kit

In the first two chapters of this book, you took a look at the foundations of machine learning and deep learning to build some basic models. For the rest of the book, you're going to switch gears and explore how to implement models on mobile devices. A powerful toolkit that allows you to implement preexisting models (aka turnkey scenarios) as well as custom models is Google's ML Kit. In this chapter you'll explore how to use ML Kit to run Android or iOS models entirely on your device. The model will stay on-device, giving your users speed and privacy advantages.

 I would strongly recommend going through this chapter in detail, particularly if you aren't super familiar with how to implement add-on libraries for both Android and iOS. I'll go through it in a lot of detail here, and subsequent chapters will refer back to this one.

There are three main scenarios where ML Kit can be used:

- Turnkey solutions where a model *already* exists in ML Kit to implement what you need
- Rapid prototyping using a generic model for a specific task; for example, if you want to build a vision app, don't have a model for your needs yet, but want to determine if it's possible with your device
- Building apps with custom models like those we explored in Chapter 2

In this chapter I'll explore some turnkey solutions, so you can understand how to get up and running quickly with ML models in your apps. In the subsequent chapters, we'll explore how to use ML Kit initially to prototype vision and natural language processing (NLP) scenarios before building custom models and implementing them.

I think it's easier to learn hands-on than it is to discuss lots of background information, so let's just get right into it and explore how to build some apps using ML Kit, starting with a face detection app on Android and iOS.

Building a Face Detection App on Android

Over the next few pages you'll look at building an app that performs face detection using an ML model that is pretrained and immediately available to you to use without further training. You can see an example of a face detection for a single face in Figure 3-1.

Figure 3-1. Detecting a single face in a picture

The same model (and thus the simple app) can also recognize *multiple* faces in a picture; you can see this in Figure 3-2. I find this particularly impressive because if you look at the woman in the foreground, her face is turned away from the camera, and we see it only in profile, but the model can still detect it!

Figure 3-2. Detecting multiple faces in an image

Let's take a look at how to get started with creating an app like this on Android!

Step 1: Create the App with Android Studio

The rest of this tutorial will use Android Studio and will expect you to have at least a basic knowledge of this tool, along with Android app development using Kotlin. If you're not familiar with these, I'd recommend taking Google's free course on Android Development in Kotlin (*https://oreil.ly/bOja4*). If you don't have Android Studio already, you can download it from *https://developer.android.com/studio/*.

The first step will be to create an app using Android Studio. So, when you use the File → New command, you'll get a dialog asking you to select a project template (Figure 3-3).

Select the Empty Activity template and click Next.

The next dialog (Configure Your Project) will ask you for the name, location, and language of your project. Use whatever suits you here, but for the namespaces to be the same as my code, you might want to use the name FD and the package name *com.example.fd* as shown in Figure 3-4.

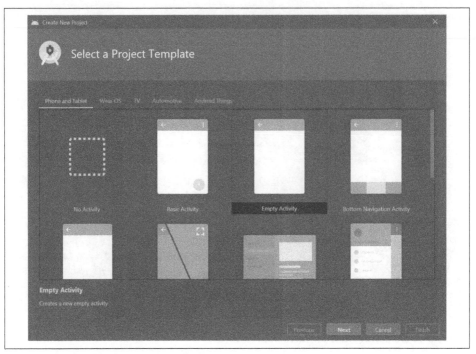

Figure 3-3. Starting a new app in Android Studio

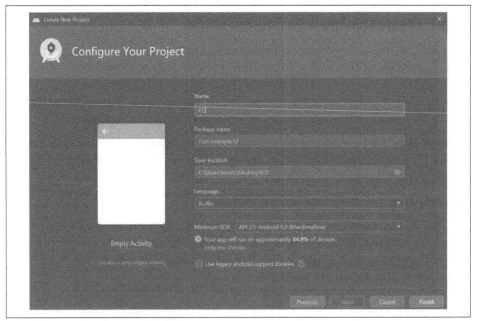

Figure 3-4. Configuring the project

Click Finish and Android Studio will create a boilerplate application with a single empty activity. We can use this going forward to build the face detector.

Step 2: Add and Configure ML Kit

Android Studio allows you to add external libraries using the Gradle build tool (*https://gradle.org*). It can be a little confusing at first because there are *two* Gradle files in your project, one which defines the overall build infrastructure for the project and one for your app. To add ML Kit you use the latter of these—the build.gradle for your app. In the IDE, you'll see something like Figure 3-5 for your Gradle scripts folder, so note that the second entry is for Module: app.

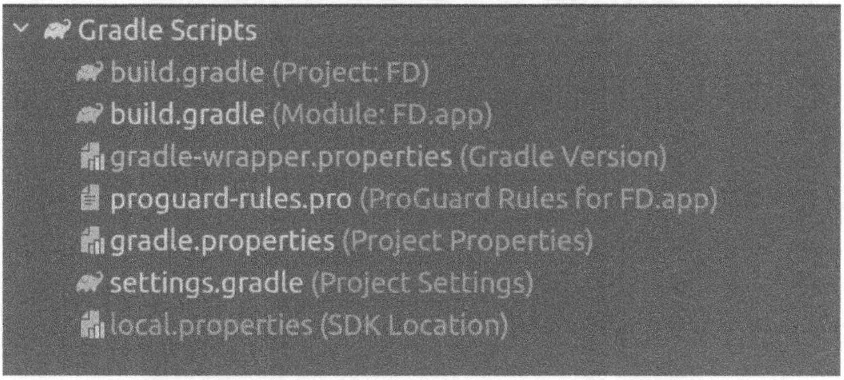

> ∨ 🐘 Gradle Scripts
> 🐘 build.gradle (Project: FD)
> 🐘 build.gradle (Module: FD.app)
> 📊 gradle-wrapper.properties (Gradle Version)
> 📓 proguard-rules.pro (ProGuard Rules for FD.app)
> 📊 gradle.properties (Project Properties)
> 🐘 settings.gradle (Project Settings)
> 📊 local.properties (SDK Location)

Figure 3-5. Exploring your Gradle scripts

Open the build.gradle file for Module: app, and you'll see a number of configuration entries. Right at the bottom of it you'll see a section called dependencies. This will contain a number of `implementation`, `testImplementation`, and `androidTestImplementation` entries. You add your dependencies here, and for ML Kit face detection you can add the implementation details shown here:

```
dependencies {
    implementation fileTree(dir: 'libs', include: ['*.jar'])
    implementation "org.jetbrains.kotlin:kotlin-stdlib-jdk7:$kotlin_version"
    implementation 'androidx.appcompat:appcompat:1.2.0'
    implementation 'androidx.core:core-ktx:1.3.1'
    implementation 'androidx.constraintlayout:constraintlayout:2.0.1'
    testImplementation 'junit:junit:4.12'
    androidTestImplementation 'androidx.test.ext:junit:1.1.2'
    androidTestImplementation 'androidx.test.espresso:espresso-core:3.3.0'
    // Use this dependency to bundle the model with your app
    implementation 'com.google.mlkit:face-detection:16.0.2'
}
```

Versions may be different for you—these are the latest versions at time of writing—and note that you are only adding the *last* line in the preceding listing, which defines the implementation for ML Kit face detection.

Step 3: Define the User Interface

We'll keep this as simple as possible so that we can get to the face detection code as quickly as possible! So, in Android Studio, find the res folder, and within it, see layout and then *activity_main.xml* as shown in Figure 3-6. This is an XML file that declares what your user interface will look like!

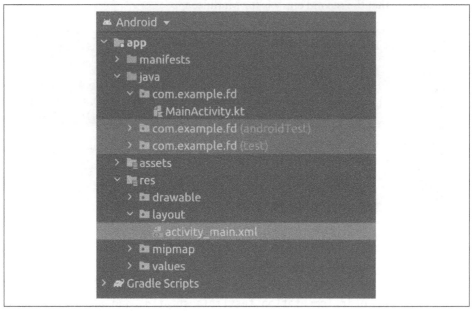

Figure 3-6. Finding the activity declaration

When you open it, you'll probably see a layout editor with a simple layout containing the text "Hello World." Switch to the Code view for the editor by selecting the "code" icon at the top right of the screen. You should then see XML code for the layout that looks something like this:

```
<?xml version="1.0" encoding="utf-8"?>
<androidx.constraintlayout.widget.ConstraintLayout
    xmlns:android="http://schemas.android.com/apk/res/android"
    xmlns:app="http://schemas.android.com/apk/res-auto"
    xmlns:tools="http://schemas.android.com/tools"
    android:layout_width="match_parent"
    android:layout_height="match_parent"
    tools:context=".MainActivity">
```

```
<TextView
    android:layout_width="wrap_content"
    android:layout_height="wrap_content"
    android:text="Hello World!"
    app:layout_constraintBottom_toBottomOf="parent"
    app:layout_constraintLeft_toLeftOf="parent"
    app:layout_constraintRight_toRightOf="parent"
    app:layout_constraintTop_toTopOf="parent" />

</androidx.constraintlayout.widget.ConstraintLayout>
```

Delete the TextView entry in the middle, and update it with a new Button and Image-View so that the listing will look like this:

```
<?xml version="1.0" encoding="utf-8"?>
<androidx.constraintlayout.widget.ConstraintLayout
    xmlns:android="http://schemas.android.com/apk/res/android"
    xmlns:app="http://schemas.android.com/apk/res-auto"
    xmlns:tools="http://schemas.android.com/tools"
    android:layout_width="match_parent"
    android:layout_height="match_parent"
    tools:context=".MainActivity">

    <Button
        android:id="@+id/btnTest"
        android:layout_width="wrap_content"
        android:layout_height="wrap_content"
        android:text="Button" />

    <ImageView
        android:id="@+id/imageFace"
        android:layout_width="match_parent"
        android:layout_height="match_parent" />

</androidx.constraintlayout.widget.ConstraintLayout>
```

You now have a very basic user interface containing a button and an image. You can load your image to the ImageView, and when you press the button, it will call ML Kit to detect the faces in the image contained in the ImageView and then draw the rectangles indicating their location.

Step 4: Add the Images as Assets

Android Studio doesn't create an assets folder for you by default, so you'll have to manually create one yourself to load images from it. The easiest way to do this is on the file structure for your project. Find the folder your code is located in, and within the *app/src/main* folder, create a directory called *assets*. Android Studio will then recognize this as your assets directory. Copy some pictures to this (or just use the ones from my GitHub) and they'll be ready to use.

When you are done and it's configured correctly, Android Studio will recognize the folder as an assets folder, and you'll be able to browse it. See Figure 3-7.

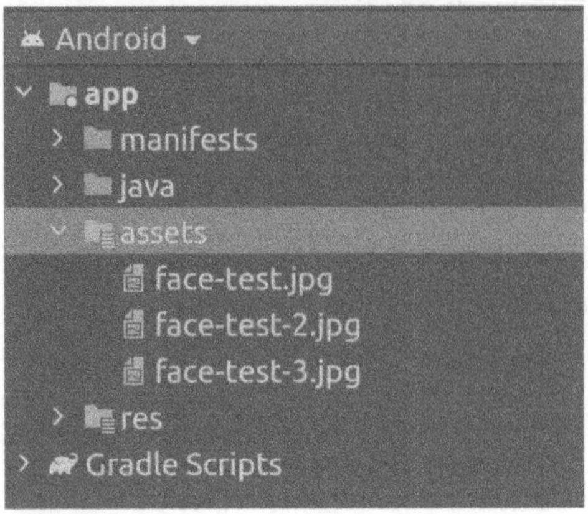

Figure 3-7. Setting up your assets

You're now ready to begin coding, so let's start by setting up the user interface with a default picture.

Step 5: Load the UI with a Default Picture

In your *MainActivity.kt* file, you should see a function called onCreate. This gets called when the activity is created. In here, add the following code at the bottom, under the setContentView line:

```
val img: ImageView = findViewById(R.id.imageFace)
// assets folder image file name with extension
val fileName = "face-test.jpg"

// get bitmap from assets folder
val bitmap: Bitmap? = assetsToBitmap(fileName)
bitmap?.apply{
    img.setImageBitmap(this)
}
```

This creates a handle to the ImageView control that you added to the layout and calls it img. It then gets the file called *face-test.jpg* and loads it from the assets folder using a helper function called assetsToBitmap, which you'll see in a moment. Once the bitmap is ready it will call apply, which allows you to execute code upon the bitmap being loaded, and it sets the image bitmap property of img to the bitmap, thus loading the image into the ImageView.

The helper function to load the bitmap from the assets folder is here:

```
// helper function to get bitmap from assets
fun Context.assetsToBitmap(fileName: String): Bitmap?{
    return try {
        with(assets.open(fileName)){
            BitmapFactory.decodeStream(this)
        }
    } catch (e: IOException) { null }
}
```

For this sample, the helper function is within the activity. Good programming practice for larger apps would have a helper class with functions like this one available.

This simply opens the assets and uses a `BitmapFactory` to stream the content of the image into a nullable `Bitmap`. If you run the app, it will now look like Figure 3-8.

Figure 3-8. Running the app

We can see that it's very basic, just an image and a button, but at least our image has been loaded into the ImageView! Next up we'll code the button and have it call ML Kit's face detector for us!

Step 6: Call the Face Detector

The face detection API (*https://oreil.ly/CPJWS*) has many options that you can call, and these are accessible via a `FaceDetectorOptions` object. I'm not going to go into detail here about all the options that are available—you can check the documentation for that—but before calling the API you will need to set up the options that you'll use to call it with. This is done using a `FaceDetectorOptions.Builder()` object, and here's an example:

```
val highAccuracyOpts = FaceDetectorOptions.Builder()
    .setPerformanceMode(FaceDetectorOptions.PERFORMANCE_MODE_FAST)
    .build()
```

There are many options that you can set here for various landmarks on the face, or classifications such as eyes open or closed, but as we're just doing a bounding box I've selected a simple set of options where I just ask for it to be fast! (If you want it to be more accurate, you can use `PERFORMANCE_MODE_ACCURATE`, which will generally take a little longer, and may perform better when there are multiple faces in a scene.)

Next you'll create an instance of the detector using these options, and pass it the bitmap. As the bitmap was a nullable type (i.e., `Bitmap?`), and `InputImage.fromBitmap` won't take nullable types, you postfix `bitmap` with `!!` to get it to recognize it. Here's the code:

```
val detector = FaceDetection.getClient(highAccuracyOpts)
val image = InputImage.fromBitmap(bitmap!!, 0)
```

You can get the results from the detector by calling `detector.process` and passing it your image. If it succeeds, you'll get a callback to its onSuccessListener, which will contain a list of faces. If it fails you'll get an `onFailureListener`, which you can use to track the exception:

```
val result = detector.process(image)
    .addOnSuccessListener { faces ->
        // Task completed successfully
        // ...
        bitmap?.apply{
            img.setImageBitmap(drawWithRectangle(faces))
        }
    }
    .addOnFailureListener { e ->
        // Task failed with an exception
        // ...
    }
```

Within the onSuccessListener, you can then use bitmap?.apply again to call a function, but this time you can set the image bitmap to the return of a function called drawWithRectangle, passing it the list of faces. This will take the bitmap and draw the rectangles on it. You'll see that in the next step.

But first, add all this code to the onCreate as part of an onClickListener for the button. Here's the complete code:

```
val btn: Button = findViewById(R.id.btnTest)
    btn.setOnClickListener {
        val highAccuracyOpts = FaceDetectorOptions.Builder()
            .setPerformanceMode(FaceDetectorOptions.PERFORMANCE_MODE_FAST)
            .build()

        val detector = FaceDetection.getClient(highAccuracyOpts)
        val image = InputImage.fromBitmap(bitmap!!, 0)
        val result = detector.process(image)
            .addOnSuccessListener { faces ->
                // Task completed successfully
                // ...
                bitmap?.apply{
                    img.setImageBitmap(drawWithRectangle(faces))
                }
            }
            .addOnFailureListener { e ->
                // Task failed with an exception
                // ...
            }
    }
```

Step 7: Add the Bounding Rectangles

Upon success the face detection API will return a list of faces to its caller, and in the previous step you took this list and passed it to a bitmap?.apply function, requesting to set the image bitmap to the return from a function called drawWithRectangle. Let's explore that here:

```
fun Bitmap.drawWithRectangle(faces: List<Face>):Bitmap?{
    val bitmap = copy(config, true)
    val canvas = Canvas(bitmap)
    for (face in faces){
        val bounds = face.boundingBox
        Paint().apply {
            color = Color.RED
            style = Paint.Style.STROKE
            strokeWidth = 4.0f
            isAntiAlias = true
            // draw rectangle on canvas
            canvas.drawRect(
                bounds,
                this
```

```
            )
        }
    }
    return bitmap
}
```

The function will make a copy of the bitmap that was used to call it and then initialize a `Canvas` with that bitmap. Then, for each face in the list of faces, it can call the boun dingBox property to get a rectangle object for that face. What's really nice is that ML Kit has scaled this rectangle to your image already, you don't need to do any further decoding.

So, in that case you can just call a `Paint()` object, define a rectangle with its `apply` method, and use `canvas.drawRect` to draw it. The canvas was initialized with your bitmap, so the rectangles will be drawn on it.

It will repeat this for all other faces, and when it's done it will return the new, marked-up bitmap with the rectangles on it. And as this was in turn used to apply to the main bitmap that is in the ImageView (see "Step 6: Draw the Bounding Boxes" on page 67), the new bitmap will be written to the ImageView and the UI updated. You can see the results in Figure 3-9.

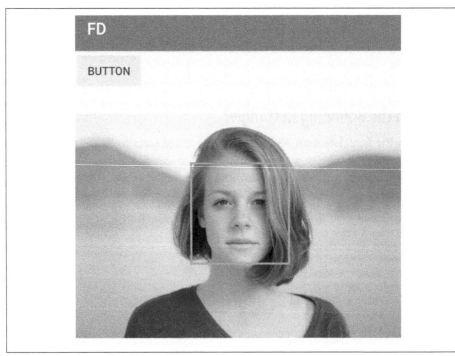

Figure 3-9. Your app with a bounding box

If you want to experiment with other images, just add them to the assets folder, and change this line from step 5 to contain the filename of the image you want to work with:

```
val fileName = "face-test.jpg"
```

You've now created your first Android app that uses a turnkey ML Kit–based model to detect faces! There's lots more that this API can do, including finding landmarks on a face such as eyes and ears, detecting contours, and classifying if the eyes are open, the person is smiling, and much more. You have everything you need to get started, so have fun enhancing this app.

For the rest of this chapter, we'll switch gears and look at how to build the same app, but on iOS!

Building a Face Detector App for iOS

Let's now explore how we would build a very similar app for iOS using ML Kit's face detection. For iOS you'll need to use a Mac computer as the developer box, as well as the Xcode environment for coding, debugging and testing.

Step 1: Create the Project in Xcode

To start, launch Xcode and select New Project. You'll see the new project templates dialog, which looks like Figure 3-10

Make sure you select iOS at the top of the screen, and then App as the app type. Click Next and you'll be asked to fill out some details. Keep all of the defaults except for the product name; in my case I called it firstFace, but it's up to you what name you use. Just be sure to keep the interface at Storyboard, the Life Cycle at UIKit App Delegate, and the language at Swift as shown in Figure 3-11.

After clicking Next, Xcode will create a template project for you. At this point you should close Xcode, as you will need to do some configuration outside of the IDE before you start coding. You'll see that in the next step where you add the ML Kit libraries using Cocoapods.

Figure 3-10. New app templates

Choose options for your new project:

Product Name:	firstFace
Team:	None
Organization Identifier:	com.lmoroney.test
Bundle Identifier:	com.lmoroney.test.firstFace
Interface:	Storyboard
Life Cycle:	UIKit App Delegate
Language:	Swift
	☐ Use Core Data
	☐ Host in CloudKit
	☐ Include Tests

Cancel   Previous   Next

Figure 3-11. Choosing project options

Step 2: Using CocoaPods and Podfiles

A common technology for managing dependencies in iOS development is CocoaPods (*https://cocoapods.org*). It's somewhat analogous to the Gradle files you saw in the Android section earlier in this chapter, and it's designed to make handling dependency files as easy as possible. You'll use CocoaPods through a Podfile, which defines the dependencies that you'll add to your app.

I won't go into a lot of detail on CocoaPods in this chapter, but please ensure that it's installed and ready to go or you won't be able to continue beyond this point for this sample, as it strongly depends on using CocoaPods to integrate ML Kit into your iOS app.

When you created the project earlier, it was stored in a directory with the project name. So, for example, in my case I called it firstFace and stored it on the Desktop. Within that folder is an Xcode project file called *firstFace.xcodeproj* and a folder, also called *firstFace*.

Within your project folder, alongside the *.xcodeproj* file, create a new text file called Podfile, with no extension. Edit the contents of this file so that it reads like this—changing `firstFace` to whatever your project is called:

```
platform :ios, '10.0'

target 'firstFace' do
        pod 'GoogleMLKit/FaceDetection'
        pod 'GoogleMLKit/TextRecognition'
end
```

Then, using Terminal, go to the project folder (it should contain the *.xcproject* file) and type **pod install**. If it executes correctly, you should see something like Figure 3-12.

 At the time of writing this book, M1-based Macs were relatively rare. Some testers encountered issues with `pod install` and it gave errors with *ffi_c.bundle*. To get around these, please ensure you are using the latest install of CocoaPods, or use the documented workaround (*https://oreil.ly/BqxCx*).

This will download the dependencies and install them in a new workspace called *firstFace.xcworkspace*. Use this to load your work going forward. So now, from within the terminal, you can type **open firstFace.xcworkspace**.

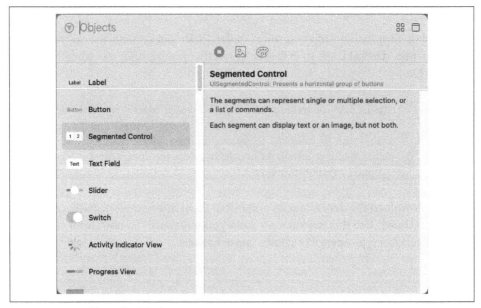

```
●  ●  ●                    🚇 firstFace — -zsh — 80×24

[laurence@laurences-mini firstFace % pod install
Analyzing dependencies
Downloading dependencies
Installing GTMSessionFetcher (1.5.0)
Installing GoogleDataTransport (8.0.1)
Installing GoogleMLKit (0.64.0)
Installing GoogleToolboxForMac (2.3.0)
Installing GoogleUtilities (7.1.1)
Installing GoogleUtilitiesComponents (1.0.0)
Installing MLKitCommon (0.64.2)
Installing MLKitFaceDetection (0.64.0)
Installing MLKitTextRecognition (0.64.0)
Installing MLKitVision (0.64.0)
Installing PromisesObjC (1.2.11)
Installing Protobuf (3.13.0)
Installing nanopb (2.30906.0)
Generating Pods project
Integrating client project

[!] Please close any current Xcode sessions and use 'firstFace.xcworkspace' for
this project from now on.
Pod installation complete! There are 2 dependencies from the Podfile and 13 tota
l pods installed.
laurence@laurences-mini firstFace % █
```

Figure 3-12. Running pod `install`

Step 3: Create the User Interface

We'll build the simplest app we can, but it will still need some UI elements. To keep it as basic as possible, these will be an ImageView and a Button. So, with Xcode open (to the *.xcworkspace* file as shown in the previous section), find the *Main.storyboard* file in the project, and open the tools library using View → Show Library.

You'll see a list of UI elements, as shown in Figure 3-13.

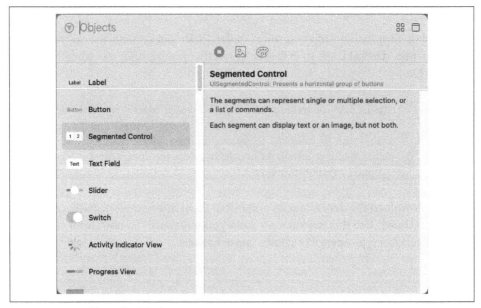

Figure 3-13. Adding the UI elements

Using this, and with the *Main.storyboard* active in the editor, drag an ImageView and a Button onto the design surface of the storyboard. Your IDE should look a little like Figure 3-14 when you are done.

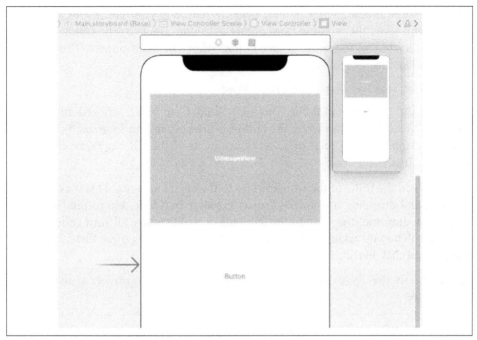

Figure 3-14. Your main storyboard

From the editor menu, you should see an entry called Assistant, which, if you select it, will open a code window alongside or below the visual editor.

Holding the Ctrl key, drag the button to the code just beneath class View Controller, and a pop-up window will appear. See Figure 3-15.

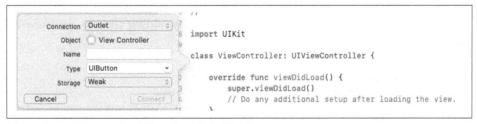

Figure 3-15. Connecting UI with code in Xcode

In the Connection setting, select Action, and in the Name field, enter buttonPressed, and then press the Connect button.

The following code will be generated for you:

```
@IBAction func buttonPressed(_ sender: Any) {
}
```

Similarly, while holding the Ctrl key, drag the UIImageView control to your code window, and when the window from Figure 3-15 pops up, keep the Connection setting to Outlet, but set the name to imageView before clicking Connect. This will generate code like this:

```
@IBOutlet weak var imageView: UIImageView!
```

Note that the IB here stands for "Interface Builder," so you've created an Interface Builder *action* that will run when the button is pressed, and an Interface Builder *outlet* that will allow you to refer to or set the contents of the UIImageView element by addressing it as imageView.

Next, let's add the JPEG of the woman's face to the app as an asset. This is as simple as dragging and dropping it onto the project explorer in Xcode. Go to Finder, get the image, and drag and drop it onto the left pane of Xcode where all your code files are. A dialog will pop up asking you to "Choose options for adding these files." Accept the defaults and click Finish.

You should see the file (in this case I called it *face1.jpg*) in your project as an asset. See Figure 3-16.

Figure 3-16. Adding a file to your project

You can now load the image into your imageView by adding code to the viewDid Load() function:

```
override func viewDidLoad() {
    super.viewDidLoad()
    // Do any additional setup after loading the view.
    imageView.image = UIImage(named: "face1.jpg")

}
```

You could run the app now and have a very boring UI with just an image and a button in it. But you'd know it worked!

The iOS Simulator provides an environment where you can emulate iOS devices. At the time of writing, some third-party libraries aren't supported in the simulator on M1 macs. As such, you can run either on a device, or you can choose the "My Mac - Designed for iPad" runtime. The screenshots for the rest of this chapter were taken from this target system, running on an M1 Mac Mini.

The final part of your user interface elements will be a view that can be used for adding annotations to the image—for example, the bounding box for the face. We'll do this using code, so, add the following to *ViewController.swift*:

```
/// An overlay view that displays detection annotations.
private lazy var annotationOverlayView: UIView = {
  precondition(isViewLoaded)
  let annotationOverlayView = UIView(frame: .zero)
  annotationOverlayView.translatesAutoresizingMaskIntoConstraints =
      false
  return annotationOverlayView
}()
```

This will just give us a view that will load after the main view containing the rest of the UI elements (note the precondition).

This overlay view can then be loaded and activated on top of your `imageView` by updating `viewDidLoad` like this:

```
override func viewDidLoad() {
    super.viewDidLoad()
    // Do any additional setup after loading the view.
    imageView.image = UIImage(named: "face1.jpg")
    imageView.addSubview(annotationOverlayView)
    NSLayoutConstraint.activate([
        annotationOverlayView.topAnchor.constraint(equalTo:
imageView.topAnchor),
        annotationOverlayView.leadingAnchor.constraint(equalTo:
imageView.leadingAnchor),
        annotationOverlayView.trailingAnchor.constraint(equalTo:
imageView.trailingAnchor),
        annotationOverlayView.bottomAnchor.constraint(equalTo:
imageView.bottomAnchor),
    ])
}
```

Now that we've created the entire user interface—consisting of the UIImageView for the picture, the button for the user to press, and the annotation overlay to render the bounding box, we're ready to start coding the logic that will use ML Kit to detect the face. You'll see that next.

Step 4: Add the Application Logic

When the user presses the button, we will want to invoke ML Kit, pass it the image, get the details for the bounding box that indicates the location of the face, and then render that on the view. Let's look at how to code this step by step.

First, you'll need to import the ML Kit libraries:

```
import MLKitFaceDetection
import MLKitVision
```

Next, let's set up the ML Kit face detector. To do this, you'll first need to create a `Face DetectorOptions` object and set up some of its properties. In this case we'll just do some basic options—getting all contours for the face, and asking it for fast performance:

```
private lazy var faceDetectorOption: FaceDetectorOptions = {
  let option = FaceDetectorOptions()
  option.contourMode = .all
  option.performanceMode = .fast
  return option
}()
```

Then, once we have the options, we can use them to instantiate a `faceDetector`:

```
private lazy var faceDetector =
    FaceDetector.faceDetector(options: faceDetectorOption)
```

You'll probably notice at this point that your code will give you an error because it can't find `FaceDetectorOptions`. That's OK. It just means they're in a library that you haven't referenced yet. You can fix that with some imports at the top of your code. These will give you the ML Kit face detection libraries, as well as the helper libraries for general computer vision:

```
import MLKitFaceDetection
import MLKitVision
```

Recall earlier that you created an Interface Builder action that would execute when the user pressed the button. Let's start there and have it run a custom function (which you'll create in a moment) when the user touches the button:

```
@IBAction func buttonPressed(_ sender: Any) {
    runFaceContourDetection(with: imageView.image!)
}
```

Now, we can code this function up—its job will be to take the image and pass it to the face detector. Once the face detector does its job, it can handle the return. So we can keep the function very simple:

```
func runFaceContourDetection(with image: UIImage) {
  let visionImage = VisionImage(image: image)
  visionImage.orientation = image.imageOrientation
```

```
    faceDetector.process(visionImage) { features, error in
      self.processResult(from: features, error: error)
    }
  }
}
```

You haven't yet written the `processResult` function, so Xcode will give you a warning. Don't worry—you'll implement that next.

To allow ML Kit to recognize many different object types, the pattern is to convert all images into a `VisionImage` object. This object supports construction from a variety of formats, and here we do so from a `UIImage`. We'll first create an instance of a `Vision Image` and set its orientation to be the same as the original image. Then, we process the image using the face detector object created earlier. This will return features and/or errors, so we can pass *these* to a function called `processResult`.

So here's the code for `processResult` (abbreviated by removing error handling, which you shouldn't do in a production app!), and its job is to get the details back from ML Kit's face detector:

```
func processResult(from faces: [Face]?, error: Error?) {
    guard let faces = faces else {
      return
    }
    for feature in faces {
      let transform = self.transformMatrix()
      let transformedRect = feature.frame.applying(transform)
      self.addRectangle(
        transformedRect,
        to: self.annotationOverlayView,
        color: UIColor.green
      )
    }
}
```

Note that the coordinates of the bounding boxes returned by ML Kit are not the same as the coordinates of the image in the iOS user interface for various reasons, including the fact that they're based on the resolution of the image, and not the number of pixels that are rendered on the screen, as well as things like the aspect ratio. So, a `transformMatrix` function needs to be created to convert between the coordinates returned from ML Kit and the onscreen ones. This is used to create the `transforme dRect`—which will be the frame of the face in screen coordinates. Finally, a rectangle will be added to the `annotationOverlayView`, which will frame the face for us.

The full code for the helper functions—transforming the rectangle's coordinates and applying it to the overlay—is here:

```
private func transformMatrix() -> CGAffineTransform {
  guard let image = imageView.image else
    { return CGAffineTransform() }
  let imageViewWidth = imageView.frame.size.width
```

```
    let imageViewHeight = imageView.frame.size.height
    let imageWidth = image.size.width
    let imageHeight = image.size.height

    let imageViewAspectRatio = imageViewWidth / imageViewHeight
    let imageAspectRatio = imageWidth / imageHeight
    let scale =
      (imageViewAspectRatio > imageAspectRatio)
      ? imageViewHeight / imageHeight : imageViewWidth / imageWidth

    let scaledImageWidth = imageWidth * scale
    let scaledImageHeight = imageHeight * scale
    let xValue = (imageViewWidth - scaledImageWidth) / CGFloat(2.0)
    let yValue = (imageViewHeight - scaledImageHeight) / CGFloat(2.0)

    var transform = CGAffineTransform.identity.translatedBy(
                                      x: xValue, y: yValue)
    transform = transform.scaledBy(x: scale, y: scale)
    return transform
}

private func addRectangle(_ rectangle: CGRect, to view: UIView, color: UIColor) {
    let rectangleView = UIView(frame: rectangle)
    rectangleView.layer.cornerRadius = 10.0
    rectangleView.alpha = 0.3
    rectangleView.backgroundColor = color
    view.addSubview(rectangleView)
}
```

And this will give you all the code you need. As you can see most of it is really for the
user interface logic—converting the coordinates, plotting the rectangles, etc. The face
detection is relatively simple—just three lines of code in the `runFaceContourDetec
tion` function!

Running the app and pressing the button should frame the face like in Figure 3-17.

Figure 3-17. Framing a face on iOS

Again, this is a super simple example, but the pattern is very typical of a far more sophisticated app. The goal with ML Kit is to make the ML part of application development as easy as possible, and hopefully the face detection part of this app proved that.

Summary

In this chapter, you had a brief introduction to using ML Kit for mobile machine learning in your apps. You saw how to use it in both Android and iOS to build a very simple app that detected a face in a given image and plotted a rectangle over that face. Importantly you saw how to include ML Kit via Gradle on Android and CocoaPods on iOS. Over the next few chapters, we'll go deeper into some common scenarios across each platform starting with vision apps in Chapter 4 using Android.

Computer Vision Apps with ML Kit on Android

Chapter 3 gave you an introduction to ML Kit and how it can be used for face detection in a mobile app. But ML Kit is far more than that—it gives you the ability to rapidly prototype common vision scenarios, host custom models, or implement other turnkey solution scenarios such as barcode detection also. In this chapter, we will explore some of the models that are available in ML Kit to provide computer vision scenarios, including image labeling and classification, and object detection in both still and moving images. We'll do this on Android, using Kotlin as the programming language. Chapter 6 will cover the equivalent content using Swift for iOS development.

Image Labeling and Classification

The concept of image classification is a well-known one in machine learning circles, and the staple of computer vision. In its simplest sense, image classification happens when you show an image to a computer and it tells you what that image contains. For example, you show it a picture of a cat, like that in Figure 4-1, and it will label it as a cat.

Image labeling in ML Kit takes this a little further and gives you a list of things seen in the image with levels of probability, so instead of Figure 4-1 just showing a cat, it might say that it sees a cat, flowers, grass, daisies, and more.

Let's explore how to create a very simple Android app that can label this image! We'll use Android Studio and Kotlin. If you don't have them already, you can download them at *https://developer.android.com/studio/*.

Figure 4-1. An image of a cat

Step 1: Create the App and Configure ML Kit

If you haven't gone through Chapter 3 yet, or if you aren't familiar with getting up and running with an Android app, I'd recommend that you do! Once you've created the app, you'll need to edit your build.gradle file as demonstrated in that chapter. However, in this case, instead of adding the face detection libraries, you'll need to add the image labeling ones, like this:

```
dependencies {
    implementation "org.jetbrains.kotlin:kotlin-stdlib:$kotlin_version"
    implementation 'androidx.core:core-ktx:1.2.0'
    implementation 'androidx.appcompat:appcompat:1.2.0'
    implementation 'com.google.android.material:material:1.1.0'
    implementation 'androidx.constraintlayout:constraintlayout:2.0.4'
    testImplementation 'junit:junit:4.+'
    androidTestImplementation 'androidx.test.ext:junit:1.1.2'
    androidTestImplementation 'androidx.test.espresso:espresso-core:3.2.0'
    implementation 'com.google.mlkit:image-labeling:17.0.1'
}
```

Once you've done this, Android Studio will likely ask you to sync given that your Gradle files have changed. This will trigger a build with the new ML Kit dependencies included.

Step 2: Create the User Interface

We'll just create a super simple UI for this app to allow us to get straight down to using the image labeling. In your res->layout directories within Android View you'll see a file called *activity_main.xml*. Refer back to Chapter 3 if this isn't familiar.

Update the UI to contain a linear layout with an ImageView, a Button, and a TextView like this:

```xml
<?xml version="1.0" encoding="utf-8"?>
<androidx.constraintlayout.widget.ConstraintLayout
    xmlns:android="http://schemas.android.com/apk/res/android"
    xmlns:app="http://schemas.android.com/apk/res-auto"
    xmlns:tools="http://schemas.android.com/tools"
    android:layout_width="match_parent"
    android:layout_height="match_parent"
    tools:context=".MainActivity">

    <LinearLayout
        android:layout_width="match_parent"
        android:layout_height="wrap_content"
        android:orientation="vertical"
        app:layout_constraintStart_toStartOf="parent"
        app:layout_constraintTop_toTopOf="parent">

        <ImageView
            android:id="@+id/imageToLabel"
            android:layout_width="match_parent"
            android:layout_height="match_parent"
            android:layout_gravity="center"
            android:adjustViewBounds="true"
        />
        <Button
            android:id="@+id/btnTest"
            android:layout_width="wrap_content"
            android:layout_height="wrap_content"
            android:text="Label Image"
            android:layout_gravity="center"/>
        <TextView
            android:id="@+id/txtOutput"
            android:layout_width="match_parent"
            android:layout_height="wrap_content"
            android:ems="10"
            android:gravity="start|top" />
    </LinearLayout>
</androidx.constraintlayout.widget.ConstraintLayout>
```

At runtime, the ImageView will load an image, and when the user presses the button, ML Kit will be invoked to get image label data back for the displayed image. The results will be rendered in the TextView. You can see this in Figure 4-3 a little later.

Step 3: Add the Images as Assets

Within your project, you'll need an assets folder. Again, if you aren't familiar with this step, check back to Chapter 3, where you'll be stepped through the process. Once you have an assets folder and have added some images to it, you'll see them in Android Studio. See Figure 4-2.

```
▼  📦 assets
        📄 face-test.jpg
        📄 face-test-2.jpg
        📄 face-test-3.jpg
        📄 figure4-1.jpg
```

Figure 4-2. Images in the assets folder

Step 4: Load an Image to the ImageView

Now let's write some code! We can go to the *MainActivity.kt* file, and within that add an extension that lets us load images from the assets folder as bitmaps:

```
fun Context.assetsToBitmap(fileName: String): Bitmap?{
    return try {
        with(assets.open(fileName)){
            BitmapFactory.decodeStream(this)
        }
    } catch (e: IOException) { null }
}
```

Then, update the onCreate function that was made for you by Android Studio to find the ImageView control based on its ID, and load one of the images from the assets folder into it:

```
val img: ImageView = findViewById(R.id.imageToLabel)
// assets folder image file name with extension
val fileName = "figure4-1.jpg"
// get bitmap from assets folder
val bitmap: Bitmap? = assetsToBitmap(fileName)
bitmap?.apply {
    img.setImageBitmap(this)
}
```

You can run your app now to test if it loads the image properly. If it does, you should see something like Figure 4-3.

Figure 4-3. Running the app with an image loaded

Pressing the button won't do anything yet because we haven't coded it. Let's do that next!

Step 5: Write the Button Handler Code

Let's start by writing code to give us variables that can represent the text view (for writing out the labels) as well as the button itself:

```
val txtOutput : TextView = findViewById(R.id.txtOutput)
val btn: Button = findViewById(R.id.btnTest)
```

Now that we have the button, we can create a button handler for it. This will be achieved by typing `btn.setOnClickListener`; autocomplete will create a stub function for you. Then, you can update it for image labeling with this complete code. We'll go through it piece by piece next:

```
btn.setOnClickListener {
        val labeler =
          ImageLabeling.getClient(ImageLabelerOptions.DEFAULT_OPTIONS)
        val image = InputImage.fromBitmap(bitmap!!, 0)
        var outputText = ""
        labeler.process(image).addOnSuccessListener { labels ->
                // Task completed successfully
                for (label in labels) {
                    val text = label.text
                    val confidence = label.confidence
```

```
                    outputText += "$text : $confidence\n"
            }
                txtOutput.text = outputText
        }
    .addOnFailureListener { e ->
                // Task failed with an exception
                // ...
        }
}
```

When the user clicks the button, this code will create an image labeler from ML Kit with default options like this:

```
val labeler = ImageLabeling.getClient(ImageLabelerOptions.DEFAULT_OPTIONS)
```

Once it has done this, it will then create an image object (which ML Kit can understand) from the bitmap (used to display the image) with this code:

```
val image = InputImage.fromBitmap(bitmap!!, 0)
```

The labeler will be called to process the image, with two listeners added to it. A *success* listener will fire if the processing was successful, and a *failure* listener if it wasn't. When an image labeler succeeds, it will return a list of *labels*. These labels will have a text property with text describing the label, and a confidence property with a value from 0 to 1 containing the probability that the labeled item is present.

So, within the success listener, the code will parse through the full list of labels, and add the text and confidence to a variable called `outputText`. Once it has completed, it can then set the text property of the TextView (now called `txtOutput`) to the value of the `outputText` variable:

```
for (label in labels) {
        val text = label.text
        val confidence = label.confidence
        outputText += "$text : $confidence\n"
}
txtOutput.text = outputText
```

It's really as simple as that. Running the app with the cat image from earlier in this chapter will then give you output like Figure 4-4.

ImageLabellingSample

LABEL IMAGE

Cat : 0.97636753
Pet : 0.85540384
Flower : 0.74621916
Plant : 0.65004134
Petal : 0.5942031
Dog : 0.53991836
Prairie : 0.51649696

Figure 4-4. Labeling the image from earlier in this chapter

Next Steps

The built-in image labeling model from ML Kit recognizes over 400 classes within an image. At the time of writing it was 447, but this may change. The full label map for ML Kit is published at *https://developers.google.com/ml-kit/vision/image-labeling/label-map*. Should you want to train a model to recognize *different* classes you'll use TensorFlow, which we'll explore in Chapter 9.

Object Detection

The previous section showed you how to do image classification and labeling where the computer was able to detect *what* was in an image, but not necessarily *where* the item was within the image. The concept of *object detection* is used here. In this case, when you pass an image to the object detector, you'll get back a list of objects, including *bounding boxes* that may be used to determine where in the image the object may be. The ML Kit default model for object detection is excellent at picking out objects in an image, but the number of classes it can classify is limited to only five before you need to use a custom model. However, when combining it with image labeling (previous section), you can get a classification of the individual objects within the image to get labels for them! You can see an example of this in Figure 4-5.

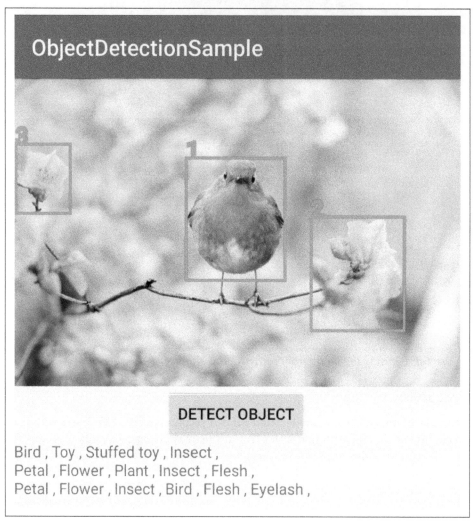

Figure 4-5. Performing object detection

Let's look at this step by step.

Step 1: Create the App and Import ML Kit

Create the app as before as a single view application. We'll try to keep this as similar to the image labeling app you've already built so that things can be familiar.

When you're done, edit your build.gradle file to use both object detection and image labeling, like this:

```
implementation 'com.google.mlkit:object-detection:16.2.2'
implementation 'com.google.mlkit:image-labeling:17.0.1'
```

 Your version numbers may be different, so check the latest at *https://developers.google.com/ml-kit*.

Step 2: Create the Activity Layout XML

The layout file for the activity is super simple and exactly the same as what we saw earlier. You'll have a LinearLayout that lays out an ImageView, a Button, and a TextView. The ImageView will display the image, the Button will run the object detection and labeling code, and the TextView will render the results of the labeling. Instead of relisting the code here, just use the same layout code as the previous example.

Step 3: Load an Image into the ImageView

As before, you'll use an extension to load an image from the assets folder into the ImageView. For convenience, I've repeated the code to do that here:

```
// extension function to get bitmap from assets
fun Context.assetsToBitmap(fileName: String): Bitmap?{
    return try {
        with(assets.open(fileName)){
            BitmapFactory.decodeStream(this)
        }
    } catch (e: IOException) { null }
}
```

Create an assets folder like before, and put some images in it. For the screenshot in Figure 4-5, I used an image from Pixabay (*https://oreil.ly/TnCR6*), which I renamed to *bird.jpg* for easier code.

Then, within the onCreate function, you can get the image from the assets using the preceding extension function and load it into your bitmap like this:

```
val img: ImageView = findViewById(R.id.imageToLabel)
// assets folder image file name with extension
val fileName = "bird.jpg"
// get bitmap from assets folder
```

```
val bitmap: Bitmap? = assetsToBitmap(fileName)
bitmap?.apply {
    img.setImageBitmap(this)
}
```

You can also set up the Button and TextView controls like this:

```
val txtOutput : TextView = findViewById(R.id.txtOutput)
val btn: Button = findViewById(R.id.btnTest)
```

Step 4: Set Up the Object Detector Options

You'll use a number of ML Kit classes in this section. Here are the imports:

```
import com.google.mlkit.vision.common.InputImage
import com.google.mlkit.vision.label.ImageLabeling
import com.google.mlkit.vision.label.defaults.ImageLabelerOptions
import com.google.mlkit.vision.objects.DetectedObject
import com.google.mlkit.vision.objects.ObjectDetection
import com.google.mlkit.vision.objects.defaults.ObjectDetectorOptions
```

The ML Kit object detector gives you a variety of ways to do object detection, and these are controlled by an `ObjectDetectorOptions` object. We will use it in one of its simplest modes, which is to detect based on a single image and enable detecting multiple objects within that image:

```
val options =
        ObjectDetectorOptions.Builder()
        .setDetectorMode(ObjectDetectorOptions.SINGLE_IMAGE_MODE)
        .enableMultipleObjects()
        .build()
```

The object detector is a powerful API, which can also do things like tracking objects in a video stream—detecting them and maintaining them from frame to frame. That's beyond the scope of what we're doing in this book, but you can learn more about it in the ML Kit documentation (*https://oreil.ly/kluVJ*).

The mode option is used to determine this—you can learn more about the `SINGLE_IMAGE_MODE` used in this example at *https://oreil.ly/WFSZD*.

Additionally, the object detector can be enabled to detect the most prominent object, or all objects within the scene. We've set it here to detect multiple objects (using `.ena bleMultipleObjects()`), so we can see multiple items as demonstrated in Figure 4-5.

Another common option is to enable classification. As the default object detector can only detect five classes of object, and it gives them a very generic label, I haven't turned it on here, and we will "roll our own" labeling of the objects using the image labeling APIs discussed earlier in the chapter. If you want to use more than the base five classes of object, you can do so with a custom TensorFlow model, and we'll explore using custom models in Chapters 9 through 11.

Step 5: Handling the Button Interaction

When the user touches the button, you'll want to invoke the object detector, get its response, and from there get the bounding boxes for the objects within the image. Later we'll also use those bounding boxes to crop the image into the subimage defined by the bounding box, so we can pass that to the labeler. But for now, let's just implement the object detection handler. It should look something like this:

```
btn.setOnClickListener {
        val objectDetector = ObjectDetection.getClient(options)
        var image = InputImage.fromBitmap(bitmap!!, 0)
        objectDetector.process(image)
            .addOnSuccessListener { detectedObjects ->
                // Task completed successfully
            }
            .addOnFailureListener { e ->
                // Task failed with an exception
                // ...
            }
    }
```

So, similar to what you did earlier with image labeling, the pattern is to create an instance of the object detection API with the options. You'll then convert the bitmap into an `InputImage`, and process this with the object detector.

This will return on success with a list of detected objects, or on failure with an exception object.

The `detectedObjects` returned to the `onSuccessListener` will contain details about the object including its bounding boxes. So let's next create a function to draw the bounding boxes on the image.

Step 6: Draw the Bounding Boxes

The easiest way is to extend the `Bitmap` object to draw rectangles on top of it using a `Canvas`. We'll pass the detected object to this, so it can establish the bounding boxes, and from there draw them on top of the bitmap.

Here's the complete code:

```
fun Bitmap.drawWithRectangle(objects: List<DetectedObject>):Bitmap?{
    val bitmap = copy(config, true)
    val canvas = Canvas(bitmap)
    var thisLabel = 0
    for (obj in objects){
        thisLabel++
        val bounds = obj.boundingBox
        Paint().apply {
            color = Color.RED
            style = Paint.Style.STROKE
```

```
                    textSize = 32.0f
                    strokeWidth = 4.0f
                    isAntiAlias = true
                    // draw rectangle on canvas
                    canvas.drawRect(
                            bounds,
                            this
                    )
                    canvas.drawText(thisLabel.toString(),
                                    bounds.left.toFloat(),
                                    bounds.top.toFloat(), this )
                }

        }
        return bitmap
    }
```

The code will first create a copy of the bitmap, and a new Canvas based on it. It will then iterate through all of the detected objects.

The bounding box returned by ML Kit for the object is in the boundingBox property, so you can get its details with:

```
val bounds = obj.boundingBox
```

This can then be used to draw a bounding box using a Paint object on the canvas like this:

```
canvas.drawRect(
        bounds,
            this
    )
```

The rest of the code just handles things like the color of the rectangle and the size and color of the text, which just contains a number, and as you saw in Figure 4-5, we write 1, 2, 3 on the boxes in the order in which they were detected.

You then call this function within the onSuccessListener like this:

```
bitmap?.apply{
    img.setImageBitmap(drawWithRectangle(detectedObjects))
}
```

So, upon a successful return from ML Kit, you'll now have bounding boxes drawn on the images. Given the limitations of the object detector, you won't get very useful labels for these boxes, so in the next step, you'll see how to use image labeling calls to get the details for what is within the bounding box.

Step 7: Label the Objects

The base model, for simplicity, only handles five very generic classes when it comes to labeling the contents of the image. You could use a custom model that is trained on more, or you could use a simple multistep solution. The process is simple—you already have the bounding boxes, so create a *new* temporary image with just what's within a bounding box, pass that to the image labeler, and then get the results back. Repeat this for each bounding box (and thus each object), and you'll get detailed labels for each detected object!

Here's the complete code:

```
fun getLabels(bitmap: Bitmap,
            objects: List<DetectedObject>, txtOutput: TextView){
    val labeler = ImageLabeling.getClient(ImageLabelerOptions.DEFAULT_OPTIONS)
    for(obj in objects) {
        val bounds = obj.boundingBox
        val croppedBitmap = Bitmap.createBitmap(
            bitmap,
            bounds.left,
            bounds.top,
            bounds.width(),
            bounds.height()
        )
        var image = InputImage.fromBitmap(croppedBitmap!!, 0)

        labeler.process(image)
            .addOnSuccessListener { labels ->
                // Task completed successfully
                var labelText = ""
                if(labels.count()>0) {
                    labelText = txtOutput.text.toString()
                    for (thisLabel in labels){
                        labelText += thisLabel.text + " , "
                    }
                    labelText += "\n"
                } else {
                    labelText = "Not found." + "\n"
                }
                txtOutput.text = labelText.toString()
            }
    }
}
```

This code loops through each of the detected objects and uses the bounding box to create a new bitmap called croppedBitmap. It will then use an image labeler (called labeler) that is set up with default options to process that new image. On a successful return it will have a number of labels, which it will then write into a comma-separated string that will be rendered in txtOutput. I've noticed occasionally that even though it succeeds in labeling, it returns an empty labeled list, so I added code to only construct the string if there are labels within the return.

To call this function, just add this code to the onSuccessListener for the *object detection* call, immediately after where you called the code to set the rectangles on the bitmap:

```
getLabels(bitmap, detectedObjects, txtOutput)
```

 When running this code, you are making a number of asynchronous calls, first to the object detector, and later to the image labeler. As a result, you'll likely see delayed behavior after pressing the button. You'll likely see the bounding boxes drawn first, and then a few moments later the list of labels will be updated. Android and Kotlin offer a lot of asynchronous functionality to make the user experience here a bit better, but they're beyond the scope of this book, as I wanted to keep the example simple and focused on what you can do with the functionality present in ML Kit.

Detecting and Tracking Objects in Video

The ML Kit object detector can also operate on video streams, giving you the ability to detect objects in a video *and* track that object in successive video frames. For example, see Figure 4-6, where I moved the camera across a scene, and the Android figurine was not only detected, and a bounding box given, but a tracking ID was assigned. While the object stayed in the field of view, subsequent frames get different bounding boxes based on the new position, but the tracking ID is maintained—i.e., it was recognized as the *same* object despite looking different because of the placement within the frame and the different camera angle.

We'll explore how an app like this can be built using ML Kit in this section. Note that to test this you should use a physical device—the nature of moving the camera around to track devices doesn't translate well to using the emulator.

There are a lot of steps in building an app like this that aren't ML-specific, like handling CameraX, using an overlay, and managing drawing of the boxes between frames, etc., that I won't go into in depth in this chapter, but the book download has the complete code that you can dissect.

Figure 4-6. Using a video-based object detector

Exploring the Layout

Naturally, the layout of an app like the preceding is a little more complex than what we've been seeing. It needs you to draw a camera preview, and then, on top of the preview, to draw bounding boxes that update in near real time as you move the camera around the frame to track the object. In this app I used CameraX, a support library in Android that is designed to make using the camera much easier—and it did! You can learn more about CameraX at *https://developer.android.com/training/camerax*.

Repeat the earlier steps for creating a new Android app. When ready, open the layout file and edit it. For an app like this, you'll need to use a FrameLayout, which is typically only used for a single item, to block out a particular area of the screen for it, but

I like using it in a circumstance like this, where I have two items but one will completely overlay the other:

```
<FrameLayout android:layout_width="fill_parent"
    android:layout_height="fill_parent"
    android:layout_weight="2"
    android:padding="5dip"
    tools:ignore="MissingConstraints">
    <androidx.camera.view.PreviewView
        android:id="@+id/viewFinder"
        android:layout_width="fill_parent"
        android:layout_height="fill_parent"
        android:layout_weight="1"
        android:layout_gravity="center" />
    <com.odmlbook.liveobjectdetector.GraphicOverlay
        android:id="@+id/graphicOverlay"
        android:layout_gravity="center"
        android:layout_width="wrap_content"
        android:layout_height="wrap_content" />
</FrameLayout>
```

Within the FrameLayout, the first control is the `androidx.camera.view.Preview View` on which the stream of video from the camera will be rendered. On top of this is a custom control called a `GraphicOverlay`, which, as its name suggests, provides an overlay on top of the Preview on which graphics can be drawn. This overlay control has been adapted from the open source ML Kit sample (*https://oreil.ly/csyn9*).

Note that in the listing I'm calling the `GraphicOverlay` `com.odmlbook.liveobjectde tector.GraphicOverlay`; this is because the `GraphicOverlay` from the preceding Google sample was added directly to my app, and I'm using my app's namespace. You'll likely have a different namespace, so be sure to use the correct naming for your `GraphicOverlay`.

I've kept the layout as simple as possible so you can focus on the aspects of object detection—so that's pretty much it—a preview for CameraX on top of which is a GraphicOverlay on which you can draw the bounding boxes. You'll see more of this a little later.

The GraphicOverlay Class

In the layout you saw a custom `GraphicOverlay` class. It's the job of this class to manage a collection of graphic objects—which will be made up of the bounding boxes and their labels—and draw them on a canvas. One thing to note is that often you'll encounter differences between coordinates between the camera preview (at the camera's resolution) and a canvas that's placed on top of it (at the screen resolution) like in this case. Thus, a coordinate translation may also be necessary for you to draw on top of the preview in the appropriate place. You can find the code for that, as well as for managing performance of drawing graphics when operating frame by frame, in

---

the `GraphicOverlay` class. The bounding boxes, represented as graphic objects, will simply be added in the `onDraw` event:

```
@Override
protected void onDraw(Canvas canvas) {
    super.onDraw(canvas);

    synchronized (lock) {
        updateTransformationIfNeeded();

        for (Graphic graphic : graphics) {
            graphic.draw(canvas);
        }
    }
}
```

Capturing the Camera

When using CameraX, you access a camera provider, which will then allow you to set various subproviders on it, including a *surface* provider that lets you define where to put the preview, as well as an *analyzer* that lets you do stuff with the frames that come in from the camera. These are perfect for our needs—the surface provider can give us the preview window, and the analyzer can be used to call the ML Kit object detector. In the `MainActivity` for the app, you will find this code (in the `startCamera()` function).

First, we set up the preview view (notice that the control in the layout listing was called `viewFinder`) to render the stream of frames from the camera:

```
val preview = Preview.Builder()
    .build()
    .also {
        it.setSurfaceProvider(viewFinder.surfaceProvider)
    }
```

Next comes the image analyzer. CameraX calls this frame by frame, giving you the ability to do some kind of processing on the image. This is perfect for our needs. When you call `setAnalyzer`, you specify a class that will handle the analysis. Here I specified a class called `ObjectAnalyzer`, which, as its name suggests, will use the object detection APIs with the frame:

```
val imageAnalyzer = ImageAnalysis.Builder()
    .setBackpressureStrategy(ImageAnalysis.STRATEGY_KEEP_ONLY_LATEST)
    .build()
    .also {
        it.setAnalyzer(cameraExecutor, ObjectAnalyzer(graphicOverlay))
    }
```

Then, once you have these, you can bind them to the life cycle of the camera so that CameraX knows to use them to render the preview and manage frame-by-frame processing respectively:

```
cameraProvider.bindToLifecycle(
    this, cameraSelector, preview, imageAnalyzer
)
```

You can learn more about the life cycle of camera applications using CameraX in the CameraX documentation. I just want to highlight the important parts when it comes to using object detection with it here.

The ObjectAnalyzer Class

The full code for this class is in the book's repo (*https://oreil.ly/WIQMR*). I recommend you clone that and use it to understand how object analysis works for tracking objects in video. This section just shows the important parts of the code, and won't really work for coding along!

Earlier you saw that you could hook into CameraX's analyzer ability to do the object detection, and we specified a class called ObjectAnalyzer to handle it. We also passed a reference to the graphic overlay to this class.

An analyzer class has to override ImageAnalysis.Analyzer, so the signature for this class should look something like:

```
public class ObjectAnalyzer(graphicOverlay: GraphicOverlay) :
                        ImageAnalysis.Analyzer {}
```

It's the job of this class to do the object detection, so we'll need to create our ObjectDetector instance as we did before:

```
val options =
            ObjectDetectorOptions.Builder()
                    .setDetectorMode(ObjectDetectorOptions.STREAM_MODE)
                    .enableMultipleObjects()
                    .enableClassification()
                    .build()
    val objectDetector = ObjectDetection.getClient(options)
```

Note the difference in the detector mode setting though—ObjectDetectorOptions.STREAM_MODE—it's now using *stream mode* because we're going to be streaming images to it. This turns on the object tracking feature that we saw in Figure 4-6 where it "remembers" the same object across different frames, even if it looks different because of camera placement.

When you create an analyzer class like this, you'll need to override the function analyze, which takes an ImageProxy object representing the image. To use a CameraX image with the image proxy, there's some processing you'll need to do to manage the rotation, etc. I won't go into the detail on that here, but the important thing to manage is if the camera is providing frames in landscape or portrait mode, in which case we need to inform the overlay about the appropriate height and width of the image, flipping them where necessary—so that the ML Kit API always receives images in the same orientation:

```
if (rotationDegrees == 0 || rotationDegrees == 180) {
    overlay.setImageSourceInfo(
        imageProxy.width, imageProxy.height, isImageFlipped
    )
} else {
    overlay.setImageSourceInfo(
        imageProxy.height, imageProxy.width, isImageFlipped
    )
}
```

Then, we can pass the frame to the object detector, and if we get success, the callback will have detected objects like before. At this point we should clear the overlay, and then add new graphic objects to the overlay for each of the detected objects. These graphic objects are a custom class within this app. You'll see them in a moment. Once we're done, we call `postInvalidate()` on the overlay, which will trigger a redraw of the overlay:

```
objectDetector.process(frame)
    .addOnSuccessListener { detectedObjects ->
    overlay.clear()
        for (detectedObject in detectedObjects){
            val objGraphic = ObjectGraphic(this.overlay, detectedObject)
            this.overlay.add(objGraphic)
        }
        this.overlay.postInvalidate()
}
```

The ObjectGraphic Class

As the bounding boxes are composed of three elements—the box, the text of the label, and the background for the label—instead of just drawing each one of these individually, a single class is used to represent each. This class will be initialized using the `detectedObject` that is returned from ML Kit, so we can get the tracking ID and the coordinates of the bounding box. The `ObjectGraphic` class manages all of this—you can see it being used in the preceding code, where a new instance of it is created using the overlay and the `detectedObject`.

Putting It All Together

That's generally how an app like this would work. Using CameraX, you specify a preview surface and an analyzer. The analyzer calls the ML Kit object detector with stream mode enabled. The detected objects that it returns are used to create objects that represent the bounding boxes, and these are added to the overlay. This uses the generic model in ML Kit, so there's not much by way of classification—just that it detected an object and that object is assigned an ID. To further classify each object detected, you'll need a custom model, and we'll discuss that in Chapter 9.

Summary

Building apps that use vision is very straightforward using ML Kit for Android. In this chapter, you explored several scenarios for this using the built-in generic models, including image classification and labeling, where a single image can have its contents determined by the computer, and then using object detection, where multiple images within an image can be detected and their location determined by a bounding box. You wrapped up the chapter with a brief exploration on how this could be extended to video—where not only would you *detect* an object, but you could also track it in real time. All these scenarios were based on the generic built-in models in ML Kit but could easily be extended with custom models. We'll explore that more in Chapter 9.

## CHAPTER 5

Text Processing Apps with ML Kit on Android

Perhaps the two largest fields in machine learning are computer vision and natural language processing. In Chapter 4, you learned about some common computer vision scenarios with models that were already defined for you in ML Kit. In this chapter, you'll explore some natural language processing ones, including how to recognize text from digital ink, perform smart replies to messages, and extract entities such as addresses from text. These are all off-the-shelf models for these specific scenarios. If you want to create apps that use other natural language processing models, such as text classification, you'll have to create your own models using TensorFlow Lite, and then implement them on mobile. We'll explore that in later chapters.

Entity Extraction

When given large amounts of text, extracting important information from it can be a difficult task. Often information that follows a particular structure, such as an address, might be predictable for one country but work very differently in another, so having a rules-based approach to acquire the information can lead to a lot of coding.

For example, consider Figure 5-1, where I've sent a message to my friend Nizhoni with some details in it. As a human we can extract valuable information about this, such as "tomorrow at 5 PM," understanding that it's a date and time. But writing code to do that can be really difficult. It's hard enough trying to write code to understand formatted dates where different countries can structure them differently—i.e., 5/2 can be May 2nd or February 5th, depending on where you live—and trying to extract from text such as "tomorrow" is even more difficult! While ML may not be a perfect solution to this, it should really help with reducing the amount of code you need to write for common scenarios.

EntityExtractor

Hi <u>Nizhoni</u>, I'll be at 19 Fifth Avenue in San Jose
tomorrow at 5PM where we can discuss my book -
978-1492078197, if you can't reach me, call me at
555 213 2121 or email <u>lmoroney@area51</u>.net

EXTRACT ENTITIES

19 Fifth Avenue:Type - Address

tomorrow at 5PM:Type - DateTime

978-1492078197:Type - ISBN

978-1492078197:Type - Phone Number

555 213 2121:Type - Phone Number

lmoroney@area51.net:Type - Email Address

Figure 5-1. Extracting entities from text

As you can see beneath the text, a list was generated with the entities that were found.
So, for example, the "tomorrow at 5PM" was extracted as a datetime. Others like
phone numbers and email addresses were also extracted correctly. Often a value will
match multiple patterns, so, for example, the ISBN of the book starts with a three-
digit number, which matches the pattern of a phone number, so it was detected as
both entities!

With this in mind, ML Kit has entity extraction APIs that can create an app that can
read data like this—including addresses, phone numbers, email, and more. We'll
explore how to create such an app in this section.

Start Creating the App

I'm assuming you've gone through the steps of creating a new app as shown in Chapter 3. If you haven't, I'd recommend starting there first. As before, create a new single view app using Android Studio. Find the app-level build.gradle file and add the entity extraction libraries with it:

```
implementation 'com.google.mlkit:entity-extraction:16.0.0-beta1'
```

Note that at time of writing entity extraction was a beta product, so there may be some bugs. Also, if you are following this, be sure to check the entity extraction site at the ML Kit documentation for the most recent version (*https://oreil.ly/DP4WI*).

Create the Layout for the Activity

We'll keep the app really simple so we can focus on the entity extraction APIs, and as a result, you can see the app from Figure 5-1 has only three controls in it—one for entering the text, a button for triggering the extraction, and a text field for rendering out what the API detected.

This will keep the XML for the layout pretty simple:

```xml
<?xml version="1.0" encoding="utf-8"?>
<androidx.constraintlayout.widget.ConstraintLayout
    xmlns:android="http://schemas.android.com/apk/res/android"
    xmlns:app="http://schemas.android.com/apk/res-auto"
    xmlns:tools="http://schemas.android.com/tools"
    android:layout_width="match_parent"
    android:layout_height="match_parent"
    tools:context=".MainActivity">

    <LinearLayout
        android:layout_width="match_parent"
        android:layout_height="match_parent"
        android:orientation="vertical">

    <EditText
        android:id="@+id/txtInput"
        android:inputType="textMultiLine"
        android:singleLine="false"
        android:layout_width="match_parent"
        android:layout_height="240dp"/>

    <Button
        android:id="@+id/btnExtract"
        android:layout_width="wrap_content"
        android:layout_height="wrap_content"
        android:text="Extract Entities" />

    <TextView
        android:id="@+id/txtOutput"
```

```
        android:text=""
        android:layout_width="match_parent"
        android:layout_height="match_parent"/>

    </LinearLayout>
</androidx.constraintlayout.widget.ConstraintLayout>
```

The EditText field is set to be multiline (by using `singleLine="false"`) so we can enter text that looks more like a text message or tweet. All three controls are encapsulated within a LinearLayout so we can see them vertically distributed.

Write the Entity Extraction Code

When using the entity extraction APIs there are four phases that you'll follow:

1. Initialize the extractor by creating a client
2. Prepare the extractor by downloading the model
3. Use the extractor by annotating text
4. Parse the inferred annotations

Let's look at these one by one.

First, you'll initialize the extractor by creating the client. Because the extractor can work across many languages, it has been designed with a model per language, so at initialization time, you can pick the correct model by specifying the language. So, for example, if you wanted to use English, you could use code like:

```
val entityExtractor = EntityExtraction.getClient(
        EntityExtractorOptions.Builder(EntityExtractorOptions.ENGLISH)
                .build())
```

For other languages, you set the `EntityExtractorOptions` to a supported language using the built-in symbols. At the time of writing, 15 languages were supported, and you can check the documentation (*https://oreil.ly/aS55g*) to see the complete set.

Note that setting the *language* doesn't set the *domicile*. These are kept separately as different places with the same language may do things differently. So, for example, the language in both the US and the UK is *English*, but they use dates differently. To revisit the date example from earlier, in the US 5/2 is May 2nd, whereas in the UK it's February 5th. You'll configure this *after* you download the model.

To download the model you'll call the `downloadModelIfNeeded()` method, which is asynchronous and will call you back with a success or failure listener. I find the easiest thing to do is have a Boolean that you set to true or false depending on success or failure of the model download.

Here's an example:

```
fun prepareExtractor(){
    entityExtractor.downloadModelIfNeeded().addOnSuccessListener {
        extractorAvailable = true
    }
    .addOnFailureListener {
        extractorAvailable = false
    }
}
```

Once you have the extractor, you can then use it by building an `EntityExtraction Params` object with your text, as well as any desired options such as the locale.

Here's an example using the default parameters:

```
val params = EntityExtractionParams.Builder(userText).build()
entityExtractor.annotate(params)
               .addOnSuccessListener { result: List<EntityAnnotation> ->
               ...
```

Or, if you would prefer to, for example, set the locale, you can do so when creating the parameters. Here's an example:

```
val locale = Locale("en-uk")
val params = EntityExtractionParams.Builder(userText)
               .setPreferredLocale(locale)
               .build()
```

 You can learn more about the `EntityExtractionParams` object and explore the available parameters on the ML Kit documentation site (*https://oreil.ly/5A3yJ*).

When you call the annotate method using the given parameters, you'll get a list of `EntityAnnotation` objects back as the result in the on-success listener. Each entity annotation object will contain a number of entities, and each entity will have a string containing the text within the original text that matches an entity type, as well as the type itself, so, for example, where the text in Figure 5-1 says "lmoroney@area51.net," the entity extractor will extract that text, and put it into an entity with type "email." There are many different entities available—you can see the complete list of supported entities (*https://oreil.ly/Tzxt7*) on the ML Kit site.

So, for example, we could process the text with code like this:

```
entityExtractor.annotate(params)
    .addOnSuccessListener { result: List<EntityAnnotation> ->
        for (entityAnnotation in result) {
            outputString += entityAnnotation.annotatedText
            for (entity in entityAnnotation.entities) {
```

```
                outputString += ":" + getStringFor(entity)
            }
            outputString += "\n\n"
        }
        txtOutput.text = outputString
    }
```

Here, the entity extractor is called to annotate the text with the params; in the on-success listener, each entity annotation will have its entities enumerated, and for each of those entities the getStringFor helper method will be called to get the string.

This method simply creates a string with the entity type and the part of the original string that defined that entity (so, for example, as earlier, it might slice out "lmoroney@area51.net" as an email), so the helper method will generate a string that says something like "Type - Email : lmoroney@area51.net."

Here's the code:

```
private fun getStringFor(entity: Entity): String{
        var returnVal = "Type - "
        when (entity.type) {
            Entity.TYPE_ADDRESS -> returnVal += "Address"
            Entity.TYPE_DATE_TIME -> returnVal += "DateTime"
            Entity.TYPE_EMAIL -> returnVal += "Email Address"
            Entity.TYPE_FLIGHT_NUMBER -> returnVal += "Flight Number"
            Entity.TYPE_IBAN -> returnVal += "IBAN"
            Entity.TYPE_ISBN -> returnVal += "ISBN"
            Entity.TYPE_MONEY -> returnVal += "Money"
            Entity.TYPE_PAYMENT_CARD -> returnVal += "Credit/Debit Card"
            Entity.TYPE_PHONE -> returnVal += "Phone Number"
            Entity.TYPE_TRACKING_NUMBER -> returnVal += "Tracking Number"
            Entity.TYPE_URL -> returnVal += "URL"
            else -> returnVal += "Address"
        }
        return returnVal
    }
```

Putting It All Together

All that remains to be done is to handle the user interface code, capturing the input text, initializing the extractor, and calling the entity extraction when the user presses the button.

So, in your MainActivity you can update the module variables and the onCreate like this:

```
val entityExtractor = EntityExtraction.getClient(
        EntityExtractorOptions.Builder(EntityExtractorOptions.ENGLISH)
                .build())
var extractorAvailable:Boolean = false
lateinit var txtInput: EditText
```

```kotlin
lateinit var txtOutput: TextView
lateinit var btnExtract: Button
override fun onCreate(savedInstanceState: Bundle?) {
    super.onCreate(savedInstanceState)
    setContentView(R.layout.activity_main)
    txtInput = findViewById(R.id.txtInput)
    txtOutput = findViewById(R.id.txtOutput)
    btnExtract = findViewById(R.id.btnExtract)
    prepareExtractor()
    btnExtract.setOnClickListener {
        doExtraction()
    }
}
```

The `prepareExtractor` helper function just ensures the extractor model is available:

```kotlin
fun prepareExtractor(){
    entityExtractor.downloadModelIfNeeded().addOnSuccessListener {
        extractorAvailable = true
    }
    .addOnFailureListener {
        extractorAvailable = false
    }
}
```

And when the user presses the button, `doExtraction()` is called, which handles the extraction process and updates the output:

```kotlin
fun doExtraction(){
        if (extractorAvailable) {
            val userText = txtInput.text.toString()
            val params = EntityExtractionParams.Builder(userText)
                .build()
            var outputString = ""
            entityExtractor.annotate(params)
                .addOnSuccessListener { result: List<EntityAnnotation> ->
                    for (entityAnnotation in result) {
                        outputString += entityAnnotation.annotatedText
                        for (entity in entityAnnotation.entities) {
                            outputString += ":" + getStringFor(entity)
                        }
                        outputString += "\n\n"
                    }
                    txtOutput.text = outputString
                }
                .addOnFailureListener {
                }
        }
    }
```

That's it for this app! This is a super simple one, where I just wanted to focus on getting you up and running with entity extraction quickly. You could use the extracted entities to create useful features—such as launching other apps on your device using

Android Intents. Examples might be to launch the Maps app when the user touches on an extracted address, or launching the Phone app to make a phone call, etc. This type of entity extraction also powers smart assistants such as Google Assistant, Siri, or Alexa.

Handwriting and Other Recognition

It's a common scenario to have handwriting recognized on touch devices, where you can draw strokes on a surface, and those strokes are then turned into text. So, for example, consider Figure 5-2, where I've created a very simple app that recognizes my terrible handwriting.

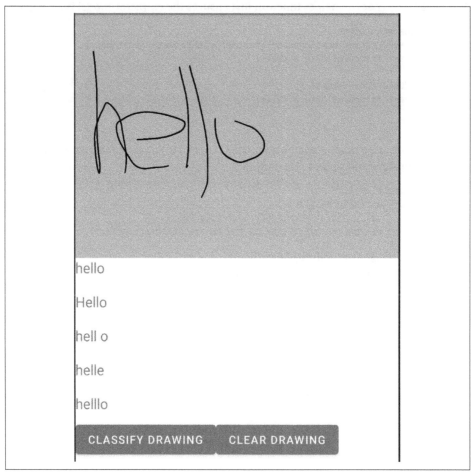

Figure 5-2. Recognizing handwriting with ML Kit

Let's explore what it would take to build an app like this.

Start the App

As before, create a new single view app (details in Chapter 3), using Android Studio. Edit the app's build.gradle file to add a dependency to ML Kit's digital ink recognition libraries:

```
implementation 'com.google.mlkit:digital-ink-recognition:16.1.0'
```

These libraries support many different languages via separate models, so they'll need to download the models in order for you to use them. This means that you'll need to update your Android Manifest to allow access to the internet and to storage, or the app won't have access to the model:

```
<uses-permission android:name="android.permission.ACCESS_NETWORK_STATE" />
<uses-permission android:name="android.permission.INTERNET" />
<uses-permission android:name="android.permission.WRITE_EXTERNAL_STORAGE" />
```

Next you will explore how to implement a surface on which you will draw your handwriting.

Creating a Drawing Surface

The easiest way to do this is to create a custom view that contains a Canvas that will be used as the drawing surface.

I won't go into detail here on how to put that all together—the code is in the GitHub for this book—but the important point is that when capturing the user's strokes on the screen, as well as drawing them on the Canvas so you can see them, you also have to add them to an ML Kit stroke builder object, which in turn can be used to construct an Ink object, which the model will accept and parse. You can also learn more about custom views at *https://developer.android.com/guide/topics/ui/custom-components*.

When drawing on a user interface there are generally three methods you need to implement—these are `touchStart()`, when the user first touches the screen, `touchMove()` , when they drag their finger or stylus across the screen, and `touchUp()` , when they remove their finger or stylus from the screen. These three methods in tandem will form a stroke. All three of them are captured by the `onTou chEvent` method on a view, so we can call them based on the action that is detected, like this:

```
override fun onTouchEvent(event: MotionEvent): Boolean {
    motionTouchEventX = event.x
    motionTouchEventY = event.y
    motionTouchEventT = System.currentTimeMillis()

    when (event.action) {
```

```
            MotionEvent.ACTION_DOWN -> touchStart()
            MotionEvent.ACTION_MOVE -> touchMove()
            MotionEvent.ACTION_UP -> touchUp()
        }
        return true
    }
```

So, when the touch starts, we want to do two things. First, start the path (that is used to draw your handwriting on the screen) and move it to the current touch point. Then, we will create a new strokeBuilder in ML Kit and capture the current point and the current time so as to create an Ink object that ML Kit can parse later:

```
private fun touchStart() {
    // For drawing on the screen
    path.reset()
    path.moveTo(motionTouchEventX, motionTouchEventY)
    // Initialize the stroke to capture the ink for MLKit
    currentX = motionTouchEventX
    currentY = motionTouchEventY
    strokeBuilder = Ink.Stroke.builder()
    strokeBuilder.addPoint(Ink.Point.create(motionTouchEventX,
                                             motionTouchEventY,
                                             motionTouchEventT))
}
```

As the user drags their finger across the screen, the touchMove() function will be called. This will first update the path variable that is used to update the screen, and then update the strokeBuilder, so that the current stroke can be turned into an Ink object that ML Kit recognizes:

```
private fun touchMove() {
    val dx = Math.abs(motionTouchEventX - currentX)
    val dy = Math.abs(motionTouchEventY - currentY)
    if (dx >= touchTolerance || dy >= touchTolerance) {
        path.quadTo(currentX, currentY, (motionTouchEventX + currentX) / 2,
                                        (motionTouchEventY + currentY) / 2)
        currentX = motionTouchEventX
        currentY = motionTouchEventY
     // Update the Stroke Builder so ML Kit can understand the ink
        strokeBuilder.addPoint(Ink.Point.create(motionTouchEventX,
                                                 motionTouchEventY,
                                                 motionTouchEventT))
        extraCanvas.drawPath(path, paint)
    }
    invalidate()
}
```

Finally, as the user removes their finger from the surface, the touch up will be called. At this point, we should reset the path, so that when drawing on the screen next time, we'll be starting afresh. For ML Kit we should finish the stroke by adding one last point at the position where the user removed their finger, and then add the finished stroke (started at touch down, drawn during touch move, and finished at touch up) to our ink with an `inkBuilder`:

```
private fun touchUp() {
    strokeBuilder.addPoint(Ink.Point.create(motionTouchEventX,
                                             motionTouchEventY,
                                             motionTouchEventT))
    inkBuilder.addStroke(strokeBuilder.build())
    path.reset()
}
```

So, over time, as you create strokes on the screen, the `inkBuilder` will stroke them in its collection of strokes.

When you want to get all of the strokes from the `inkBuilder`, you can do so by calling its `build` method, like this:

```
fun getInk(): Ink{
    val ink = inkBuilder.build()
    return ink
}
```

For the code that you can download, I implemented all of these in a `CustomDrawing Surface` view, which can then be added to the activity layout like this:

```
<com.odmlbook.digitalinktest.CustomDrawingSurface
    android:id="@+id/customDrawingSurface"
    android:layout_width="match_parent"
    android:layout_height="300dp" />
```

Parsing the Ink with ML Kit

In the previous section you saw a custom drawing surface on which the user can write, and their strokes are captured into an Ink object. This Ink object can then be used with ML Kit to interpret the strokes into text. The steps to do this are as follows:

1. Initialize a model identifier object with the specs of the model you want to use—for example, the language that the model will recognize.

2. Build a reference to the model from the model identifier.

3. Use a remote model manager object to download the model.

4. Create a recognizer object from the model.

5. Pass the ink to the recognizer and parse the returned results.

So, in the activity that hosts the custom drawing surface that generates the ink, you'll need to do all of these steps. Let's walk through what this looks like in practice.

First, the `initializeRegonition()` function will create an instance of `DigitalInkRe`
`cognitionModelIdentifier` and use this to build a reference to the model, which it
will then download:

```
fun initializeRecognition(){
    val modelIdentifier: DigitalInkRecognitionModelIdentifier? =
        DigitalInkRecognitionModelIdentifier.fromLanguageTag("en-US")
    model = DigitalInkRecognitionModel.builder(modelIdentifier!!).build()
    remoteModelManager.download(model!!, DownloadConditions.Builder().build())
}
```

Note the `fromLanguageTag` method, where I passed `en-US` as the language code. As
you might expect, this will implement the model to recognize English/US text. For a
full list of codes, check out the ML Kit sample app for digital ink (*https://oreil.ly/
tHRS3*), where they have code to connect to ML Kit to download the full list of currently supported codes.

Once the remote model manager downloads the model, you'll be able to use it to use
inference on your ink strokes. So, you'll first create a recognizer by calling the `get`
`Client` method on the `DigitalInkRecognition` object from ML Kit, and pass the
model you just specified and downloaded as the desired model from which to construct the recognizer:

```
recognizer = DigitalInkRecognition.getClient(
                    DigitalInkRecognizerOptions.builder(model!!).build() )
```

Then, you can get the ink from the drawing surface you created earlier:

```
val thisInk = customDrawingSurface.getInk()
```

You can then call the `recognize` method on your recognizer, passing it the ink. ML
Kit will call you back with the result, and you can catch this in an on-success or on-
failure listener:

```
recognizer.recognize(thisInk)
            .addOnSuccessListener { result: RecognitionResult ->
                var outputString = ""
                txtOutput.text = ""
                for (candidate in result.candidates){
                    outputString+=candidate.text + "\n\n"
                }
                txtOutput.text = outputString
            }
            .addOnFailureListener { e: Exception ->
                Log.e("Digital Ink Test", "Error during recognition: $e")
            }
```

With the success, you'll get back a "result" object containing a number of result candidates. In this case I just loop through them all and output them. They're presorted
into their likelihood of matching your strokes.

So, referring back to Figure 5-2, you can see that my strokes were most likely "hello" (with a lowercase H), followed by "Hello" and then "hell o" with a space between the second "l" and the "o."

Given the many languages supported, this gives you a really powerful tool for understanding your users' input, should you want to create an interface for handwriting!

For example, check out my wonderful attempt at writing "hello" in Chinese in Figure 5-3, and how the app was able to parse it into the correct characters!

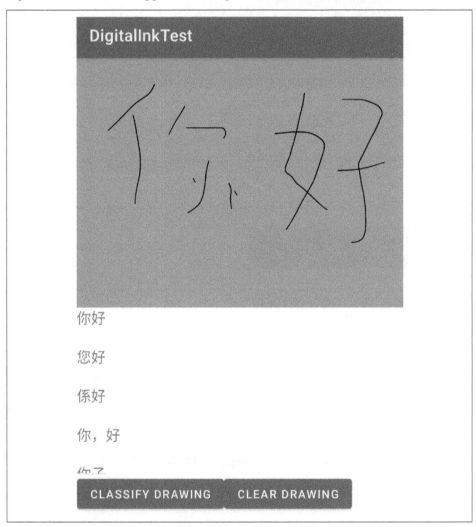

Figure 5-3. Using the Chinese language model

Smart Reply to Conversations

Another example of a turnkey model that you can use is the Smart Reply model. With this, you can give the model the contents of a conversation, and it can figure out what might be the reply to it. You've probably seen this in use now on a number of websites and apps, and if you'd wondered how to implement it, this API will give you a great head start.

You can see it in action in Figure 5-4.

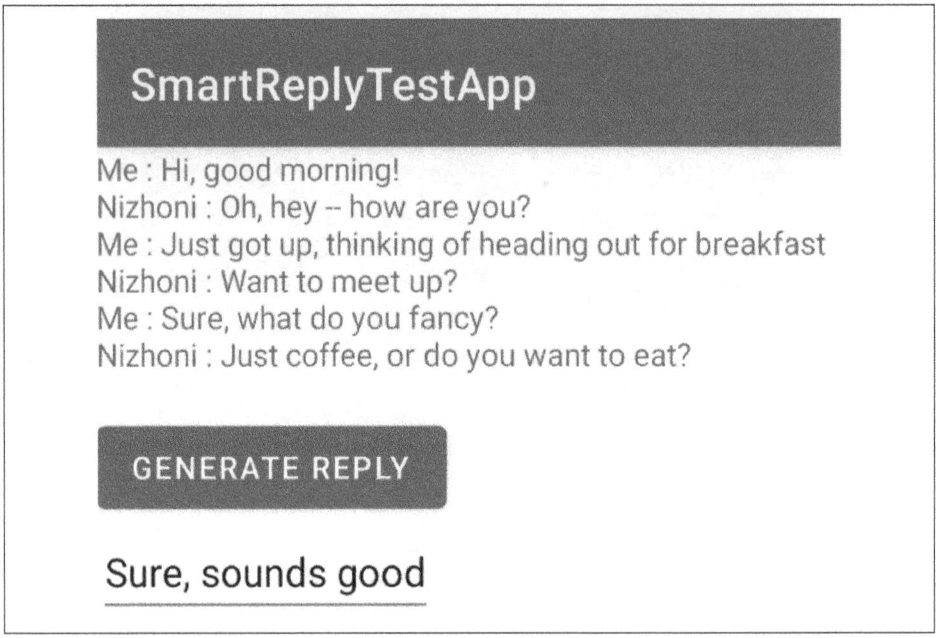

SmartReplyTestApp

Me : Hi, good morning!
Nizhoni : Oh, hey -- how are you?
Me : Just got up, thinking of heading out for breakfast
Nizhoni : Want to meet up?
Me : Sure, what do you fancy?
Nizhoni : Just coffee, or do you want to eat?

GENERATE REPLY

Sure, sounds good

Figure 5-4. Using Smart Reply

Here, I mocked up a conversation with a friend of mine, where we are talking about breakfast. She asks me a question, "Just coffee, or do you want to eat?" and when I press the Generate Reply button, the recommended answer is "Sure, sounds good." It doesn't really answer the question, but it's a decent enough reply, as it captures my vernacular—when asked if I wanted to meet up, my response was "Sure, what do you fancy?" so now the generated phrase also begins with the word "Sure."

Let's look at how this app was built.

Start the App

As before, create a new app with a single activity. Refer back to Chapter 3 for the steps if you aren't familiar.

When you are done, you can include the Smart Reply libraries by adding the following to your build.gradle file:

```
implementation 'com.google.mlkit:smart-reply:16.1.1'
```

After a Gradle sync, the libraries will be ready and you can start coding.

Mock a Conversation

The Smart Reply APIs require a conversation to be passed to them, and the last element in the conversation *not* to be you talking. To create a conversation, you use the TextMessage type for each item in the conversation and add them to an ArrayList. The type can be created either for a local user (you) or a remote user (your friend) by calling createForLocalUser or createForRemoteUser, respectively. It's important to call the right ones so the API can know the difference between you and other people, and it can generate the smart reply based on your vernacular.

I wrote code like this to initialize the mock conversation:

```
// Class level variables
var outputText = ""
var conversation : ArrayList<TextMessage> = ArrayList<TextMessage>()

fun initializeConversation(){
        val friendName: String = "Nizhoni"
        addConversationItem("Hi, good morning!")
        addConversationItem("Oh, hey -- how are you?", friendName)
        addConversationItem("Just got up, thinking of heading out for breakfast")
        addConversationItem("Want to meet up?",friendName)
        addConversationItem("Sure, what do you fancy?")
        addConversationItem("Just coffee, or do you want to eat?", friendName)
        conversationView.text = outputText
    }

    private fun addConversationItem(item: String){
        outputText += "Me : $item\n"
        conversation.add(TextMessage.createForLocalUser(
                                item, System.currentTimeMillis()))
    }

    private fun addConversationItem(item: String, who: String){
        outputText += who + " : " + item + "\n"
        conversation.add(TextMessage.createForRemoteUser(
                                item, System.currentTimeMillis(),who))
    }
```

The `initializeConversation()` method simply calls `addConversationItem` with the string, and an optional second parameter with my friend's name in it. I then overloaded `addConversationItem` so that if only one string is passed, then a `TextMessage` for the current user is added, or if two strings are passed, then a `TextMessage` for the remote user is added.

`outputText` is the text of the conversation that will be added to a TextView later.

So, now that we have a conversation that is made up of `TextMessages` that were created either for local or remote users, we can use it to generate a predicted next text.

Generating a Smart Reply

The app shown in Figure 5-4 is available in the GitHub repo for this book. In that screenshot you can see a Generate Reply button—to get a smart reply, you'll simply initialize a Smart Reply client with `SmartReply.getClient()` within the `OnClickLis` tener for this button.

You pass your conversation to its `suggestReplies` method, and if there's a successful inference, you'll get a result object back:

```
val smartReplyGenerator = SmartReply.getClient()

smartReplyGenerator.suggestReplies(conversation)
                   .addOnSuccessListener { result ->
}
```

This result object contains a list of suggestions, each of which contains a text property with the text of the suggestion. So you could, for example, set the contents of an `Edit Text` control with the top-rated reply like this:

```
txtInput.setText(result.suggestions[0].text.toString())
```

Or, if you prefer, you could iterate through each of them and generate some kind of picker where the user can choose which of the suggestions they want to take.

Summary

In this chapter, you looked at how to get started with a number of scenarios where an ML model, or a set of models, was already available to you to handle text. You started with looking at a full string and parsing common entities out of it, like addresses and phone numbers. You then explored how an app could capture a user's handwriting, and an ML Kit model could then convert that handwriting into text. Finally you had a quick look at Smart Reply, so you could create an app that uses ML to give suggested replies to a conversation!

These are all off-the-shelf models, but they can give you a really nice head start into machine learning in your apps. The logical next step is to extend this into using custom models that you create from your own data—we'll begin exploring that in Chapter 8. In Chapters 6 and 7, you'll cover the same ground that you covered in the previous two chapters, but with a focus on getting started with the same vision and text scenarios on iOS using Swift!

## CHAPTER 6

Computer Vision Apps with ML Kit on iOS

Chapter 3 gave you an introduction to ML Kit and how it could be used to do face detection in a mobile app. In Chapter 4 you then took a look at how to do some more sophisticated scenarios on Android devices—image labeling and classification and object detection in both still images and video. In this chapter, we'll see how to use ML Kit for the same scenarios, but on iOS using Swift. Let's start with image labeling and classification.

Image Labeling and Classification

A staple of computer vision is the concept of image classification, where you give a computer an image, and the computer will tell you what the image contains. At the highest level, you could give it a picture of a dog, like that in Figure 6-1, and it will tell you that the image contains a dog.

ML Kit's image labeling takes this a bit further—and it will give you a list of things it "sees" in the image, each with levels of probability. So, for the image in Figure 6-1, not only will it see a dog, it may also see a pet, a room, a jacket, and more. Building an app to do this on iOS is pretty simple, so let's explore that step by step.

 At the time of writing, ML Kit's pods give some issues when running on a Mac with the iOS simulator. Apps will still run on devices, and also with the "My Mac (designed for iPad)" runtime setting in Xcode.

Figure 6-1. Sample image for iPhone image classification

Step 1: Create the App in Xcode

You'll use Xcode to create the app. Use the App template in Xcode and ensure that your interface type is Storyboard and the language is Swift. If you aren't familiar with these steps, refer back to Chapter 3 where we went through them in more detail. Call your app whatever you want, but in my case, I used the name MLKitImageClassifier. When you're done, close Xcode. In the next step, you'll add a pod file, and when you install this, it gives you a new file to open Xcode with.

Step 2: Create the Podfile

This step requires that you have CocoaPods installed on your development box. CocoaPods is a dependency management tool that makes it easy for you to add third-party libraries to your iOS app. As ML Kit ships from Google, it's not built-in to Xcode, and as a result, you'll need to add it to any apps as a "pod" from CocoaPods. You can find CocoaPods install instructions at *http://cocoapods.org*, and I'll give you the code that shows you how to pick the appropriate pod as we walk through each example.

In the directory where you created your project, add a new file. Call it *podfile* with no extension. After you save it, your directory structure with your project should look like Figure 6-2.

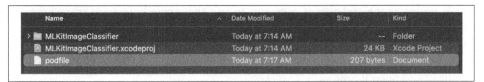

Figure 6-2. Adding a Podfile to the project folder

Edit the contents of this file to look like this:

```
platform :ios, '10.0'

target 'MLKitImageClassifier' do
        pod 'GoogleMLKit/ImageLabeling'
end
```

Note the line beginning with target. After target, the name of your project should be in the quotes, which in the preceding case is MLKitImageClassifier, but if you used something else, make sure you change the code to fit your project name.

Once you've done and saved this, use Terminal and navigate to the folder. Type the command **pod install**. You should see output like Figure 6-3.

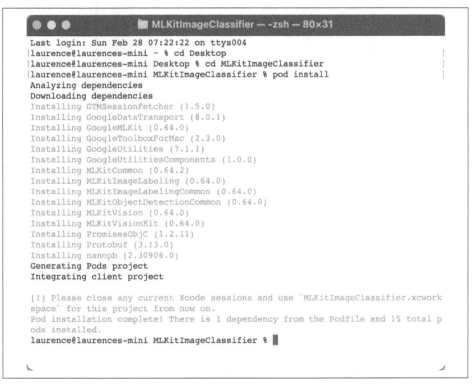

Figure 6-3. Installing the image classifier CocoaPod

You'll notice at the end that it asks you to use the *.xcworkspace* file from now on. When you created your project in step 1, you would open it in Xcode using the *.xcproject* file. Those files cannot handle external libraries that are included via pods, but *.xcworkspace* ones can. As such, you should use that file going forward. So go ahead and open it now with Xcode!

Step 3: Set Up the Storyboard

The storyboard file called *main.storyboard* will contain the user interface for your app. Add a UIImage view to it and set its property to Aspect Fit. Then, add a button control, and change its text to "Do Inference." Finally add a UILabel and use the attributes inspector to set its Lines property to "0" to ensure it will have multiple lines of text. Resize the label to give it plenty of space. When you're done, your storyboard should look like Figure 6-4.

Figure 6-4. Creating the simple storyboard

Next up you'll need to create outlets for the image and label controls, and an action for the button. You do this by opening a separate window and control-dragging the control onto the *ViewController.swift* file. If you aren't familiar with this, please refer back to Chapter 3 for a detailed example.

It might be confusing as to when you need outlets and when you need actions, so I like to think of it like this. If you want to read or set properties on the control, you need an "outlet." So, for example, we will need to *read* the contents of the image view control to pass to ML Kit to have it classified. You will also need to *write* to the contents of the Label to render the results. So, as a result, they will both need an outlet set up, and the name of that outlet is how you'll refer to these controls in your code. When you need to respond to the user doing something with the control—like pressing the button—you'll need an "action." When you drag the controls onto your code editor, you'll be given the option to use an outlet or action, so use that to create outlets for the UIImageView and the Label now, and call them imageView and lblOut put, respectively. Then create an action for the button. You can call this action doInference.

When you're done, your *ViewController.swift* file should look like this:

```swift
import UIKit

class ViewController: UIViewController {

    @IBOutlet weak var imageView: UIImageView!
    @IBOutlet weak var lblOutput: UILabel!
    @IBAction func doInference(_ sender: Any) {
    }
    override func viewDidLoad() {
        super.viewDidLoad()
        // Do any additional setup after loading the view.
    }


}
```

You'll edit that next to implement the image classification code. Before you can do that, though, you'll need an image to classify! You can pick any image from your filesystem and drag it onto Xcode. Drop it into your project, in the same folder as your storyboard. You'll get a dialog asking you to choose options. Keep the defaults here, but ensure that "Add to targets" is set with the checkbox beside your project name checked. This will ensure that the image is compiled into your app so at runtime it can be loaded.

Step 4: Edit the View Controller Code to Use ML Kit

Right now your app can't do anything, the image hasn't been loaded, and no code for handling the button press has been written. Let's go through building that functionality in this section.

First of all, to load the image, you can add code to the `viewDidLoad` function that gets loaded when the app first starts. This is as simple as just setting the `.image` property on `imageView`:

```
// On view did load we only need to initialize the image,
// so we can do that here
override func viewDidLoad() {
    super.viewDidLoad()
    // Do any additional setup after loading the view.
    imageView.image = UIImage(named:"fig6-1dog.jpg")
}
```

If you were to launch the app now, the picture would render, but not much else would happen. Typically your user would press the button and you would want to respond to that action. You already have the action `doInference` set up, so let's have it call a function called `getLabels`, using the image within the `imageView` as a parameter:

```
@IBAction func doInference(_ sender: Any) {
    getLabels(with: imageView.image!)
}
```

Xcode will complain because you don't have this function implemented yet. That's OK—you'll do that next. The job of this function is to take the contents of the image and pass them to ML Kit to get a set of labels back. So, before you can write that, you'll need to ensure that you have referenced the relevant ML Kit libraries. At the top of your *ViewController.swift* file, add these lines:

```
// Import the MLKit Vision and Image Labeling libraries
import MLKitVision
import MLKitImageLabeling
```

To use ML Kit for image labeling, you'll need to do the following tasks:

- Convert the image into a VisionImage type.
- Set up options for the image labeler and initialize it with these options.
- Call the image labeler and catch the asynchronous callback.

So, to first convert the image to a `VisionImage` you'll write code like this:

```
let visionImage = VisionImage(image: image)
visionImage.orientation = image.imageOrientation
```

Then you'll initialize the labeler by setting up some options. In this case, you can keep it simple and just have the options use a confidence threshold. The goal, while it can label many things in an image, is to return the ones above a certain probability. So, for example, the image in Figure 6-1, despite being a dog, will actually have a little over a 0.4 probability (i.e., 40%) that it's also a cat! So to see this, you can set the confidence threshold to 0.4:

```
let options = ImageLabelerOptions()
options.confidenceThreshold = 0.4
let labeler = ImageLabeler.imageLabeler(options: options)
```

Now that you have a labeler and an image in the desired format, you can pass it to the labeler. This is an asynchronous operation, so you won't lock up your user interface while it processes. Instead, you can specify a callback function that it will call when the inference is complete. The labeler will return two objects: "labels" for the inferences, and "error" if it fails. You can then pass these to a function of your own (called processResult in this case) to handle them:

```
labeler.process(visionImage) { labels, error in
    self.processResult(from: labels, error: error)
}
```

For convenience, here's the entire getLabels func:

```
// This is called when the user presses the button
func getLabels(with image: UIImage){
    // Get the image from the UI Image element
    // and set its orientation
    let visionImage = VisionImage(image: image)
    visionImage.orientation = image.imageOrientation

    // Create Image Labeler options, and set the
    // threshold to 0.4 so we will ignore all classes
    // with a probability of 0.4 or less
    let options = ImageLabelerOptions()
    options.confidenceThreshold = 0.4

    // Initialize the labeler with these options
    let labeler = ImageLabeler.imageLabeler(options: options)

    // And then process the image, with the
    // callback going to self.processresult
    labeler.process(visionImage) { labels, error in
        self.processResult(from: labels, error: error)
    }
}
```

After the labeler has done its job, it will call the processResult function. If you've entered the preceding code, Xcode is probably complaining because it can't find this function. So, let's implement that next!

The labels collection returned by ML Kit is an array of `ImageLabel` objects. So you'll need your function to use that as the type for the `from` parameter. These objects have a `text` property, with the label description (i.e., `cat`) and a confidence property containing the probability that the image matches that label (i.e., 0.4). So you can iterate through the collection and build a string with these values with this code. It will then set the `lblOutput` text to the string you constructed. Here's the complete code:

```
// This gets called by the labeler's callback
func processResult(from labels: [ImageLabel]?, error: Error?){
    // String to hold the labels
    var labeltexts = ""
    // Check that we have valid labels first
    guard let labels = labels else{
        return
    }
    // ...and if we do we can iterate through
    // the set to get the description and confidence
    for label in labels{
        let labelText = label.text + " : " +
                        label.confidence.description + "\n"
        labeltexts += labelText
    }
    // And when we're done we can update the UI
    // with the list of labels
    lblOutput.text = labeltexts
}
```

And that's everything you need! When you run the app and press the button, you'll see something like Figure 6-5.

And you can see that while ML Kit was 99% sure it was looking at a dog, it was also 40% sure that it might be a cat!

Understandably this is a super simple app, but hopefully it demonstrates how you can use image labeling quickly and easily on iOS in just a few lines of code using ML Kit!

8:25

Do Inference

Dog : 0.99002767
Pet : 0.96211964
Room : 0.6968201
Fur : 0.67044264
Pattern : 0.52595145
Chair : 0.4811045
Jacket : 0.43941522
Cat : 0.40040797

Figure 6-5. Running inference with this app on the dog picture

Object Detection in iOS with ML Kit

Next, let's explore a similar scenario to image classification, where we go a step further. Instead of having the device recognize *what* it sees in an image, let's also have it recognize *where* in the image it sees the object, using a bounding box to draw that for the user.

So, as an example, see Figure 6-6. The app saw this picture and detected three objects within it.

Figure 6-6. Object detector app in iOS

Step 1: Get Started

Creating this app is pretty straightforward. Create a new iOS app as before. Give it whatever name you like but ensure that you're using Swift and storyboards in the new project settings dialog. In this case I called my project *MLKitObjectDetector*.

In the project directory, you'll create a Podfile as you did in the previous section, but this time you'll want to specify that you want to use ML Kit's object detection libraries instead of the image labeling ones. Your Podfile should look something like this:

```
platform :ios, '10.0'
# Comment the next line if you're not using Swift and don't want to use dynamic
# frameworks
use_frameworks!


target 'MLKitObjectDetector' do
        pod 'GoogleMLKit/ObjectDetection'
end
```

Note that the target setting should be the name of the project as you created it in Xcode (in my case, I used *MLKitObjectDetector*) and the pod should be *GoogleMLKit/ObjectDetection*.

When you're done, run **pod install** to download the required dependencies, and you'll have a new *.xcworkspace* file created for you. Open this to continue.

Step 2: Create Your UI on the Storyboard

This app is even simpler than the image labeling one in that you'll have only two UI elements—an image that you want to perform object detection on, and on which you'll draw the bounding boxes, and a button that the user will press to trigger the object detection. So, add a UIImageView and a button to the storyboard. Edit the button to change its text to "Detect Objects." Your storyboard should look something like Figure 6-7 when you're done.

Figure 6-7. The storyboard for the object detection app

You'll want to create an outlet for the image view and an action for the button. If you're not familiar with these, I'd recommend going back to Chapter 3 and working through the example there, as well as doing the image labeling one earlier in this chapter.

When you're done, your *ViewController.swift* file will have the outlet and action defined and should look like this:

```
import UIKit

class ViewController: UIViewController {
    @IBOutlet weak var imageView: UIImageView!
    @IBAction func doObjectDetection(_ sender: Any) {
    }

    override func viewDidLoad() {
        super.viewDidLoad()
        // Do any additional setup after loading the view.
    }


}
```

In the preceding code, I named the outlet for the UIImageView `imageView`, and the action for pressing the button `doObjectDetection`.

You'll need to add an image to your project, so that you can load it into the UIImage-View. In this case I have one called *bird.jpg*, and the code to load it in `viewDidLoad()` will look like this:

```
imageView.image = UIImage(named: "bird.jpg")
```

Step 3: Create a Subview for Annotation

This app draws bounding boxes on top of the image when it gets detected objects back from ML Kit. Before we do the inference, let's make sure that we can draw on the image. To do this, you'll need to have a subview drawn on top of the image. This subview will be transparent and will have the rectangles for the bounding boxes drawn on it. As it's on top of the image and transparent except for the rectangles, it will appear as if the rectangles are drawn on the image.

Declare this view in your *ViewController.swift* as a UIView type. With Swift, you can specify how to instantiate the view with things like a precondition that the view has already loaded, ensuring that this view will load *after* the UIImageView containing your picture and making it easier to load it on top of it! See the following:

```
/// An overlay view that displays detection annotations.
private lazy var annotationOverlayView: UIView = {
  precondition(isViewLoaded)
  let annotationOverlayView = UIView(frame: .zero)
  annotationOverlayView
      .translatesAutoresizingMaskIntoConstraints = false
  return annotationOverlayView
}()
```

Once you've declared it, you can now instantiate and configure it within your view
DidLoad function, adding it as a subview to the imageView. You can also activate
it using NSLayoutConstraint to make sure that it matches the dimensions of
imageView:

```
override func viewDidLoad() {
        super.viewDidLoad()
        // Do any additional setup after loading the view.
        imageView.image = UIImage(named: "bird.jpg")
        imageView.addSubview(annotationOverlayView)
        NSLayoutConstraint.activate([
          annotationOverlayView.topAnchor.constraint(
              equalTo: imageView.topAnchor),
          annotationOverlayView.leadingAnchor.constraint(
              equalTo: imageView.leadingAnchor),
          annotationOverlayView.trailingAnchor.constraint(
              equalTo: imageView.trailingAnchor),
          annotationOverlayView.bottomAnchor.constraint(
              equalTo: imageView.bottomAnchor),
        ])

    }
```

Step 4: Perform the Object Detection

Before you can use the object detection APIs from ML Kit, you need to include them
in your code file. You can do this with:

```
import MLKitVision
import MLKitObjectDetection
```

Then, within the action you created for when the user presses the button, add this
code:

```
runObjectDetection(with: imageView.image!)
```

Xcode will complain that this function hasn't yet been created. That's OK. You'll create it now! Create the runObjectDetection function within your *ViewController.swift*
file:

```
func runObjectDetection(with image: UIImage){
}
```

Similar to the image labeling earlier in the chapter, the process of performing object detection with ML Kit is very straightforward:

- Convert your image into a `VisionImage`.

- Create an options object with the options you choose and instantiate an object detector with these options.

- Pass the image to the object detector and catch its response in a callback.

Let's walk through how you can do each of these steps within the function you just created. First, to convert your image to a `VisionImage`:

```
let visionImage = VisionImage(image: image)
```

Then create the options object and instantiate an object detector with them:

```
let options = ObjectDetectorOptions()
options.detectorMode = .singleImage
options.shouldEnableClassification = true
options.shouldEnableMultipleObjects = true
let objectDetector = ObjectDetector.objectDetector(
                            options: options)
```

Explore the ML Kit documentation for the option types; the ones I have used here are very commonly used. `EnableClassification` not only gives you the bounding boxes but ML Kit's classification of the object. The base model (that you're using here) only recognizes five very generic object types like "Fashion Item" or "Food Item," so manage your expectations accordingly! The `EnableMultipleObjects` option, when set, as its name suggests, will allow you to detect multiple objects as in Figure 6-6, where three items—the bird and two flowers—were detected and bounding boxes plotted.

Finally, you'll pass the image to the object detector to get it to infer the labels and bounding boxes for objects it spots within the image. This is an asynchronous function, so you'll need to specify the function to call back when the inference is complete. ML Kit will return a `detectedObjects` list and an error object, so you can simply pass these to a function that you'll create next:

```
objectDetector.process(visionImage)
    { detectedObjects, error in
        self.processResult(from: detectedObjects, error: error)
    }
```

Step 5: Handle the Callback

In the previous step we defined the callback function, `processResult`. So let's first create that. It takes `detectedObjects`, which is an array of `Objects`, as the `from:` parameter, and an `Error` object as the `error:` parameter. Here's the code:

```
func processResult(from detectedObjects: [Object]?,
                    error: Error?){
}
```

Next, we'll exit if the `detectedObjects` array is empty, so that we don't waste time trying to draw or update the overlay:

```
guard let detectedObjects = detectedObjects else{
    return
}
```

Next, you'll iterate through all of the detected objects and draw the bounding boxes that were detected.

Handling the callback to collect the bounding boxes is a little bit more complicated than the image classification scenario you explored earlier in this chapter. This is because the image *as rendered on the screen* likely has different dimensions than the underlying image. When you pass the image to ML Kit, you are passing the entire image, so the bounding boxes you get returned are relative to the image. If this doesn't make sense, consider it this way. Imagine your image is 10,000 × 10,000 pixels. What gets rendered on your screen might be 600 × 600 pixels. When the bounding boxes are returned from ML Kit, they will be relative to the image at 10,000 × 10,000, so you will need to transform them to the coordinates that are correct for the displayed image.

So, you'll first calculate a transformation matrix for the image, which you can apply to get a transformed rectangle.

Here's the complete code. I won't go through it in detail, but the main point is to get the size of the underlying image and scale it to the size of the image as rendered in the UIImage control:

```
private func transformMatrix() -> CGAffineTransform {
    guard let image = imageView.image else {
            return CGAffineTransform() }
    let imageViewWidth = imageView.frame.size.width
    let imageViewHeight = imageView.frame.size.height
    let imageWidth = image.size.width
    let imageHeight = image.size.height

    let imageViewAspectRatio =
      imageViewWidth / imageViewHeight
    let imageAspectRatio = imageWidth / imageHeight
    let scale =
      (imageViewAspectRatio > imageAspectRatio)
        ? imageViewHeight / imageHeight :
          imageViewWidth / imageWidth

    // Image view's `contentMode` is `scaleAspectFit`,
    // which scales the image to fit the size of the
    // image view by maintaining the aspect ratio.
```

```
    //  Multiple by `scale` to get image's original size.
    let scaledImageWidth = imageWidth * scale
    let scaledImageHeight = imageHeight * scale

     let xValue =
      (imageViewWidth - scaledImageWidth) / CGFloat(2.0)

     let yValue =
      (imageViewHeight - scaledImageHeight) / CGFloat(2.0)

    var transform = CGAffineTransform.identity.translatedBy(
                      x: xValue, y: yValue)
    transform = transform.scaledBy(x: scale, y: scale)
    return transform
}
```

So now that you can transform the image, the next thing is to iterate through each of the objects, pulling the results and transforming them with it. You'll do this by looping through the detected objects and using their frame property, which contains the frame of the bounding box.

The loop for this is now simple thanks to the transform matrix you just created:

```
for obj in detectedObjects{
    let transform = self.transformMatrix()
    let transformedRect = obj.frame.applying(transform)
}
```

Given that you now have a transformed rectangle that matches the rendered image, you will next want to draw this rectangle. Earlier you created the annotation overlay view that matched the image. So you can draw on it by adding a rectangle subview to that overlay. Here's the code:

```
self.addRectangle(transformedRect,
                  to: self.annotationOverlayView)
```

You don't have an addRectangle function yet, but creating one is now pretty straightforward. You simply need to create a new view with the dimensions of the rectangle and add it to the specified view. In this case that's the annotationOverlayView.

Here's the code:

```
private func addRectangle(_ rectangle: CGRect,
                          to view: UIView) {

    let rectangleView = UIView(frame: rectangle)
    rectangleView.layer.cornerRadius = 2.0
    rectangleView.layer.borderWidth = 4
    rectangleView.layer.borderColor = UIColor.red.cgColor
    view.addSubview(rectangleView)
}
```

And that's it! You've now created an app that will recognize elements within your image, and give you back bounding boxes for them. Explore with different images.

The classification that it gave was very limited, but now that you have the bounding boxes, you can clip the original image based on the bounding box and pass that clip to the image labeler to get a more granular description of what it sees! You'll explore that next.

Combining Object Detection with Image Classification

The previous example showed you how you could do object detection and get bounding boxes for the objects that were detected in the image. The base model with ML Kit can only classify a few classes such as "Fashion good," "Food good," "Home good," "Place," or "Plant." However it is able to detect distinct objects in an image, as we saw in the preceding example, where it spotted the bird and two flowers. It just could not *categorize* them as such.

If you want to do that, there's an option in combining object detection with image classification. As you already have the bounding boxes for the items in the image, you could crop the image to them, and then use image labeling to get the details of that subimage.

So, you could update your process results to use the frame property of each object to crop the image and load the cropped image into a new UIImage, called croppedImage, like this:

```
guard let cutImageRef: CGImage =
    theImage?.cgImage?.cropping(to: obj.frame)
    else {break}

let croppedImage: UIImage = UIImage(cgImage: cutImageRef)
```

The image labeling API uses a VisionImage object as you saw earlier in this chapter. So, the UIImage that represents the cropped image can be converted like this:

```
let visionImage = VisionImage(image: croppedImage)
```

You'll then need to instantiate an image labeler. This code will instantiate one with a confidence threshold of 0.8:

```
let options = ImageLabelerOptions()
options.confidenceThreshold = 0.8
let labeler = ImageLabeler.imageLabeler(options: options)
```

Then you'll just pass the VisionImage object to the labeler, and specify the callback to handle the results:

```
labeler.process(visionImage) {labels, error in
    self.processLabellingResult(from: labels, error: error)
}
```

Your callback can then process the labels inferred from each object as you did earlier in this chapter.

Object Detection and Tracking in Video

While it's beyond the scope of this book to demonstrate how live video overlay works, the "Chapter6ObjectTracking" sample app in the repo implements it for you. It uses CoreVideo from Apple to implement an `AVCaptureVideoPreviewLayer` and an `AVCaptureSession`.

Capturing is then delegated to an extension of the `ViewController`, which will capture frames from an `AVCaptureConnection` derived from the `AVCaptureSession`.

What's important to show here is how you can use frames from this video, pass them to ML Kit, and get object detections back. You can then use these to overlay bounding boxes on top of the live video.

When you create an app that uses a live video preview using Apple's AVFoundation, you'll have a delegate function called `captureOutput` that receives a buffer containing details of the frame. This can be used to create a `VisionImage` object, which you can then use with the object detection API in ML Kit like this:

```
func captureOutput(_ output: AVCaptureOutput,
                   didOutput sampleBuffer: CMSampleBuffer,
                   from connection: AVCaptureConnection) {

    guard let imageBuffer = CMSampleBufferGetImageBuffer(sampleBuffer)
        else {
            print("Failed to get image buffer from sample buffer.")
            return
        }

    lastFrame = sampleBuffer
    let visionImage = VisionImage(buffer: sampleBuffer)
    let orientation = UIUtilities.imageOrientation(
        fromDevicePosition: .back
    )

    visionImage.orientation = orientation
    let imageWidth = CGFloat(CVPixelBufferGetWidth(imageBuffer))
    let imageHeight = CGFloat(CVPixelBufferGetHeight(imageBuffer))
    let shouldEnableClassification = false
    let shouldEnableMultipleObjects = true
    let options = ObjectDetectorOptions()
    options.shouldEnableClassification = shouldEnableClassification
    options.shouldEnableMultipleObjects = shouldEnableMultipleObjects
    detectObjectsOnDevice(
        in: visionImage,
        width: imageWidth,
        height: imageHeight,
```

```
        options: options)
    }
```

When you get the captured output from the delegate, it will contain a sample buffer. This can then be used to get the image buffer containing a frame.

From this, you can convert the buffer to a `VisionImage` type using:

```
let visionImage = VisionImage(buffer: sampleBuffer)
```

To track objects in video, you need to disable classification of the objects and enable multiple object detection. You can achieve that with:

```
let shouldEnableClassification = false
let shouldEnableMultipleObjects = true
let options = ObjectDetectorOptions()
options.shouldEnableClassification = shouldEnableClassification
options.shouldEnableMultipleObjects = shouldEnableMultipleObjects
```

Now, given that you have the image, the options, and the dimensions of the image, you can call a helper function to do the object detection:

```
detectObjectsOnDevice(
    in: visionImage,
    width: imageWidth,
    height: imageHeight,
    options: options)
}
```

The job of this function will be to call ML Kit to get the detected objects in the frame, and then calculate bounding boxes for them, displaying those boxes with the tracking IDs.

So, first, to detect the objects:

```
let detector = ObjectDetector.objectDetector(options: options)
    var objects: [Object]
    do {
      objects = try detector.results(in: image)
    } catch let error {
      print("Failed with error: \(error.localizedDescription).")
      return
    }
```

Then, once they're detected, their bounding boxes will be returned in the `object.frame`. This needs to be normalized to be drawn on the preview overlay, and it's simply normalized by dividing its value by the width of the frame:

```
for object in objects {
    let normalizedRect = CGRect(
          x: object.frame.origin.x / width,
          y: object.frame.origin.y / height,
          width: object.frame.size.width / width,
```

```
        height: object.frame.size.height / height
    )
```

The preview layer provides a method to turn a normalized rectangle into one that matches the preview layer's coordinate system, so you can add it to the preview layer like this:

```
let standardizedRect = strongSelf.previewLayer.layerRectConverted(
    fromMetadataOutputRect: normalizedRect
).standardized

 UIUtilities.addRectangle(
   standardizedRect,
   to: strongSelf.annotationOverlayView,
   color: UIColor.green
 )
```

(UIUtilities is a class of helper utilities you can find in the repo.) You can see it in action on an iPhone in Figure 6-8.

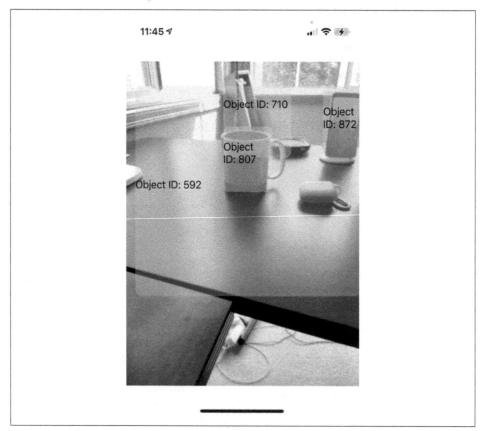

Figure 6-8. Object detection and tracking in a video

With these tools you should be able to create basic computer vision applications using ML Kit on iOS in Swift. In Chapter 11, you'll see how to use custom models instead of relying on the base models from ML Kit!

Summary

In this chapter you saw how to use computer vision algorithms with ML Kit, including image labeling and object detection. You saw how you can combine these to extend the basic model that ships with ML Kit, so you can classify the contents of the bounding boxes returned from object detection. You also saw how you can use object detection within a live video and got a sample for how you could do bounding boxes on live video! This provides you with the foundation to go forward in building apps that use images, either for classification or object detection purposes.

## CHAPTER 7

Text Processing Apps with ML Kit on iOS

In Chapter 6, you saw how to use ML Kit in your iOS apps for some computer vision scenarios including image recognition and object detection. Perhaps the next largest segment of ML apps are those which perform natural language processing tasks. So in this chapter we'll look at a few examples of how models from ML Kit provide some common machine learning tasks for you, including extracting entities from text, such as recognizing an email address or a date; performing handwriting recognition, turning strokes into text; and analyzing a conversation to generate a smart reply. If you want to create apps that use other natural language processing concepts with custom models, such as classifying text, you'll need to build your own models, and we'll explore that in later chapters.

Entity Extraction

Often you'll want to extract vital information from text. You've no doubt seen apps that can determine when there's an address in a piece of text and automatically generate a link to a map of that address, or others that understand an email address and generate a link that lets you launch your email app to send mail to that address. This concept is called *entity extraction*, and in this section you'll explore a turnkey model that performs this for you. This is a really cool implementation of ML, because if you consider how a rules-based approach would solve this problem, you would expect to write a lot of code!

So, consider Figure 7-1, where I've sent a message to my friend Nizhoni with some details in it. As a human reading, this you'll automatically extract valuable information from it and parse it. You'll see words like "tomorrow at 5PM" and automatically infer a date and time. Code for that would have lots of if...then statements!

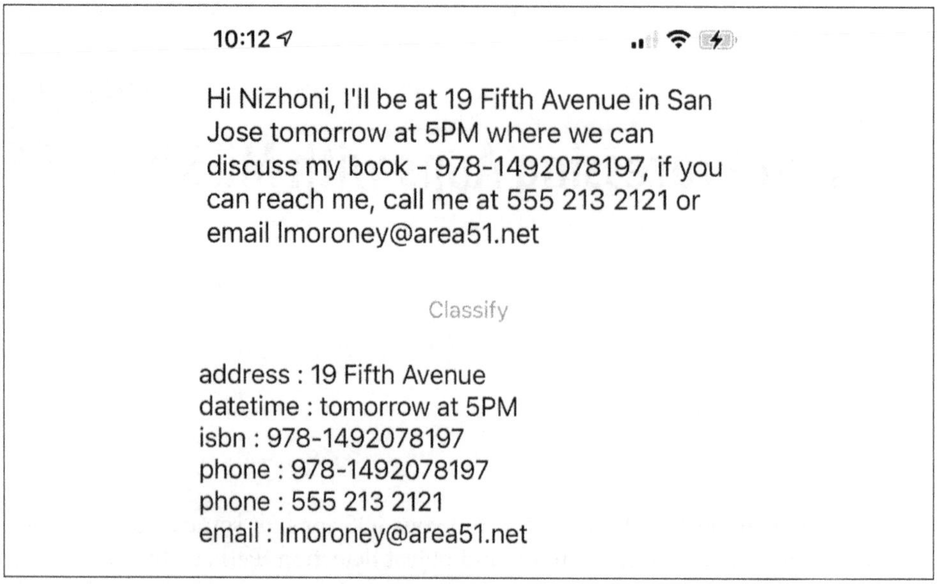

Figure 7-1. Running entity extraction on iOS

As you can see beneath the text, a list was generated with the entities that were found. So, for example, the "tomorrow at 5PM" was extracted as a datetime. Others like phone numbers and email addresses were also extracted correctly. Often a value will match multiple patterns; for example, the ISBN of the book starts with a three-digit number, which matches the pattern of a phone number, so it was detected as both entities!

Let's now explore how you can create this app!

Step 1: Create the App and Add the ML Kit Pods

Using Xcode, create a new app. When you're done, close Xcode and create a Podfile in the directory where the *.xcproject* resides.

Edit the Podfile to include the *GoogleMLKit/EntityExtraction* pod like this:

```
platform :ios, '10.0'
# Comment the next line if you're not using Swift and don't want to use dynamic
# frameworks
use_frameworks!

target 'MLKitEntityExample' do
        pod 'GoogleMLKit/EntityExtraction'
end
```

The value after `target` should be the name of your project, so in this case I created a project called *MLKitEntityExample*.

Once you're done, run **pod install**; CocoaPods will update your project to use the ML Kit dependencies and generate a *.xcworkspace* file that you should open to go to the next step.

Step 2: Create the Storyboard with Actions and Outlets

As you saw in Figure 7-1, the user interface for this app is really simple. Add a Text-View, a Button, and a Label control in a layout similar to what you can see in Figure 7-1. Make sure that the TextView is editable by checking the editable box in the properties inspector after you put it on the storyboard.

Your storyboard designer should look like Figure 7-2 when you're done.

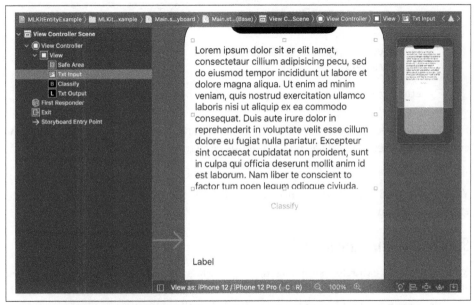

Figure 7-2. Designing the user interface in the storyboard editor

Next you should create outlets for the TextView and Label, called `txtInput` and `txtOutput`, respectively. Also create an action for the button and call it `doExtrac tion`. If you're not familiar with the process of outlets and actions, check back to Chapters 3 and 6 for more guided examples.

When you're done, the following code should be in your `ViewController` class:

```
@IBOutlet weak var txtInput: UITextView!
@IBOutlet weak var txtOutput: UILabel!
@IBAction func doExtraction(_ sender: Any) {
}
```

Step 3: Allow Your View Controller to be Used for Text Entry

When the user taps on the text view at the top, they'll be able to edit its contents via their device keyboard. However, the keyboard won't go away by default when they're done. To give this functionality, you need to update your ViewController to be a UITextViewDelegate like this:

```
class ViewController: UIViewController, UITextViewDelegate {
```

Once that's done, you can add this function to make the keyboard leave when the user presses Enter:

```
func textView(_ textView: UITextView,
              shouldChangeTextIn range: NSRange,
              replacementText text: String) -> Bool {

    if (text == "\n") {
        textView.resignFirstResponder()
        return false
    }
    return true
}
```

Finally, you have to inform iOS that the txtInput control will delegate TextView events to this ViewController by adding this code to your viewDidLoad function:

```
txtInput.delegate = self
```

You're now ready to allow the user to input text. So, next up, let's look at how to extract entities in this text!

Step 4: Initialize the Model

ML Kit's entity extractor supports many language models, so the first thing you should do is to define which one you want by using EntityExtractorOptions. In this case, I'm specifying that I want to use an English entity extractor:

```
var entityExtractor =
  EntityExtractor.entityExtractor(options:
    EntityExtractorOptions(
modelIdentifier:EntityExtractionModelIdentifier.english))
```

There are a number of different languages supported, with the complete list at *https://developers.google.com/ml-kit/language/entity-extraction*.

The model isn't guaranteed to be on the device when your user presses the button, so you can use code like this in your viewDidLoad to download it, and set a Boolean flag indicating that it's available which you'll check later:

```
entityExtractor.downloadModelIfNeeded(completion: { error in
    guard error == nil else {
        self.txtOutput.text = "Error downloading model, please restart app."
        return
    }
    self.modelAvailable = true
})
```

Step 5: Extract Entities from Text

Earlier, when you created the action for the button, you got a function called doEx
traction. Within this you want to call extractEntities, which you'll create shortly,
but only if the model is available. You downloaded the model in step 3, and set mode
lAvailable to true when it was done, so you can use this code:

```
@IBAction func doExtraction(_ sender: Any) {
    if(modelAvailable){
        extractEntities()
    } else {
        txtOutput.text = "Model not yet downloaded, please try later."
    }
}
```

You can now create the extractEntities function, and within it, you can use the
entityExtractor you just created with the text within txtInput to get the entities
within the text.

Start by creating the code to extract the entities like this:

```
func extractEntities(){
    let strText = txtInput.text
    entityExtractor.annotateText(
        strText!,
        completion: {
        }
}
```

Here you've passed the text to the entityExtractor within its annotateText method.
It will give you a callback on completion, and the callback will contain results and
error data structures. Results will be a list of annotations, and each annotation will be
a list of entities.

An entity has an entityType property defining the annotation type, such as email,
address or ISBN. The entity has a range property containing the location and length
of the text. So, if an email address is at the 20th character, and it is 15 characters long,
then annotation.range.location will be 20, and annotation.range.length will be
15. You can use this to slice the string to get the desired text.

Here's the complete code:

```
func extractEntities(){
  let strText = txtInput.text
  entityExtractor.annotateText(strText!,
    completion: {
      results, error in
      var strOutput = ""
      for annotation in results! {
        for entity in annotation.entities{
          strOutput += entity.entityType.rawValue + " : "
          let startLoc = annotation.range.location
          let endLoc = startLoc + annotation.range.length - 1
          let mySubString = strText![startLoc...endLoc]
          strOutput += mySubString + "\n"
        }
      }
      self.txtOutput.text = strOutput
    })
}
```

Swift string slicing is more complicated than you might think! The reason for this is that a common way of attacking apps is with strings and with code that naively slices strings, potentially causing a buffer underflow or a buffer overflow. As a result, Swift is designed to guard against naive string slicing with Mid() or Left() type functions that you may be familiar with. In the preceding code we calculate a startLoc and an endLoc, and then set mySubString to be the slice from the start to the end. This is *not* supported in Swift and an extension was necessary to get it to work. Do not use this code in any kind of production app and check how you manage your strings before publishing any app!

Here's the code for the string slicing extension:

```
extension String {
  subscript(_ i: Int) -> String {
    let idx1 = index(startIndex, offsetBy: i)
    let idx2 = index(idx1, offsetBy: 1)
    return String(self[idx1..<idx2])
  }

  subscript (r: Range<Int>) -> String {
    let start = index(startIndex, offsetBy: r.lowerBound)
    let end = index(startIndex, offsetBy: r.upperBound)
    return String(self[start ..< end])
  }

  subscript (r: CountableClosedRange<Int>) -> String {
    let startIndex =  self.index(self.startIndex,
                        offsetBy: r.lowerBound)
    let endIndex = self.index(startIndex,
                        offsetBy: r.upperBound - r.lowerBound)
```

```
      return String(self[startIndex...endIndex])
   }
}
```

And that's pretty much everything that you need to get started with entity extraction with ML Kit on iOS. This is just scratching the surface, but hopefully this gives you an idea of how easy ML Kit can make this task!

Handwriting Recognition

Another example of where it would be complex to write code to solve a task is in handwriting recognition, where the user draws on their screen with a stylus or finger and it's your job to turn their scribbles into text. Fortunately ML Kit makes this a lot easier too, and you'll explore how to do that in this section. So, for example, consider Figure 7-3, where I've drawn some letters with my finger, and the app detected them to say the word "hello."

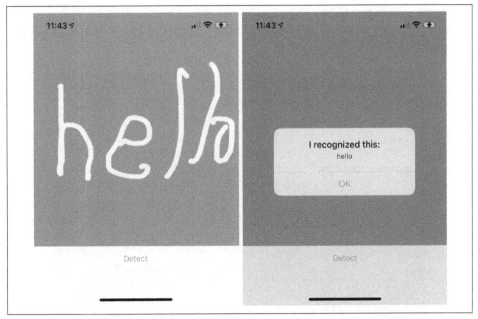

Figure 7-3. App that recognizes handwriting

Using ML Kit to create this type of app is really straightforward! Let's explore.

Step 1: Create the App and Add the ML Kit Pods

As before, create a simple single view app, and when you're done, add a Podfile to the same directory as the *.xcproject*. Edit the Podfile to include the ML Kit Digital Ink libraries:

```
platform :ios, '10.0'
# Comment the next line if you're not using Swift and don't want to use dynamic
# frameworks
use_frameworks!


target 'MLKitInkExample' do
        pod 'GoogleMLKit/DigitalInkRecognition'
end
```

 If you aren't calling your project *MLKitInkExample*, then the name of your project should be specified as the `target` instead. Run **pod install** and then open the *.xcworkspace* that gets generated for you.

Step 2: Create the Storyboard, Actions, and Outlets

The drawing surface will be a UIImageView, so draw a big one that covers most of the screen on the storyboard. Also add a button and change its label to Detect, as shown in Figure 7-4.

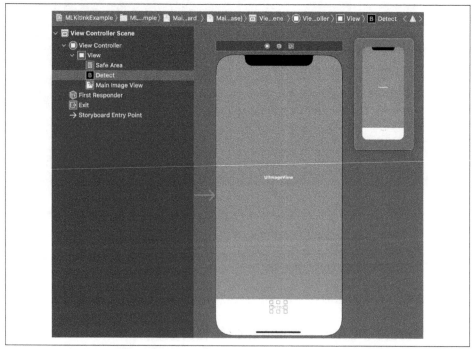

Figure 7-4. Creating the storyboard

When you're done, create an outlet for the image view (call it `mainImageView`) and an action for the button ((call it `recognizeInk`). To the action add a call to a function called `doRecognition()`. Don't worry if Xcode complains that that function doesn't exist yet. You'll create it soon.

Your code should look like this:

```
@IBAction func recognizeInk(_ sender: Any) {
    doRecognition()
}

@IBOutlet weak var mainImageView: UIImageView!
```

Step 3: Strokes, Points, and Ink

When using ML Kit to recognize handwriting, you will pass it an ink object. This object is made up of a number of strokes, and each stroke is a number of points. For example, consider the letter Z. This could be made up of three strokes: one for the top line, one for the diagonal, and one for the bottom line. The ink would be the collection of strokes, and each stroke would be a number of points that were gathered as the user drew the lines.

So, before we capture the user's input when they drag their finger around the screen, we'll need these data structures set up for us:

```
private var strokes: [Stroke] = []
private var points: [StrokePoint] = []
```

You'll see the ink object set up later.

Step 4: Capture User Input

Next you'll want to gather the user's input when they draw on the UIImage with their finger or stylus. This is done by overriding three different functions—touchesBegan, touchesMoved, and touchesEnded.

The first, touchesBegan, is fired when the user starts drawing something. Their finger first touches the screen. Here, we want to initialize the array of points and start it with the point where our drawing begins:

```
override func touchesBegan(_ touches: Set<UITouch>,
                           with event: UIEvent?) {

    guard let touch = touches.first else { return }
    lastPoint = touch.location(in: mainImageView)
    let t = touch.timestamp
    points = [StrokePoint.init(x: Float(lastPoint.x),
                               y: Float(lastPoint.y),
                               t: Int(t * 1000))]
}
```

Because the sequence in which strokes and stroke points are recorded is important to the model, we also need a timestamp, so you can see that it is collected here also and used to initialize the StrokePoint.

The next event to capture is the touchesMoved event, which occurs when the user's finger passes across the surface before they lift it. In this case we want to get the current point from the touch location, but this time we append it to the points array, instead of creating a new array. We'll also need a timestamp like before. The drawLine function will draw from the last (aka previous) point to the current point, and then set the last point to the current point.

Here's the code:

```
override func touchesMoved(_ touches: Set<UITouch>,
                    with event: UIEvent?) {
    guard let touch = touches.first else { return }
    let currentPoint = touch.location(in: mainImageView)
    let t = touch.timestamp
    points.append(StrokePoint.init(x: Float(currentPoint.x),
                                   y: Float(currentPoint.y),
                                   t: Int(t * 1000)))
    drawLine(from: lastPoint, to: currentPoint)
    lastPoint = currentPoint
}
```

When the user removes their finger from the screen at the end of the stroke, the tou chesEnded event will fire. There is no "new" point here to add, so the lastPoint that you've been keeping track of becomes the final point to have in the list. You can create a new StrokePoint using it, and add that to the list of points in this stroke, finalizing the stroke.

The finalized stroke will then be added to the list of strokes by initializing a new Stroke object using the points that have been collected since this touch began:

```
override func touchesEnded(_ touches: Set<UITouch>,
                    with event: UIEvent?) {
    guard let touch = touches.first else { return }
    let t = touch.timestamp
    points.append(StrokePoint.init(x: Float(lastPoint.x),
                                   y: Float(lastPoint.y),
                                   t: Int(t * 1000)))
    strokes.append(Stroke.init(points: points))
    drawLine(from: lastPoint, to: lastPoint)
}
```

I won't show the code for drawing the line here, but you can find it in the GitHub repo for this book.

Step 5: Initialize the Model

Now that you have an app that can capture the user's drawings on the UIImage and have those represented as a list of strokes, you have everything you need to pass to the model to get an inference about them, which should hopefully be an accurate conversion of handwriting into text!

Before you can do that, of course, you need a model! In this step, you'll download and initialize the model so that later you can turn your strokes into Ink and have it infer from them.

First, you'll need to check if the model is available. You can do this by specifying your language and using DigitalInkRecognitionModelIdentifier to see if it's available. Here's the code:

```
let languageTag = "en-US"
let identifier = DigitalInkRecognitionModelIdentifier(
                         forLanguageTag: languageTag)
```

If this identifier is nil, you have a problem and need to check your setup or internet connection. Make sure also that it's a supported language; the list of supported languages can be found in the *ML Kit documentation (https://oreil.ly/4ZoiJ)*.

Once you have a working model, you can download it. You do this by initializing a DigitalInkRecognitionModel object with the identifier, and then by using a model manager to download it. To set up the model manager, you'll need to initialize a con ditions object, which controls properties about how the model can or can not be downloaded. So, in this example, I've set one up that allows for cellular access (and not just WiFi), as well as allowing the model to download in the background:

```
let model = DigitalInkRecognitionModel.init(
               modelIdentifier: identifier!)
var modelManager = ModelManager.modelManager()

modelManager.download(model,
     conditions: ModelDownloadConditions.init(
            allowsCellularAccess: true,
            allowsBackgroundDownloading: true))
```

Once the model is downloaded, you can create a recognizer object from it. Following the familiar pattern, you define an options object (DigitalInkRecognizerOptions), which in this case you initialize with the model you just downloaded. Once you have that, you can then instantiate a recognizer from DigitalInkRecognizer using these options.

Here's the code:

```
let options: DigitalInkRecognizerOptions =
                DigitalInkRecognizerOptions.init(
                                model: model)

recognizer = DigitalInkRecognizer.digitalInkRecognizer(
                                options: options)
```

If you've gotten this far, you should now have a working recognizer. I've taken a little bit of a shortcut here and just expected the model download to work and to be finished before I instantiated the `DigitalInkRecognizerOptions`. There is a chance that this could fail (poor network conditions, for example), and as a result, this isn't the best pattern. It would be better to do some kind of asynchronous callback that only initializes the recognizer upon successful model download, but for the purposes of this tutorial, I wanted to keep it simple.

Step 6: Do the Ink Recognition

Now that you have a recognizer, it's simply a matter of converting your strokes into ink, passing them to the recognizer, and parsing the results you get back. Let's explore the code for this.

First, here's how to turn the strokes into ink:

```
let ink = Ink.init(strokes: strokes)
```

Next, you can use the recognizer with its recognize method, passing it the ink and catching a completion callback:

```
recognizer.recognize(
  ink: ink,
  completion: {
}
```

The completion callback will contain a result and an error, so be sure to set them up to begin your completion callback. The result will be a `DigitalInkRecognitionRe sult`:

```
(result: DigitalInkRecognitionResult?, error: Error?) in
```

A valid result will have many candidates, where it has multiple potential matches. So for example, if you look back to Figure 7-3, my "h" might be mistaken for an "n," and the final "lo" might be mistaken for a "b." The engine will return back various candidates in order of priority, so it might have "hello," "nello," "helb," "nelb," etc. To keep things simple, this code will just take the first candidate using `results.candi dates.first`:

```
if let result = result, let candidate = result.candidates.first {
    alertTitle = "I recognized this:"
    alertText = candidate.text
} else {
    alertTitle = "I hit an error:"
    alertText = error!.localizedDescription
}
```

The `alertTitle` and `alertText` values are strings that will be used to set up the alert dialog. You saw this on the righthand side of Figure 7-3. The important property to note is `candidate.text`, which is the text interpretation of the current candidate. As we're just taking the first candidate, it's the one that ML Kit determined to be the most likely match.

After this, you just want to display the alert box, clear the image, and reset the strokes and points so you can try again:

```
let alert = UIAlertController(title: alertTitle,
                message: alertText,
                preferredStyle: UIAlertController.Style.alert)

alert.addAction(
  UIAlertAction(
    title: "OK", style: UIAlertAction.Style.default, handler: nil))
self.present(alert, animated: true, completion: nil)
self.mainImageView.image = nil
self.strokes = []
self.points = []
```

And that's it! Try it out and experiment! I'd love to see how it works with other languages too!

Smart Reply to Conversations

Another fun example of a turnkey model you can use in your apps is the Smart Reply model. You've probably used sites like LinkedIn where, as you are chatting with somebody, you have suggested responses. Or if you're an Android user, many of the messaging apps include smart replies, as you can see in Figure 7-5, where I'm being invited for breakfast and the smart reply has given some suggested responses. It's also done an entity extraction to get the date "tomorrow at 9:30AM" and turned it into a link to create a calendar entry!

Other than that, there are smart reply options for "'Sure," "What time?" and "Yes." These have been generated with the context of the statement (it's a question), as well as the vernacular I have used while chatting in the past. I say "sure" a lot when invited to stuff!

Building an app that uses the ML Kit Smart Reply APIs to get similar functionality is very straightforward. Let's explore how to do that next.

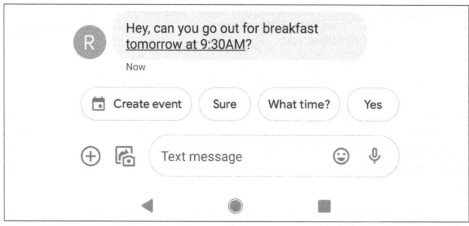

Figure 7-5. Smart reply in Android instant messages

Step 1: Create an App and Integrate ML Kit

As before, using Xcode creates a simple single view app. When it's done, put the following Podfile in the same directory as your *.xcproject*:

```
platform :ios, '10.0'

target 'MLKitSmartReplyExample' do
        pod 'GoogleMLKit/SmartReply'
end
```

In this case, my project was called *MLKitSmartReplyExample*, so be sure to use whatever your project name is as the `target` in place of mine. Run **pod install**, and after it's done, open the *.xcworkspace* to continue.

Step 2: Create Storyboard, Outlets, and Actions

To keep this app simple, create a storyboard that has two labels and a button. The topmost label will contain a simulated conversation between me and a friend. When the user presses the button the Smart Reply model will be used to generate a likely reply. The reply will be rendered in the second label. So, from a storyboard perspective, your UI should look something like Figure 7-6.

Once you're done with this, create outlets called `conversationLabel` and `txtSugges tions` for the upper and lower labels, respectively. For the button, create an action called `generateReply` and put a call to the function `getSmartReply()` within it. Don't worry if Xcode complains—you'll write that function shortly.

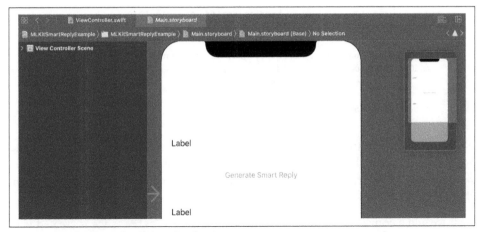

Figure 7-6. Creating the Smart Reply view

When you're done, your code should look like this:

```
@IBOutlet weak var conversationLabel: UILabel!
@IBOutlet weak var txtSuggestions: UILabel!
@IBAction func generateReply(_ sender: Any) {
    getSmartReply()
}
```

Step 3: Create a Simulated Conversation

The quickest way to see the model in action is to have a conversation that we can pass to it, so let's create a simple one here. I've created an `initializeConversation()` function that creates conversation items and adds them to an array of `TextMessage` types.

So, at the class level you should initialize the array:

```
var conversation: [TextMessage] = []
```

Then, `initializeConversation` will begin to populate the array. A `TextMessage` type contains details about a message including its contents, timestamp, who it's from, and most importantly, if it is a local user (i.e., you) or a remote user (i.e., someone else). So, to create a conversation, I wrote a helper function that overloads `addConversatio nItem` based on whether it's me or my friend sending the message. Here's the function in full:

```
private func initializeConversation(){
    let friendName = "Nizhoni"
    addConversationItem(item: "Hi, good morning!")
    addConversationItem(item: "Oh, hey -- how are you?",
                        fromUser: friendName)
    addConversationItem(item: "Just got up, thinking of
```

```
                             heading out for breakfast")
        addConversationItem(item: "Want to meet up?",
                            fromUser: friendName)
        addConversationItem(item: "Sure, what do you fancy?")
        addConversationItem(item: "Just coffee, or do you want to
                                  eat?",
                            fromUser: friendName)
        conversationLabel.text = outputText
    }
```

Notice that some of the calls to addConversation have a fromUser: parameter, and some do not. Those that do not are simulated to be from me, while those that do will be simulated from a remote user. So, the addConversation overloads that implement this are here.

First we add a conversation item from me. Note that the TextMessage is created with userID as "Me", and not something that is passed to the function, and the isLoca lUser property is set to true:

```
    private func addConversationItem(item: String){
        outputText += "Me : \(item)\n"
        let message = TextMessage(text: item,
                        timestamp:Date().timeIntervalSince1970,
                        userID: "Me",
                        isLocalUser: true)

        conversation.append(message)
    }
```

Here's the overload for when the fromUser: property is set. In this case, note that the TextMessage is created with the userID that is passed in from that property, and isLo calUser is set to false:

```
    private func addConversationItem(item: String,
                              fromUser: String){
        outputText += "\(fromUser) : \(item)\n"
        let message = TextMessage(text: item,
                        timestamp:Date().timeIntervalSince1970,
                        userID: fromUser,
                        isLocalUser: false)

        conversation.append(message)
    }
```

In both cases the conversationLabel is updated with the message and the user, and the conversation is updated with the message. You can see what this looks like in Figure 7-7.

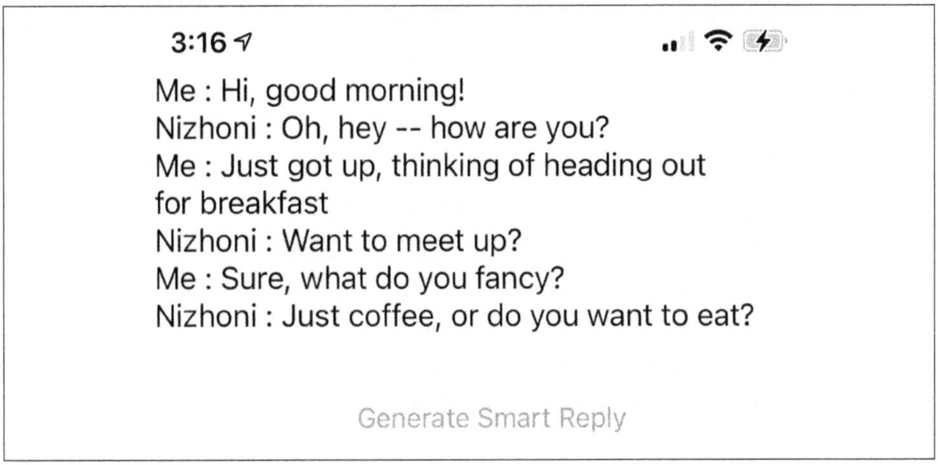

Figure 7-7. Simulating a conversation

Step 4: Get Smart Reply

Now that you have a conversation and it's stored as an array of `TextMessage` types, you can simply call `SmartReply.smartReply()` and use the `suggestReplies` method for that conversation to get a set of smart replies. Earlier, in the button action, you coded it to call `getSmartReply()`. You can create that function now, and have it call the Smart Reply model:

```
private func getSmartReply(){
    SmartReply.smartReply().suggestReplies(for: conversation)
    { result, error in
        guard error == nil, let result = result else { return }
```

This will get the suggested replies for your conversation, and if there's no error, they'll be in the result variable. `result` will be a list of suggestion types, and these contain a `suggestion.text` property with the contents of the suggestion. So, if you want to create a text list of all the suggested replies, you simply need this code:

```
var strSuggestedReplies = "Suggested Replies:"
if (result.status == .notSupportedLanguage) {
    // The conversation's language isn't supported, so
    // the result doesn't contain any suggestions.
    // You should output something helpful in this case
} else if (result.status == .success) {
    // Successfully suggested smart replies.
    for suggestion in result.suggestions {
        strSuggestedReplies = strSuggestedReplies +
                              suggestion.text + "\n"
    }
}
self.txtSuggestions.text = strSuggestedReplies
```

Here, if the result status is a success, you can see that we loop through `result.sugges`
`tions`, building the suggested replies list. When you run the app, you'll see a list of
suggested replies. This is shown in Figure 7-8.

Me : Hi, good morning!
Nizhoni : Oh, hey -- how are you?
Me : Just got up, thinking of heading out
for breakfast
Nizhoni : Want to meet up?
Me : Sure, what do you fancy?
Nizhoni : Just coffee, or do you want to eat?

Generate Smart Reply

Suggested Replies:
Sure, sounds good
Sounds good
Sure

Figure 7-8. Viewing the suggested replies

In a real app you could make these a pickable list, and when the user selects one it
populates the reply box with the suggested text, just like the Android SMS app shown
in Figure 7-5!

This is just a simple example of what's possible with Smart Reply, and hopefully this
will show you how easy it is to incorporate into your apps!

Summary

This chapter took you through a number of scenarios where you could use a turnkey
model in ML Kit to get ML functionality in an iOS app. You started with entity detection where you could quickly and easily parse common entities such as email or time/
date out of a string. You then looked at using digital ink to capture a user's strokes on
the screen and parse that into text—effectively recognizing handwriting! Finally, you
dug into the Smart Reply APIs that help you speed up conversations with suggested
replies. All of these models run using TensorFlow Lite on the backend (and if you
were eagle eyed you might have seen mentions of this in the debugger!), so in Chapter 8 we'll switch gears and get an overview of how this technology works to bring
ML to mobile.

Going Deeper: Understanding TensorFlow Lite

Underlying all of the machine learning technology that you've seen so far in this book is TensorFlow. This is a framework that allows you to architect, train, and test machine learning models; we had an introduction to this in Chapter 1 and Chapter 2.

TensorFlow models are usually *not* designed for mobile scenarios where one has to consider size, battery consumption, and everything else that can impact the mobile user experience. To that end, TensorFlow Lite was created with two main aims. The first—it could be used to *convert* existing TensorFlow models into a format that was smaller and more compact, with an eye on optimizing them for mobile. The second is to have an efficient runtime for various mobile platforms that could be used for model inference. In this chapter, we'll explore TensorFlow Lite and take a deeper look at the tooling that's available for you to convert models trained with TensorFlow as well as how to use tools to optimize them.

We'll start with a brief tour of why it's important, and then we can roll our sleeves up and get down to the bits and bytes...

What Is TensorFlow Lite?

The rationale behind the need for something like TensorFlow Lite was driven by several factors. The first is the explosion in the number of personal devices. Mobile devices running iOS or Android already outnumber traditional desktop or laptops as primary computing devices, and embedded systems outnumber mobile devices. The need for these to run machine learning models grows with them.

But let's focus on the smartphone here, and the user experience for the smartphone. If machine learning models are in the realm of the server, and there is no mobile runtime, one would have to wrap their functionality in some form of interface that the mobile device could call. For example, for an image classifier, the mobile device would have to send the picture to the server, have the server do the inference, and return the results. There's an obvious *latency* issue here beyond the fact that *connectivity* is essential. Not everywhere may have connectivity that would allow for a quick and easy upload of an image, which can be several megabytes of data.

And of course, there's *privacy*. Many scenarios involve using very personal data—such as the aforementioned photos—and requiring them to be uploaded to a server in order for functionality to work can violate the user's privacy, and they probably would reject using your app as a result.

Having a framework that allows models to work on the device so that there's no lag in transferring the data to a third party and no connectivity dependency, while also maintaining the user's privacy, is paramount for machine learning to be a viable scenario on mobile.

Enter TensorFlow Lite. As mentioned in the introduction, it's designed for you to convert your TensorFlow model to a compact format for mobile, as well as the runtime for inference on that mobile platform.

What's exciting about this in particular is that it can allow for a whole new generation of products and scenarios. Think about what happens when new platforms appear, and the innovation that follows. Consider, for example, when the smartphone first came on the scene—a device that was loaded with sensors like GPS or a camera and connected to the internet. Think about how difficult it was to find your way around a new location, particularly one that primarily used different languages, using a paper map! Now, you can use your device to pinpoint your location, give it your destination, and it can smartly route you to the quickest way there with step-by-step instructions—even if you are walking, using an augmented reality interface that shows you the route to follow. While you *could* have done that with your laptop if you were able to connect it to the internet somehow, it wasn't really feasible. With the emergence of ML models on mobile, a whole new platform awaits for interesting scenarios to be implemented—these may be things that *could* be implemented without ML, but are likely too difficult to do when not using models.

Consider, for example, Figure 8-1, where there's text in Chinese that I can't read. I'm in a restaurant and have some food allergies. With Google Translate, using ML models on-device for translation, and with another model able to do text recognition for what's in the camera's field of view, I can now have a live, visual, translation of what's in front of me.

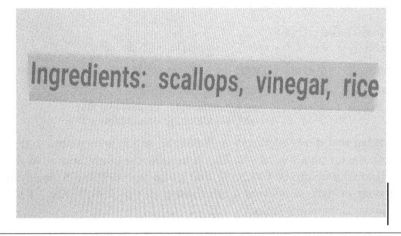

成分：扇貝，醋，米飯

Figure 8-1. *Live translation on a camera screen*

Consider how difficult it would be to do something like this *without* machine learning. How to write code to do optical character recognition of any character in any language. And then, once you've done that, how to then translate those without a round trip to a translation server. It simply wouldn't be feasible. But ML, and in particular ML on the device, is making this possible.

Getting Started with TensorFlow Lite

To understand TensorFlow Lite, I think it's easiest to get hands-on and work with it right away. Let's start by exploring the *converter* that takes a TensorFlow model and converts it to the TensorFlow Lite format. We'll then take the model it creates and implement it in a simple Android app.

In Chapter 1, we did some code that we called the "Hello World" of machine learning, with a very simple linear regression to build a model that could predict the relationship between two numbers x and y as y = 2x − 1. As a recap, here's the Python code for training the model in TensorFlow:

```
import tensorflow as tf
import numpy as np
from tensorflow.keras import Sequential
from tensorflow.keras.layers import Dense
```

```
layer_0 = Dense(units=1, input_shape=[1])
model = Sequential([layer_0])
model.compile(optimizer='sgd', loss='mean_squared_error')

xs = np.array([-1.0, 0.0, 1.0, 2.0, 3.0, 4.0], dtype=float)
ys = np.array([-3.0, -1.0, 1.0, 3.0, 5.0, 7.0], dtype=float)

model.fit(xs, ys, epochs=500)

print(model.predict([10.0]))
print("Here is what I learned: {}".format(layer_0.get_weights()))
```

After training for 500 epochs, it gave the following output on the print statements:

```
[[18.984955]]
Here is what I learned: [array([[1.9978193]], dtype=float32),
                         array([-0.99323905], dtype=float32)]
```

So it predicted that if x is 10, then y is 18.984955, which is very close to the 19 we'd expect with the formula $y = 2x - 1$. This is because the single neuron in the neural network learned a weight of 1.9978193, and a bias of -0.99323905. So, given a very small amount of data, it inferred a relationship of $y = 1.9978193x - 0.99323905$, which is pretty close to our desired $y = 2x - 1$.

So, can we now get this working on Android, instead of running it in the cloud or on our developer workstation? The answer, of course, is yes. And the first step is to save our model.

Save the Model

TensorFlow uses several different methods of saving models, but the most standardized across the TensorFlow ecosystem is the SavedModel format. This will save the model in the *.pb* (for protobuf) file format, as a representation of the frozen model, with associated directories containing any model assets or variables. This has the decided advantage of separation of architecture from state, so that other states could be added later if we wanted, or updates to the model could be shipped without needing to reship any on-model assets, which themselves may be quite large.

To save with this format, you just specify the output directory and then call `tf.saved_model.save()` like this:

```
export_dir = 'saved_model/1'
tf.saved_model.save(model, export_dir)
```

You can see the directory structure that gets saved out in Figure 8-2.

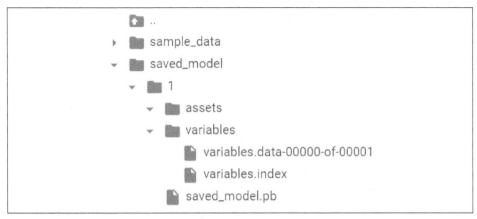

Figure 8-2. The directory structure after saving a model

As this is a very simple model, the *variables* file has only one shard. Larger models will be split into multiple ones, hence the naming *variables.data-00000-of-00001*. This model doesn't use any assets, so that folder will be empty.

Convert the Model

Converting the model is as easy as creating an instance of the converter from the saved model, and calling its convert method. This will give you a model in the TFLite format that you can then save out by writing its bytes to a file stream.

Here's the code:

```
converter = tf.lite.TFLiteConverter.from_saved_model(export_dir)
tflite_model = converter.convert()

import pathlib
tflite_model_file = pathlib.Path('model.tflite')
tflite_model_file.write_bytes(tflite_model)
```

The process of writing the bytes will return a number, and this is the number of bytes written. With different versions of the converter this might change, but the one at the time of writing wrote out a file called *model.tflite* that was 896 bytes in size. This encapsulates the entire trained model, including architecture and learned weights.

 While using the Python APIs as shown earlier is the recommended way to perform the model conversion, the TensorFlow team also offers a command-line interpreter should you want to use that instead. You can learn more about it at *https://www.tensorflow.org/ lite/convert*.

Testing the Model with a Standalone Interpreter

Before trying the model on iOS or Android, you should use the standalone interpreter from TensorFlow Lite to see if it works well. This interpreter runs in the Python environment, so it can also be used in embedded systems that can run Python, such as the Linux-based Raspberry Pi!

The next step is to load the model into the interpreter, allocate tensors that will be used for inputting data to the model for prediction, and then read the predictions that the model outputs. This is where using TensorFlow Lite, from a programmer's perspective, greatly differs from using TensorFlow. With TensorFlow you can just say model.predict(*something*) and get the results, but because TensorFlow Lite won't have many of the dependencies that TensorFlow does, particularly in non-Python environments, you now have to get a bit more low level and deal with the input and output tensors, formatting your data to fit them and parsing the output in a way that makes sense for your device.

First, load the model and allocate the tensors:

```
interpreter = tf.lite.Interpreter(model_content=tflite_model)
interpreter.allocate_tensors()
```

Then you can get the input and output details from the model, so you can begin to understand what data format it expects and what data format it will provide back to you:

```
input_details = interpreter.get_input_details()
output_details = interpreter.get_output_details()
print(input_details)
```

You'll get a lot of output!

First, let's inspect the input parameter. Note the shape setting, which is an array of type [1,1]. Also note the class, which is numpy.float32. These settings will dictate the shape of the input data and its format:

```
[{'name': 'serving_default_dense_input:0', 'index': 0,
   'shape': array([1, 1], dtype=int32),
   'shape_signature': array([1, 1], dtype=int32),
   'dtype': <class 'numpy.float32'>,
   'quantization': (0.0, 0),
   'quantization_parameters': {'scales': array([],
                                 dtype=float32),
                                 'zero_points': array([], dtype=int32),
                                 'quantized_dimension': 0},
   'sparsity_parameters': {}}]
```

So, in order to format the input data, you'll need to use code like this to define the input array shape and type if you want to predict the y for x = 10.0:

```
to_predict = np.array([[10.0]], dtype=np.float32)
print(to_predict)
```

The double brackets around the 10.0 can cause a little confusion—the mnemonic I use for the `array[1,1]` here is to say that there is one list, giving us the first set of [], and that list contains just one value, which is [10.0], thus giving [[10.0]]. It can also be confusing that the shape is defined as `dtype=int32`, whereas you're using `numpy.float32`. The `dtype` parameter is the datatype defining the shape, not the contents of the list that is encapsulated in that shape. For that, you'll use the class.

You can also print the output details with `print(output_details)`.

These are very similar, and what you want to keep an eye on here is the shape. As it's also an array of type [1,1], you can expect the answer to be [[y]] in much the same way as the input was [[x]]:

```
[{'name': 'StatefulPartitionedCall:0',
  'index': 3,
  'shape': array([1, 1], dtype=int32),
  'shape_signature': array([1, 1], dtype=int32),
  'dtype': <class 'numpy.float32'>,
  'quantization': (0.0, 0),
  'quantization_parameters': {'scales': array([], dtype=float32),
                              'zero_points': array([], dtype=int32),
                              'quantized_dimension': 0},
  'sparsity_parameters': {}}]
```

To get the interpreter to do the prediction, you set the input tensor with the value to predict, telling it what input value to use:

```
interpreter.set_tensor(input_details[0]['index'], to_predict)
interpreter.invoke()
```

The input tensor is specified using the index of the array of input details. In this case, you have a very simple model that only has a single input option, so it's `input_details[0]`, and you'll address it at the index. Input details item 0 has only one index, indexed at 0, and it expects a shape of [1,1] as defined earlier. So, you put the `to_predict` value in there. Then you invoke the interpreter with the `invoke` method.

You can then read the prediction by calling `get_tensor` and supplying it with the details of the tensor you want to read:

```
tflite_results = interpreter.get_tensor(output_details[0]['index'])
print(tflite_results)
```

Again, there's only one output tensor, so it will be `output_details[0]`, and you specify the index to get the details beneath it, which will have the output value.

So, for example, assume you run this code:

```
to_predict = np.array([[10.0]], dtype=np.float32)
print(to_predict)
interpreter.set_tensor(input_details[0]['index'], to_predict)
interpreter.invoke()
tflite_results = interpreter.get_tensor(output_details[0]['index'])
print(tflite_results)
```

You should see output like:

```
[[10.]]
[[18.975412]]
```

where 10 is the input value and 18.97 is the predicted value, which is very close to 19, which is 2x – 1 when x = 10. For the reasons why it's not 19, look back to Chapter 1!

Note that you might have seen slightly different results (such as 18.984) in Chapter 1, and these will occur for two main reasons. First, the neurons start from a different random initialization state, so their final value will be slightly different. Also, when compressing to a TFLite model, optimizations will be made that impact the final results. Keep this in mind when creating more complex models later—it's important to keep an eye on any accuracy impact by mobile conversion.

Now that we've tested the model using the standalone interpreter, and it looks to be performing as expected, for the next step, let's build a simple Android application and see what using the model looks like there!

Create an Android App to Host TFLite

Create an Android app using Android Studio using the single activity template. If you're not familiar with this, go through all the steps in Chapter 3. Check them out there!

Edit your *build.gradle* file to include the TensorFlow Lite runtime:

```
implementation 'org.tensorflow:tensorflow-lite:2.4.0'
```

Here I've used version 2.4.0. To get the latest version, you can check out the current versions available on the Bintray website (*https://oreil.ly/Y3kb0*).

You'll also need a new setting within the android{} section, as follows:

```
android{
...
    aaptOptions {
        noCompress "tflite"
    }
...
}
```

This step prevents the compiler from compressing your *.tflite* file. Android Studio compiles assets to make them smaller, so that the download time from the Google Play Store will be reduced. However, if the *.tflite* file is compressed, the TensorFlow Lite interpreter won't recognize it. To ensure that it doesn't get compressed, you need to set aaptOptions to noCompress for *.tflite* files. If you used a different extension (some people just use *.lite*), make sure you have that here.

You can now try building your project. The TensorFlow Lite libraries will be downloaded and linked.

Next, update your activity file (you can find this in your layout directory) to create a simple UI. This will have an edit text in which you can type a value, and a button that you press in order to trigger the inference:

```xml
<?xml version="1.0" encoding="utf-8"?>
<LinearLayout xmlns:tools="http://schemas.android.com/tools"
    android:orientation="vertical"
    xmlns:android="http://schemas.android.com/apk/res/android"
    android:layout_height="match_parent"
    android:layout_width="match_parent">

    <LinearLayout
        android:layout_width="match_parent"
        android:layout_height="wrap_content">

        <TextView
            android:id="@+id/lblEnter"
            android:layout_width="wrap_content"
            android:layout_height="wrap_content"
            android:text="Enter X:   "
            android:textSize="18sp"></TextView>

        <EditText
            android:id="@+id/txtValue"
            android:layout_width="180dp"
            android:layout_height="wrap_content"
            android:inputType="number"
            android:text="1"></EditText>

        <Button
            android:id="@+id/convertButton"
            android:layout_width="wrap_content"
            android:layout_height="wrap_content"
            android:text="Convert">

        </Button>
    </LinearLayout>
</LinearLayout>
```

Before you start coding you'll need to import the TFLite file to your app. You can see how to do that next.

Import the TFLite File

The first thing to do is create an *assets* folder in your project. To do this, navigate to the *app/src/main* folder in the project explorer, right-click on the *main* folder and select New Directory. Call it *assets*. Drag the *.tflite* file that you downloaded after training the model into that directory. If you didn't create this file earlier, you can find it in the book's GitHub repository.

If you get a warning about the file not being in the right directory, so Model Binding is disabled, it's safe to ignore it. Model Binding is something we'll explore later that works for a number of fixed scenarios: it allows you to easily import a *.tflite* model without many of the manual steps illustrated in this example. Here we're going a little lower level into the nuts and bolts of how to use a TFLite file within Android Studio.

After adding the asset to Android Studio, your project explorer should look a little like Figure 8-3.

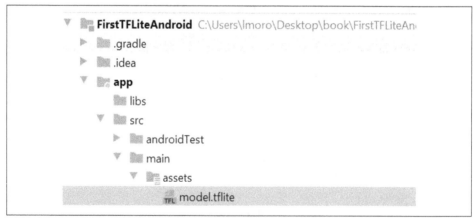

Figure 8-3. Adding a TFLite file as an assets file

Now that everything is set up, we can start coding!

Write Kotlin Code to Interface with the Model

Despite the fact that you're using Kotlin, your source files are in the *java* directory!. Open this, and you'll see a folder with your package name. Within that you should see your *MainActivity.kt* file. Double-click this file to open it in the code editor.

First, you'll need a helper function that loads the TensorFlow Lite model from the *assets* directory:

```
private fun loadModelFile(assetManager: AssetManager,
                          modelPath: String): ByteBuffer {
    val fileDescriptor = assetManager.openFd(modelPath)
    val inputStream = FileInputStream(fileDescriptor.fileDescriptor)
    val fileChannel = inputStream.channel
    val startOffset = fileDescriptor.startOffset
    val declaredLength = fileDescriptor.declaredLength
    return fileChannel.map(FileChannel.MapMode.READ_ONLY,
startOffset, declaredLength)
}
```

As the *.tflite* file is effectively a binary blob of weights and biases that the interpreter will use to build an internal neural network model, it's a `ByteBuffer` in Android terms. This code will load the file at `modelPath` and return it as a `ByteBuffer`. (Note that earlier you made sure not to compress this file type at compile time so that Android could recognize the contents of the file.)

Then, within your activity, at the class level (i.e., just below the class declaration, not within any class functions), you can add the declarations for the model and interpreter:

```
private lateinit var tflite : Interpreter
private lateinit var tflitemodel : ByteBuffer
```

So, in this case, the interpreter object that does all the work will be called `tflite` and the model that you'll load into the interpreter as a `ByteBuffer` is called `tflitemodel`.

Next, in the `onCreate` method, which gets called when the activity is created, add some code to instantiate the interpreter and load `model.tflite` into it:

```
try{
    tflitemodel = loadModelFile(this.assets, "model.tflite")
    tflite = Interpreter(tflitemodel)
} catch(ex: Exception){
    ex.printStackTrace()
}
```

Also, while you're in `onCreate`, add the code for the two controls that you'll interact with—the `EditText` where you'll type a value, and the `Button` that you'll press to get an inference:

```
var convertButton: Button = findViewById<Button>(R.id.convertButton)
convertButton.setOnClickListener{
    doInference()
}
txtValue = findViewById<EditText>(R.id.txtValue)
```

You'll also need to declare the `EditText` at the class level alongside `tflite` and `tflitemodel`, as it will be referred to within the next function. You can do that with:

```
private lateinit var txtValue : EditText
```

Finally, it's time to do the inference. You can do this with a new function called doInference:

```
private fun doInference(){
}
```

Within this function you can gather the data from the input, pass it to TensorFlow Lite to get an inference, and then display the returned value.

 In this case, the inference is very simple. For complex models it can be a long-running process that can block the UI thread, which you'll need to keep in mind when building your own apps.

The EditText control, where you'll enter the number, will provide you with a string, which you'll need to convert to a float:

```
var userVal: Float = txtValue.text.toString().toFloat()
```

As you'll recall from Chapter 1 and Chapter 2, when feeding data into the model you'll typically need to format it as a NumPy array. Being a Python construct, NumPy isn't available in Android, but you can just use a FloatArray in this context. Even though you're only feeding in one value, it still needs to be in an array, roughly approximating a tensor:

```
var inputVal: FloatArray = floatArrayOf(userVal)
```

The model will return a stream of bytes to you that will need to be interpreted. As you know you're getting a float value out of the model, and given that a float is 4 bytes, you can set up a ByteBuffer of 4 bytes to receive the output. There are several ways that bytes can be ordered, but you just need the default, native order:

```
var outputVal: ByteBuffer = ByteBuffer.allocateDirect(4)
outputVal.order(ByteOrder.nativeOrder())
```

To perform the inference, you call the run method on the interpreter, passing it the input and output values. It will then read from the input value and write to the output value:

```
tflite.run(inputVal, outputVal)
```

The output is written to the ByteBuffer, whose pointer is now at the end of the buffer. To read it, you have to reset it to the beginning of the buffer:

```
outputVal.rewind()
```

And now you can read the contents of the ByteBuffer as a float:

```
var inference:Float = outputVal.getFloat()
```

If you want to display this to the user, you can then use an AlertDialog:

```
val builder = AlertDialog.Builder(this)
with(builder)
{
    setTitle("TFLite Interpreter")
    setMessage("Your Value is:$inference")
    setNeutralButton("OK", DialogInterface.OnClickListener {
            dialog, id -> dialog.cancel()
    })
    show()
}
```

You can now run the app and try it for yourself! You can see the results in Figure 8-4, where I entered a value of 10 and the model gave me an inference of 18.984955, which is displayed in an alert box. Note that your value may be different for the reasons discussed earlier. When you train a model, the neural network begins by being randomly initialized, so when it converges it may be doing so from a different starting point, and as such your model may have slightly different results.

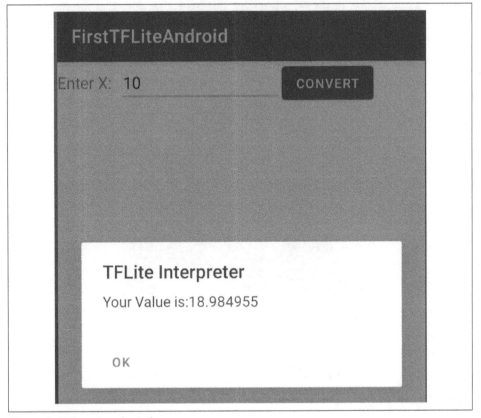

Figure 8-4. Running the inference

Going Beyond the Basics

This example was very trivial—you had a model that took a single input value and provided a single output value. Both of these were floats, which take 4 bytes to store, so you could create byte buffers with just 4 bytes in each and know that they contained the single value. So, when using more complex data, you'll have to work to get your data into the format that the model expects, which will require a lot of engineering on your part. Let's look at an example using an image. In Chapter 9 we'll look at Model Maker, which is a really useful tool for abstracting the complexity of using TFLite on Android or iOS for common scenarios—including image classification like this—but I think it's still a useful exercise to explore an under-the-hood scenario for how to manage data in and out of a model for when you go outside the common scenarios!

For example, let's start with an image like that in Figure 8-5, which is a simple image of a dog that happens to be 395 × 500 pixels. This is used in a model that can tell the difference between cats and dogs. I won't go into detail on how to *create* that model, but there's a notebook in the repository for this book that does that for you, as well as a sample app to handle the inference. You can find the training code in *Chapter8_Lab2.ipynb* (*https://oreil.ly/mohak*), and the app is called "cats_vs_dogs."

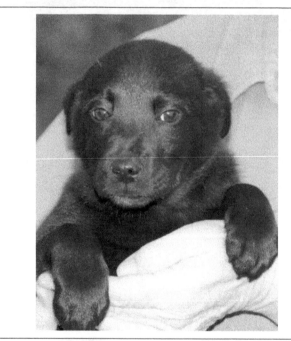

Figure 8-5. Image of a dog to interpret

The first thing you need to do is resize it to 224 × 224 pixels, the image dimensions that the model was trained on. This can be done in Android using the Bitmap libraries. For example, you can create a new 224 × 224 bitmap with:

```
val scaledBitmap = Bitmap.createScaledBitmap(bitmap, 224, 224, false)
```

(In this case, bitmap contains the raw image loaded as a resource by the app. The full app is available in the book's GitHub repo.)

Now that it's the right size, you have to reconcile how the image is structured in Android with how the model expects it to be structured. If you recall, when training models in earlier chapters in the book, you fed in images as normalized tensors of values. For example, an image like this would be (224, 224, 3): 224 × 224 is the image size, and 3 is the color depth. The values were also all normalized to between 0 and 1.

So, in summary, you need 224 × 224 × 3 float values between 0 and 1 to represent the image. To store that in a ByteArray, where 4 bytes make a float, you can use this code:

```
val byteBuffer = ByteBuffer.allocateDirect(4 * 224 * 224 * 3)
byteBuffer.order(ByteOrder.nativeOrder())
```

Our Android image, on the other hand, has each pixel stored as a 32-bit integer in an ARGB value. This might look something like 0x0010FF10 for a particular pixel. The first two values are the transparency, which you can ignore, and the rest are for RGB (i.e., 0x10 for red, 0xFF for green, and 0x10 for blue). The simple normalization you've been doing to this point is just to divide the R, G, B channel values by 255, which would give you .06275 for red, 1 for green, and .06275 for blue.

So, to do this conversion, let's first turn our bitmap into an array of 224 × 224 integers, and copy the pixels in. You can do this using the getPixels API:

```
val intValues = IntArray(224 * 224)

scaledbitmap.getPixels(intValues, 0, 224, 0, 0, 224, 224)
```

You can find details on the getPixels API explaining these parameters in the Android developer documentation (*https://oreil.ly/EFs1Q*).

Now you'll need to iterate through this array, reading the pixels one by one and converting them into normalized floats. You'll use bit shifting to get the particular channels. For example, consider the value 0x0010FF10 from earlier. If you shift that by 16 bits to the right, you'll get 0x0010 (with the FF10 being "lost"). If you then "and" that by 0xFF, you'll get 0x10, keeping just the bottom two numbers. Similarly, if you had shifted by 8 bits to the right you'd have 0x0010FF, and performing an "and" on that would give you 0xFF. This technique (typically called *masking*) allows you to quickly and easily strip out the relevant bits that make up the pixels. You can use the shr operation on an integer for this, with input.shr(16) reading "shift input 16 pixels to the right":

```
var pixel = 0
for (i in 0 until INPUT_SIZE) {
  for (j in 0 until INPUT_SIZE) {
    val input = intValues[pixel++]
    byteBuffer.putFloat(((input.shr(16)  and 0xFF) / 255))
    byteBuffer.putFloat(((input.shr(8) and 0xFF) / 255))
    byteBuffer.putFloat(((input and 0xFF)) / 255))
  }
}
```

As before, when it comes to the output, you need to define an array to hold the result. It doesn't *have* to be a `ByteArray`; indeed, you can define something like a `FloatAr ray` if you know the results are going to be floats, as they usually are. In this case, with the dogs versus cats model, you have two labels, and the model architecture is defined with two neurons in the output layer, containing the respective properties for the classes `cat` and `dog`. Reading back the results, you can define a structure to contain the output tensor like this:

```
val result = Array(1) { FloatArray(2) }
```

Note that it's a single array that contains an array of two items. Remember back when using Python you might see a value like [[1.0 0.0]]—it's the same here. The `Array(1)` is defining the containing array [], while the `FloatArray(2)` is the [1.0 0.0]. It can be a little confusing, for sure, but it's something that I hope you'll get used to as you write more TensorFlow apps!

As before, you interpret using `interpreter.run`:

```
interpreter.run(byteBuffer, result)
```

And now your result will be an array, containing two values (one for each of the probabilities that the image is a cat or a dog). You can see what it looks like in the Android debugger in Figure 8-6—where you can see this image had a 0.01 probability of being a cat and a 0.99 one of being a dog!

```
►   ▤  this = {Classifier@9590}
►   ▤  bitmap = {Bitmap@9591} "" ... View Bitmap
►   ⓟ  scaledBitmap = {Bitmap@9592} "" ... View Bitmap
►   ▤  byteBuffer = {DirectByteBuffer@9593} "java.nio.DirectByteBuffer[pos=602112 lim=602112 cap=602112]"
▼   ⓟ  result = {float[1][]@9594}
    ▼  ▤  0 = {float[2]@9599}
          01  0 = 0.012712446
          01  1 = 0.9872875
```

Figure 8-6. Parsing the output value

As you create mobile apps with Android, this is the most complex part—other than creating the model, of course—that you'll have to take into account. How Python represents values, particularly with NumPy, can be very different from how Android does. You'll have to create converters to reformat your data for how neural networks expect the data to be input, and you'll have to understand the output schema that the neural network uses so that you can parse the results.

Create an iOS App to Host TFLite

Earlier we explored creating an app to host the simple y = 2x – 1 model in Android. Let's see how to do the same in iOS next. You'll need a Mac if you want to follow along with this example, as the development tool to use is Xcode (which is only available on Mac). If you don't have it already, you can install it from the App Store. It will give you everything you need, including an iOS Simulator on which you can run iPhone and iPod apps without the need for a physical device.

Step 1: Create a Basic iOS App

Open Xcode and select File → New Project. You'll be asked to pick the template for your new project. Choose Single View App, which is the simplest template (Figure 8-7), and click Next.

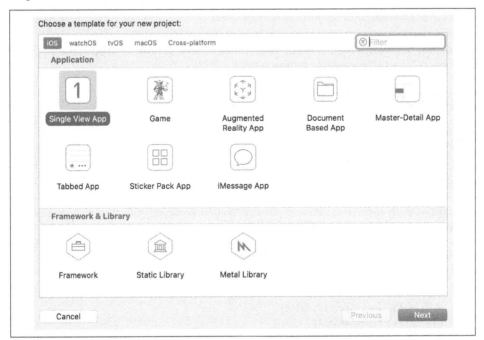

Figure 8-7. Creating a new iOS application in Xcode

After that you'll be asked to choose options for your new project, including a name for the app. Call it *firstlite*, and make sure that the language is Swift and the user interface is Storyboard (Figure 8-8).

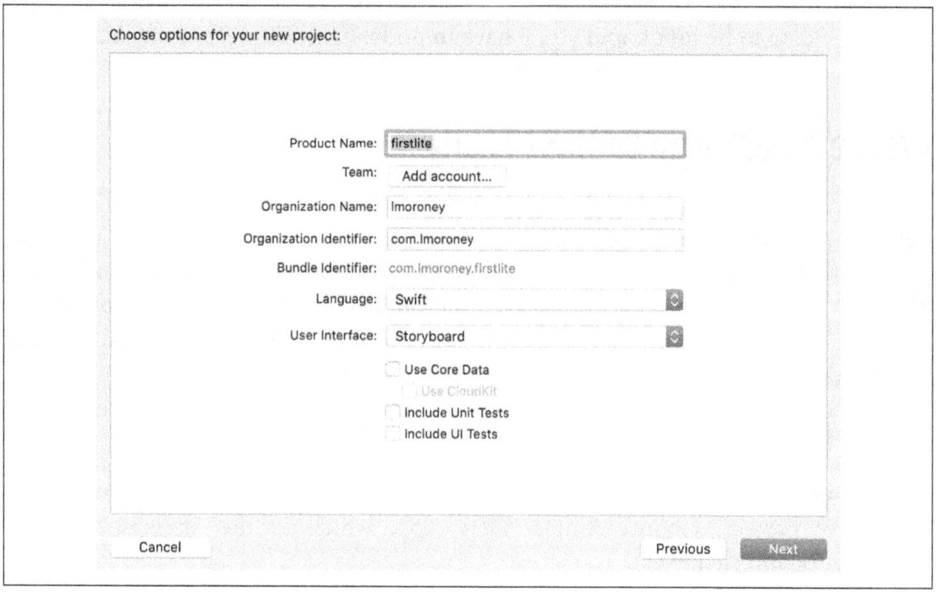

Figure 8-8. Choosing options for your new project

Click Next to create a basic iOS app that will run on an iPhone or iPad simulator. The next step is to add TensorFlow Lite to it.

Step 2: Add TensorFlow Lite to Your Project

To add dependencies to an iOS project, you can use a technology called CocoaPods (*https://cocoapods.org*), a dependency management project with many thousands of libraries that can be easily integrated into your app. To do so, you create a specification called a Podfile, which contains details about your project and the dependencies you want to use. This is a simple text file called *Podfile* (no extension), and you should put it in the same directory as the *firstlite.xcodeproj* file that was created for you by Xcode. Its contents should be as follows:

```
# Uncomment the next line to define a global platform for your project
platform :ios, '12.0'

target 'firstlite' do
  # Pods for ImageClassification
  pod 'TensorFlowLiteSwift'
end
```

The important part is the line that reads pod 'TensorFlowLiteSwift', which indicates that the TensorFlow Lite Swift libraries need to be added to the project.

Next, using Terminal, change to the directory containing the Podfile and issue the following command:

```
> pod install
```

The dependencies will be downloaded and added to your project, stored in a new folder called *Pods*. You'll also have an *.xcworkspace* file added, as shown in Figure 8-9. Use this one in the future to open your project, and not the *.xcodeproj* file.

Figure 8-9. Your file structure after running pod install

You now have a basic iOS app, and you have added the TensorFlow Lite dependencies. The next step is to create your user interface.

Step 3: Create the User Interface

The Xcode storyboard editor is a visual tool that allows you to create a user interface. After opening your workspace, you'll see a list of source files on the left. Select *Main.storyboard*, and using the controls palette, drag and drop controls onto the view for an iPhone screen (Figure 8-10).

If you can't find the controls palette, you can access it by clicking the + at the top right of the screen (highlighted in Figure 8-10). Using it, add a Label, and change the text to "Enter a Number." Then add another one with the text "Result goes here." Add a Button and change its caption to "Go," and finally add a TextField. Arrange them similarly to what you can see in Figure 8-10. It doesn't have to be pretty!

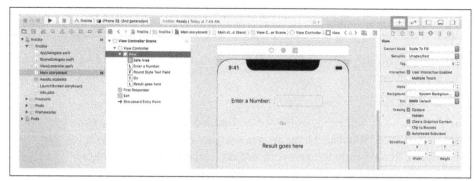

Figure 8-10. Adding controls to the storyboard

Now that the controls are laid out, you want to be able to refer to them in code. In storyboard parlance, you do this using either *outlets* (when you want to address the control to read or set its contents) or *actions* (when you want to execute some code when the user interacts with the control).

The easiest way to wire this up is to have a split screen, with the storyboard on one side and the *ViewController.swift* code that underlies it on the other. You can achieve this by selecting the split screen control (highlighted in Figure 8-11), clicking on one side and selecting the storyboard, and then clicking on the other side and selecting *ViewController.swift*.

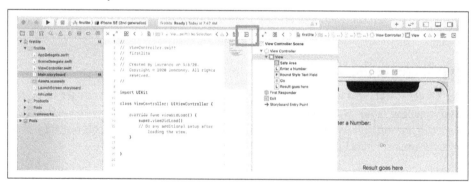

Figure 8-11. Splitting the screen

Once you've done this, you can start creating your outlets and actions by dragging and dropping. This app will have the user type a number into the text field and press the Go button, and then run inference on the value that they typed. The result will be rendered in the label that says "Result goes here."

This means you'll need to read or write to two controls, reading the contents of the text field to get what the user typed in and writing the result to the "Results goes here" label. Thus, you'll need two outlets. To create them, hold down the Ctrl key and drag the control on the storyboard onto the *ViewController.swift* file, dropping it just below the class definition. A pop-up will appear asking you to define it (Figure 8-12).

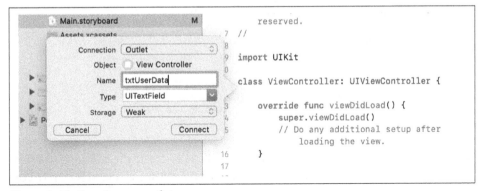

Figure 8-12. Creating an outlet

Ensure the connection type is Outlet, and create an outlet for the text field called `txtUserData` and one for the label called `txtResult`.

Next, drag the button over to the *ViewController.swift* file. In the pop-up, ensure that the connection type is Action and the event type is Touch Up Inside. Use this to define an action called `btnGo` (Figure 8-13).

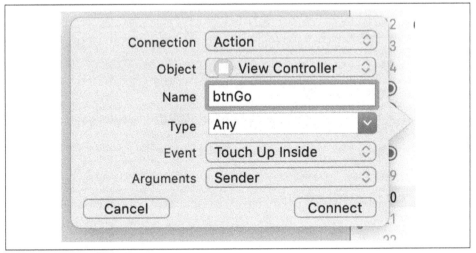

Figure 8-13. Adding an action

At this point your *ViewController.swift* file should look like this—note the `IBOutlet` and `IBAction` code:

```
import UIKit

class ViewController: UIViewController {
    @IBOutlet weak var txtUserData: UITextField!

    @IBOutlet weak var txtResult: UILabel!
    @IBAction func btnGo(_ sender: Any) {
    }
    override func viewDidLoad() {
        super.viewDidLoad()
        // Do any additional setup after loading the view.
    }
}
```

Now that the UI is squared away, the next step will be to create the code that will handle the inference. Instead of having this in the same Swift file as the ViewController logic, you'll place it in a separate code file.

Step 4: Add and Initialize the Model Inference Class

To keep the UI separate from the underlying model inference, you'll create a new Swift file containing a ModelParser class. This is where all the work of getting the data into the model, running the inference, and then parsing the results will happen. In Xcode, choose File → New File and select Swift File as the template type (Figure 8-14).

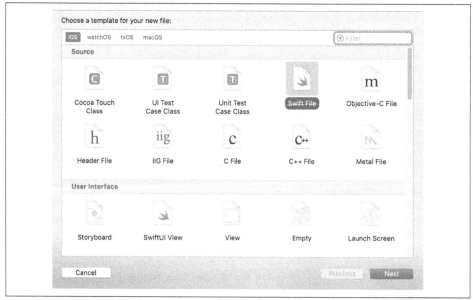

Figure 8-14. Adding a new Swift file

Call this *ModelParser* and ensure that the checkbox targeting it to the *firstlite* project is checked (Figure 8-15).

Figure 8-15. Adding ModelParser.swift to your project

This will add a *ModelParser.swift* file to your project that you can edit to add the inference logic. First, ensure that the imports at the top of the file include `Tensor FlowLite`:

```
import Foundation
import TensorFlowLite
```

You'll pass a reference to the model file, *model.tflite*, to this class—you haven't added it yet, but you will soon:

```
typealias FileInfo = (name: String, extension: String)

enum ModelFile {
    static let modelInfo: FileInfo = (name: "model", extension: "tflite")
}
```

This `typealias` and `enum` make the code a little more compact. You'll see them in use in a moment. Next you'll need to load the model into an interpreter, so first declare the interpreter as a private variable to the class:

```
private var interpreter: Interpreter
```

Swift requires variables to be initialized, which you can do within an `init` function. The following function will take two input parameters. The first, `modelFileInfo`, is the `FileInfo` type you just declared. The second, `threadCount`, is the number of threads to use to initialize the interpreter, which we'll set to 1. Within this function, you'll create a reference to the model file that you described earlier (*model.tflite*):

```
init?(modelFileInfo: FileInfo, threadCount: Int = 1) {
    let modelFilename = modelFileInfo.name

    guard let modelPath = Bundle.main.path
    (
        forResource: modelFilename,
        ofType: modelFileInfo.extension
    )
    else {
        print("Failed to load the model file")
        return nil
    }
```

When you compile your app and assets into a package that gets deployed to the device, the term used in iOS parlance is a "bundle." So your model needs to be in the bundle, and once you have the path to the model file, you can load it:

```
do
{
    interpreter = try Interpreter(modelPath: modelPath)
}
catch let error
{
    print("Failed to create the interpreter")
    return nil
}
```

Step 5: Perform the Inference

Within the `ModelParser` class, you can then do the inference. The user will type a string value in the text field, which will be converted to a float, so you'll need a function that takes a float, passes it to the model, runs the inference, and parses the return value.

Start by creating a function called `runModel`. Your code will need to catch errors, so start it with a do{:

```
func runModel(withInput input: Float) -> Float? {
    do{
```

Next, you'll need to allocate tensors on the interpreter. This initializes the model and prepares it for inference:

```
try interpreter.allocateTensors()
```

Then you'll create the input tensor. As Swift doesn't have a `Tensor` datatype, you'll need to write the data directly to memory in an `UnsafeMutableBufferPointer`. These are covered in Apple's developer documentation (*https://oreil.ly/EfDus*).

You can specify the type of this, which will be Float, and write one value (as you only have one float), starting from the address of the variable called data. This will effectively copy all the bytes for the float into the buffer:

```
var data: Float = input
let buffer: UnsafeMutableBufferPointer<Float> =
        UnsafeMutableBufferPointer(start: &data, count: 1)
```

With the data in the buffer, you can then copy it to the interpreter at input 0. You only have one input tensor, so you can specify it as the buffer:

```
try interpreter.copy(Data(buffer: buffer), toInputAt: 0)
```

To execute the inference, you invoke the interpreter:

```
try interpreter.invoke()
```

There's only one output tensor, so you can read it by taking the output at 0:

```
let outputTensor = try interpreter.output(at: 0)
```

Similar to when inputting the values, you're dealing with low-level memory, which is referred to as *unsafe* data. When using typical datatypes, their location in memory is tightly controlled by the operating system so that you don't overflow and overwrite other data. When doing this, you are writing the data to memory directly yourself, and as such are taking the risk that bounds may not be respected (hence the term *unsafe*).

It's in an array of `Float32` values (it only has one element but still needs to be treated as an array), which can be read like this:

```
let results: [Float32] =
                    [Float32](unsafeData: outputTensor.data) ?? []
```

If you're not familiar with the `??` syntax, this says to make the results an array of `Float32` by copying the output tensor into it, and if that fails (usually a null pointer error), then create an empty array instead. For this code to work, you'll need to implement an `Array` extension; the full code for that will be shown in a moment.

Once you have the results in an array, the first element will be your result. If this fails, just return `nil`:

```
guard let result = results.first else {
  return nil
}
return result
}
```

The function began with a do{, so you'll need to catch any errors, print them, and return nil in that event:

```
catch {
  print(error)
  return nil
  }
 }
}
```

Finally, still in *ModelParser.swift*, you can add the Array extension that handles the unsafe data and loads it into an array:

```
extension Array {
  init?(unsafeData: Data) {
    guard unsafeData.count % MemoryLayout<Element>.stride == 0
        else { return nil }
    #if swift(>=5.0)
    self = unsafeData.withUnsafeBytes {
      .init($0.bindMemory(to: Element.self))
    }
    #else
    self = unsafeData.withUnsafeBytes {
      .init(UnsafeBufferPointer<Element>(
        start: $0,
        count: unsafeData.count / MemoryLayout<Element>.stride
      ))
    }
    #endif  // swift(>=5.0)
  }
}
```

This is a handy helper that you can use if you want to parse floats directly out of a TensorFlow Lite model. Now that the class for parsing the model is done, the next step is to add the model to your app.

Step 6: Add the Model to Your App

To add the model to your app, you'll need a *models* directory within the app. In Xcode, right-click on the *firstlite* folder and select New Group (Figure 8-16). Call the new group *models*.

You can get the model by training the simple y = 2x – 1 sample from earlier in this chapter. If you don't have it already, you can use the Colab in the book's GitHub repository.

Once you have the converted model file (called *model.tflite*), you can drag and drop it into Xcode on the models group you just added. Select "Copy items if needed" and ensure you add it to the target *firstlite* by checking the box beside it (Figure 8-17).

Figure 8-16. Adding a new group to your app

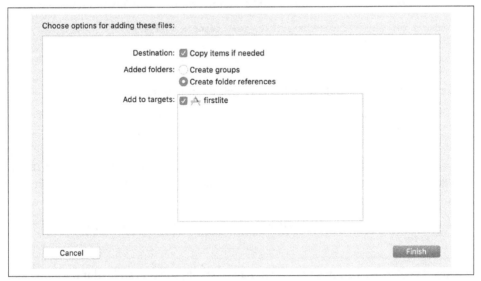

Figure 8-17. Adding the model to your project

The model will now be in your project and available for inference. The final step is to complete the user interface logic—then you'll be ready to go!

Step 7: Add the UI Logic

Earlier, you created the storyboard containing the UI description and began editing the *ViewController.swift* file containing the UI logic. As most of the work of inference has now been offloaded to the `ModelParser` class, the UI logic should be very light.

Start by adding a private variable declaring an instance of the `ModelParser` class:

```
private var modelParser: ModelParser? =
    ModelParser(modelFileInfo: ModelFile.modelInfo)
```

Previously, you created an action on the button called `btnGo`. This will be called when the user touches the button. Update that to execute a function called `doInference` when the user takes that action:

```
@IBAction func btnGo(_ sender: Any) {
  doInference()
}
```

Next, you'll construct the `doInference` function:

```
private func doInference() {
```

The text field that the user will enter data into is called `txtUserData.` Read this value, and if it's empty just set the result to 0.00 and don't bother with any inference:

```
guard let text = txtUserData.text, text.count > 0 else {
  txtResult.text = "0.00"
  return
}
```

Otherwise, convert it to a float. If this fails, exit the function:

```
guard let value = Float(text) else {
  return
}
```

If the code has reached this point, you can now run the model, passing it that input. The `ModelParser` will do the rest, returning you either a result or `nil`. If the return value is `nil`, then you'll exit the function:

```
guard let result = self.modelParser?.runModel(withInput: value) else {
  return
}
```

Finally, if you've reached this point, you have a result, so you can load it into the label (called `txtResult`) by formatting the float as a string:

```
txtResult.text = String(format: "%.2f", result)
```

That's it! The complexity of the model loading and inference has been handled by the ModelParser class, keeping your ViewController very light. For convenience, here's the complete listing:

```
import UIKit

class ViewController: UIViewController {
  private var modelParser: ModelParser? =
      ModelParser(modelFileInfo: ModelFile.modelInfo)
  @IBOutlet weak var txtUserData: UITextField!

  @IBOutlet weak var txtResult: UILabel!
  @IBAction func btnGo(_ sender: Any) {
    doInference()
  }
  override func viewDidLoad() {
    super.viewDidLoad()
    // Do any additional setup after loading the view.
  }
  private func doInference() {

    guard let text = txtUserData.text, text.count > 0 else {
      txtResult.text = "0.00"
      return
    }
    guard let value = Float(text) else {
      return
    }
    guard let result = self.modelParser?.runModel(withInput: value) else {
      return
    }
    txtResult.text = String(format: "%.2f", result)
  }

}
```

You've now done everything you need to get the app working. Run it, and you should see it in the simulator. Type a number in the text field, press the button, and you should see a result in the results field, as shown in Figure 8-18.

While this was a long journey for a very simple app, it should provide a good template to help you understand how TensorFlow Lite works. In this walkthrough, you saw how to:

- Use pods to add the TensorFlow Lite dependencies
- Add a TensorFlow Lite model to your app
- Load the model into an interpreter
- Access the input tensors and write directly to their memory

- Read the memory from the output tensors and copy that to high-level data structures like float arrays

- Wire it all up to a user interface with a storyboard and view controler.

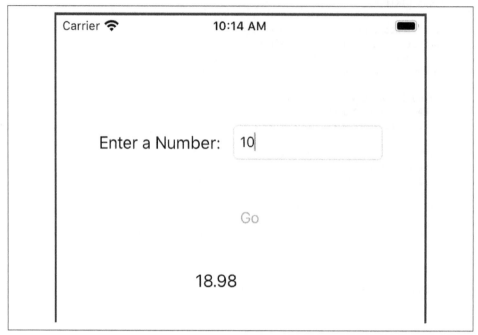

Figure 8-18. Running the app in the iPhone Simulator

In the next section, you'll move beyond this simple scenario and look at handling more complex data.

Moving Beyond "Hello World": Processing Images

In the previous example, you saw how to create a full app that uses TensorFlow Lite to do very simple inferences. However, despite the simplicity of the app, the process of getting data into the model and parsing data out of the model can be a little unintuitive because you're handling low-level bits and bytes. As you get into more complex scenarios, such as managing images, the good news is that the process isn't that much more complicated.

Consider a model that you'd create to distinguish between cats versus dogs. In this section you'll see how to create an iOS app in Swift with a trained model that, given an image of a cat or a dog, will be able to infer what is in the picture. The full app code is available in the GitHub repo for this book, as well as a Colab notebook to train and convert the model to TFLite format.

First, recall that the tensor for an image has three dimensions: width, height, and color depth. So, for example, when using the MobileNet architecture that the dogs versus cats mobile sample is based on, the dimensions are 224 × 224 × 3—each image is 224 × 224 pixels and has three channels for color depth. Note that each pixel, after normalization, will be represented by a value between 0 and 1 in each channel, indicating the intensity of that pixel on the red, green, and blue channels.

In iOS, images are typically represented as instances of the `UIImage` class, which has a useful `pixelBuffer` property that returns a buffer of all the pixels in the image.

Within the `CoreImage` libraries, there's a `CVPixelBufferGetPixelFormatType` API that will return the type of the pixel buffer:

```
let sourcePixelFormat = CVPixelBufferGetPixelFormatType(pixelBuffer)
```

This will typically be a 32-bit image with channels for alpha (aka transparency), red, green, and blue. However, there are multiple variants, generally with these channels in different orders. You'll want to ensure that it's one of these formats, as the rest of the code won't work if the image is stored in a different format:

```
assert(sourcePixelFormat == kCVPixelFormatType_32ARGB ||
    sourcePixelFormat == kCVPixelFormatType_32BGRA ||
    sourcePixelFormat == kCVPixelFormatType_32RGBA)
```

As the desired format is 224 × 224, which is square, the best thing to do next is to crop the image to the largest square in its center, using the `centerThumbnail` property, and then scale this down to 224 × 224:

```
let scaledSize = CGSize(width: 224, height: 224)
guard let thumbnailPixelBuffer =
    pixelBuffer.centerThumbnail(ofSize: scaledSize)
    else {
        return nil
    }
```

Now that you have the image resized to 224 × 224, the next step is to remove the alpha channel. Remember that the model was trained on 224 × 224 × 3, where the 3 is the RGB channels, so there is no alpha.

Now that you have a pixel buffer, you need to extract the RGB data from it. This helper function achieves that for you by finding the alpha channel and slicing it out:

```
private func rgbDataFromBuffer(_ buffer: CVPixelBuffer,

                              byteCount: Int) -> Data? {

    CVPixelBufferLockBaseAddress(buffer, .readOnly)
    defer { CVPixelBufferUnlockBaseAddress(buffer, .readOnly) }
    guard let mutableRawPointer =
        CVPixelBufferGetBaseAddress(buffer)
        else {
```

```
            return nil
        }

    let count = CVPixelBufferGetDataSize(buffer)
    let bufferData = Data(bytesNoCopy: mutableRawPointer,
                          count: count, deallocator: .none)

    var rgbBytes = [Float](repeating: 0, count: byteCount)
    var index = 0

    for component in bufferData.enumerated() {
        let offset = component.offset
        let isAlphaComponent =
            (offset % alphaComponent.baseOffset) ==
        alphaComponent.moduloRemainder

        guard !isAlphaComponent else { continue }

        rgbBytes[index] = Float(component.element) / 255.0
        index += 1
    }

    return rgbBytes.withUnsafeBufferPointer(Data.init)


}
```

This code uses an extension called `Data` that copies the raw bytes into an array:

```
extension Data {
  init<T>(copyingBufferOf array: [T]) {
    self = array.withUnsafeBufferPointer(Data.init)
  }
}
```

Now you can pass the thumbnail pixel buffer you just created to `rgbDataFromBuffer`:

```
guard let rgbData = rgbDataFromBuffer(
      thumbnailPixelBuffer,
      byteCount: 224 * 224 * 3
      ) else {
          print("Failed to convert the image buffer to RGB data.")
          return nil
      }
```

At this point you have the raw RGB data that is in the format the model expects, and you can copy it directly to the input tensor:

```
try interpreter.allocateTensors()
try interpreter.copy(rgbData, toInputAt: 0)
```

You can then invoke the interpreter and read the output tensor:

```
try interpreter.invoke()
outputTensor = try interpreter.output(at: 0)
```

In the case of dogs versus cats, you have as output a float array with two values, the first being the probability that the image is of a cat and the second that it's a dog. This is the same results code that you saw earlier, and it uses the same array extension from the previous example:

```
let results = [Float32](unsafeData: outputTensor.data) ?? []
```

As you can see, although this is a more complex example, the same design pattern holds. You must understand your model's architecture, and the raw input and output formats. You must then structure your input data in the way the model expects—which often means getting down to raw bytes that you write into a buffer, or at least simulate using an array. You then have to read the raw stream of bytes coming out of the model and create a data structure to hold them. From the output perspective, this will almost always be something like we've seen in this chapter—an array of floats. With the helper code you've implemented, you're most of the way there!

We'll look into this example in more detail in Chapter 11.

Exploring Model Optimization

TensorFlow Lite includes tools to optimize your model using representative data as well as processes such as quantization. We'll explore those in this section.

Quantization

The idea of quantization comes from understanding that neurons in a model default to using float32 as representation, but often their values fall within a much smaller range than the range of a float32. Consider Figure 8-19 as an example.

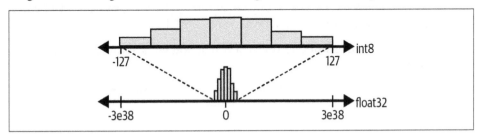

Figure 8-19. Quantizing values

In this case, at the bottom of the diagram is a histogram of the possible values that a particular neuron might have. They're normalized, so they're spread around 0, but the min is far greater than the min of a float32, and the max value is far less than the max of a float32. What if, instead of having all of this "empty space," the histogram could be converted into a much smaller range—say −127 to +127, with the values mapped accordingly. Note that by doing this you are significantly reducing how many *possible* values can be represented, so you will risk a loss in precision. Studies of this method have shown that while precision can be lost, the loss is often small, but the benefits in model size, as well as inference time, because of the simpler data structure, greatly outweigh the risks.

Then, the range of values could be implemented in a single byte (256 values) instead of the 4 bytes of a float32. And given that neural networks can have many neurons, often using hundreds of thousands or millions of parameters, using only one-quarter of the space to store their parameters can have significant time savings.

 This can also be coupled with hardware that's optimized to use data storage in int8 instead of float32, giving even further benefits of hardware accelerated inference.

This process is called *quantization* and is available in TensorFlow Lite. Let's explore how it works.

Note that there are multiple methods for quantization, including quantization-aware training, where you take it into account while the model learns; pruning, which is used to reduce connectivity in a model to simplify it; and post-training quantization, which we'll explore here, where you reduce the data storage in a model for weights and biases as described earlier.

In the source code for this chapter, there's a notebook called *Chapter8Lab2* that trains a neural network to recognize the difference between cats and dogs. I strongly recommend you work through it as you follow along here. You can access it using Colab (*https://oreil.ly/xpEd0*) if it's available in your country; otherwise, you'll need a Python environment or Jupyter notebook environment to work in.

You may notice as you're working through it that you get a summary of the model that looks like this:

```
Layer (type)                 Output Shape              Param #
=================================================================
keras_layer (KerasLayer)     (None, 1280)              2257984

_____
dense (Dense)                (None, 2)                 2562
=================================================================
Total params: 2,260,546
Trainable params: 2,562
Non-trainable params: 2,257,984
```

Note the number of parameters: over two million! If you're reducing the storage of these by 3 bytes apiece, you can reduce your model size by over 6 MB with quantization!

So let's explore how to do quantization on the model—it's very easy to do! Earlier you saw how to instantiate the converter from a saved model like this:

```
converter = tf.lite.TFLiteConverter.from_saved_model(CATS_VS_DOGS_SAVED_MODEL)
```

But before converting, you can set an optimizations parameter on the converter, which accepts a parameter specifying the type of optimization. It was originally designed so that there were three different types of optimization (default or balanced, for size, and for speed), but the option to choose a type of quantization has been deprecated, so for now, you can only use "default" quantization.

For compatibility reasons, and future flexibility, the method signature remains, but you only have one option (default) that you can use like this:

```
converter.optimizations = [tf.lite.Optimize.DEFAULT]
```

When I created the cats versus dogs model *without* optimization, I had a model that was 8.8 Mb. When the optimization was applied, it shrank to 2.6 Mb, a significant savings!

You might wonder about any impact this has on accuracy. Given the change in size of the model, it's good to investigate.

There's code in the notebook that you can try for yourself, but when I investigated, I found that the unoptimized version of the model would do about 37 iterations per second in Colab (which uses a GPU, so it's optimized for floating point operations!), whereas the shrunken version did about 16 iterations per second. Without the GPU, the performance degraded by about half, but importantly, the speed is still terrific for image classification, and it's not likely you'll need this kind of performance when classifying images on a device!

More important is the accuracy—on a set of 100 images I tested, the unoptimized model got 99 of them correct, while the optimized one got 94. Here's where you'll have a trade-off decision about whether or not you want to optimize the model at the cost of accuracy. Experiment with this for your own models! Do note that in this case I just did basic quantization. There are other methods to reduce the size of your model that may have less of an impact, and all should be explored. Let's look next at using representative data.

Using Representative Data

The preceding example showed quantization by reducing values from float32 to int8 by effectively removing "white space" from the data, but the algorithm generally assumed that the data was uniformly spread around 0, because that's what it learned from the training data, which could lead to a loss of accuracy if your test or real-world data isn't represented like this. We saw that the accuracy dropped from 99/100 to 94/100 with a small set of test images.

You can give the optimization process a helping hand by providing some representative data from your dataset so it can predict better how to optimize for the type of data that the neural network will be expected to "see" going forward. This will give you a trade-off of size against accuracy—the size might be a bit larger, because the optimization process won't convert all the values from float32 to int8, detecting, from the dataset, that some might involve too much lost data.

Doing this is pretty simple—simply take a subset of your data as the representative data:

```
def representative_data_gen():
    for input_value, _ in test_batches.take(100):
        yield [input_value]
```

Then, specify this as the representative dataset for the convertor:

```
converter.representative_dataset = representative_data_gen
```

Finally, specify the desired ops to target. You'll generally use the built-in `INT8` ones like this:

```
converter.target_spec.supported_ops = [tf.lite.OpsSet.TFLITE_BUILTINS_INT8]
```

Note that at the time of writing, the full set of supported ops selections is experimental. You can find details on the TensorFlow website (*https://oreil.ly/Kn1Xj*).

After converting with this process, the model size increased slightly (to 2.9 Mb, but still significantly smaller than the original 8.9 Mb), but the iteration speed dropped sharply (to about one iteration per second). However the accuracy improved to 98/100, much closer to the original model.

For more techniques, and to explore results in model optimization, check out *https://www.tensorflow.org/lite/performance/model_optimization*.

Try it out for yourself, but do note that the Colab environment can change a lot, and your results may be different from mine, in particular if you use different models. I'd strongly recommend seeing what the inference speed and accuracy look like on a device to get more appropriate results.

Summary

This chapter provided an introduction to TensorFlow Lite, and how it works to bring models trained using Python to mobile devices such as Android or iOS. You saw the toolchain and the converter scripts that let you shrink your model and optimize for mobile, before exploring some scenarios in how to code Android/Kotlin or iOS/Swift applications to use these models. Going beyond a simple model, you also began to see some of the considerations you need to take on as an app developer when converting data from the internal representation of a mobile environment to the tensor-based one in a TensorFlow model. Finally, you explored some scenarios for optimizing and shrinking your model further. In Chapter 9, you'll study some scenarios to create more sophisticated models than "Hello World," and in Chapters 10 and 11, you'll bring those models into Android and iOS!

Creating Custom Models

In earlier chapters you saw how to use turnkey models for image labeling, object detection, entity extraction, and more. What you didn't see was how you might be able to use models that you had created yourself, and indeed *how* you might be able to create them by yourself. In this chapter, we'll look at three scenarios for creating models, and then in Chapters 10 and 11, we'll look at incorporating those models into Android or iOS apps.

Creating models from scratch can be difficult and very time consuming. It's also the realm of pure TensorFlow development and is covered in lots of other books such as my book *AI and Machine Learning for Coders* (O'Reilly). If you aren't creating from scratch, and in particular if you're focused on mobile apps, there are some tools to assist you, and we'll look at three of them in this chapter:

- *TensorFlow Lite Model Maker* is the preferred choice *if* you are building an app that fits a scenario that Model Maker supports. It's *not* a generic tool for building any type of model, but is designed to support common use cases such as image classification, object detection, and more. It involves little to no neural-network-specific coding, and as such is a great place to start if you don't want to learn that stuff yet!

- Creating models using *Cloud AutoML*, and in particular the tools in Cloud AutoML designed to minimize the amount of code you have to write and maintain. Similar to TensorFlow Model Maker, the scenarios here are focused on the core common ones, and if you want to step off the trail, you'll need to do some custom model coding.

- Creating models with TensorFlow using *transfer learning*. In this scenario, you don't create a model from scratch, but reuse an existing model, repurposing part of it for your scenario. As you will be getting a little closer to neural network modeling, this will require you to do some neural network coding. If you're look-ing to dip your toes into the world of creating deep learning models, it's a terrific way to start; much of the complexity is already implemented for you, but you can be flexible enough to build new model types.

A further iOS-only scenario is to create models using Create ML, which also uses transfer learning; we'll explore that in Chapter 13. We'll also explore language models, where as well as the model, your mobile app will need to understand metadata about the model such as the dictionary of words used in creating the model. In order to get a gentle start, let's explore TensorFlow Lite Model Maker first.

Creating a Model with TensorFlow Lite Model Maker

A core scenario that TensorFlow Lite Model Maker was designed for is image classifi-cation, and it claims to be able to help you create a basic model with only four lines of code. Furthermore the model will work with Android Studio's import functionality so you don't have to mess around in the assets folder, and it will generate code to get you started. As you'll see in Chapter 10, models made with Model Maker are much easier to use in your apps, because the difficult task of translating from your Android repre-sentation of data to the tensors required by models has been abstracted for you into helper classes that are automatically generated when you import the model using Android Studio. Unfortunately, at the time of writing, equivalent tools are not avail-able for Xcode, so you'll need to do much of the model data input/output with code you write yourself, but we'll go through some examples to give you a head start in Chapter 11.

Creating a model with the Model Maker is really simple. You'll use Python, and I've created a Python notebook for you already; it's available in the code repository for this book (*https://oreil.ly/9ImxO*).

Start by installing the `tflite-model-maker` package:

```
!pip install -q tflite-model-maker
```

Once that's done, you can import `tensorflow`, `numpy`, and the various modules in TensorFlow Lite Model Maker like this:

```
import numpy as np
import tensorflow as tf

from tflite_model_maker import configs
from tflite_model_maker import ExportFormat
from tflite_model_maker import image_classifier
from tflite_model_maker import ImageClassifierDataLoader
from tflite_model_maker import model_spec
```

To train a model with the Model Maker, you'll need data, which can be folders of images or TensorFlow datasets. So, for this example, there's a downloadable containing pictures of five different types of flower. When you download and unzip this, subdirectories will be created for the flowers.

Here's the code, where url is the location of the archive containing the flowers. It uses the tf.keras.utils libraries to download and extract the file:

```
image_path = tf.keras.utils.get_file('flower_photos.tgz',
                                      url, extract=True)

image_path = os.path.join(os.path.dirname(image_path), 'flower_photos')
```

If you want to inspect what it downloaded, you can do so with:

```
os.listdir(image_path)
```

This will output the contents of that path, including subdirectories, and should look something like this:

```
['roses', 'daisy', 'dandelion', 'LICENSE.txt', 'sunflowers', 'tulips']
```

Model Maker will train a classifier using these subdirectories as the label names. Remember in image classification that training data is labeled (i.e., this is a daisy, this is a rose, this is a sunflower, etc.), and the neural network matches distinct features in each image to a label, so that over time it learns to "see" the difference between the labeled objects. It's akin to "when you see this feature, it's a sunflower, and when you see this, it's a dandelion," etc.

You shouldn't use *all* your data to train the model. It's a best practice to hold some back to see if the model really understands the differences between the different types of flower in a general sense, or if it is specialized to everything that it sees. That sounds abstract, so consider it like this: you want your model to recognize roses *that it hasn't yet seen* and not just recognize roses based on the images you train it on. A simple technique to see if you are successful at this is to only use a portion of your data—say 90%—to train on. The other 10% is not *seen* while training. This 10% could then be a representation of what the network will be asked to classify in the future, and measuring its effectiveness on that is better than measuring its effectiveness on what it was trained on.

To achieve this, you'll need to create a data loader for Model Maker from a folder. As the images are already in the *image_page* folder, you can use the from_folder method on the ImageClassifierDataLoader object to get a dataset. Then, once you have your dataset, you can split it using the split method; to get train_data with 90% of your images, and test_data with the other 10%, you can use code like this:

```
data = ImageClassifierDataLoader.from_folder(image_path)
train_data, test_data = data.split(0.9)
```

You'll likely get an output like the following. Note that 3,670 is the number of total images in the dataset, and not the 90% used for training. The number of labels is the number of distinct types—in this case five—labeled with the five types of flower:

```
INFO:tensorflow:Load image with size: 3670, num_label: 5,
labels: daisy, dandelion, roses, sunflowers, tulip
```

Now, in order to train your model, all you have to do is call the `create` method on the image classifier and it will do the rest:

```
model = image_classifier.create(train_data)
```

This probably looks a little too simple—it's because a lot of the complexity such as defining the model architecture, performing transfer learning from an existing model, specifying a loss function and optimizer, and finally doing the training is all encapsulated within the `image_classifier` object. It's open source, so you can peek under the hood by checking out the TensorFlow Lite Model Maker repo (*https://oreil.ly/WYfXO*).

There'll be a lot of output and while it might look a little alien to you at first, it's good to take a quick look at it to understand. Here's the complete output:

```
Model: "sequential_1"
```

Layer (type)	Output Shape	Param #
hub_keras_layer_v1v2_1 (HubK	(None, 1280)	3413024
dropout_1 (Dropout)	(None, 1280)	0
dense_1 (Dense)	(None, 5)	6405

```
Total params: 3,419,429
Trainable params: 6,405
Non-trainable params: 3,413,024
```

```
None
Epoch 1/5
103/103 [====================] - 18s 151ms/step - loss: 1.1293 - accuracy: 0.6060
Epoch 2/5
103/103 [====================] - 15s 150ms/step - loss: 0.6623 - accuracy: 0.8878
Epoch 3/5
103/103 [====================] - 15s 150ms/step - loss: 0.6200 - accuracy: 0.9149
Epoch 4/5
103/103 [====================] - 15s 149ms/step - loss: 0.6011 - accuracy: 0.9219
Epoch 5/5
103/103 [====================] - 15s 149ms/step - loss: 0.5884 - accuracy: 0.9369
```

The first part of the output is the *model architecture*, telling us how the model has been designed. This model has three layers: the first layer is called `hub_keras_layer_v1v2_1`, which looks a bit mysterious. We'll get back to that in a second. The second is called dropout_1, and the third (and final) is called dense_1. What's important is to note the shape of the final layer—it's (None, 5), which in TensorFlow terms means that the first dimension can be any size, and the second is 5. Where have we seen 5 before? That's right, it's the number of classes in this dataset— we have five flowers. So the output of this will be a number of items each with five elements. The first number is for handling what's called *batch* inference. So if you throw a number of images, say 20, at the model, then it will give you a single 20 × 5 output, containing the inferences for the 20 images.

Why are there five values, you might wonder, and not a single value? Look back to Chapter 2, and in particular the cats versus dogs example (Figure 2-5), and you'll see that the output of a neural network that recognizes *n* classes has *n* neurons, with each neuron representing the probability that the network sees that class. So, in this case, the output of the neurons are the probabilities of the five classes respectively (i.e., neuron 1 for daisy, neuron 2 for dandelion, etc.). And if you were wondering what determines the order—in this case, it's simply alphabetic.

So what about the other layers? Well, let's start with the first one that's called hub_keras-layer_v1v2_1. That's a weird name! But the clue is at the beginning with the word "hub." A common form of training a model is to use an existing, pretrained model and adapt it to your needs. Think of it a little like subclassing an existing class and overriding some methods. There are many models out there that are trained on *millions* of images, and as such have become really good at extracting features from those images. So, instead of starting from scratch, it's often easier to use the features that they've already learned and match those to your images. This process is called *transfer learning*, and TensorFlow Hub stores a number of pretrained models, or parts of models with learned features (also called feature vectors) that can be reused. It's almost like a library of classes of existing code that you can reuse, but instead of code, it's neural networks that already know how to do something. So, this model then takes an existing model from TensorFlow Hub and uses its features. The output from that model will be 1,280 neurons, indicating that it has 1,280 features that it tries to "spot" in your image.

This is followed by a "dropout" layer, which is a common trick in neural network design that is used to speed up training of the network. From a high level, it just means "ignore a bunch of neurons"! The logic is that something simple like flowers, where there are only five classes, don't need 1,280 features to be spotted, so it's more reliable to ignore some of them at random! Sounds weird, I know, but when you look more in depth into how models can be created (my book *AI and Machine Learning for Coders* is a good start), it will make a bit more sense.

The rest of the output should make sense if you've followed Chapters 1 and 2 in this book. It's five epochs of training, where in each epoch we make a guess as to the class of an image, and repeat across all images. How good or bad those guesses are is then used to optimize the network and prepare to make another guess. With five epochs, we only do that loop five times. Why so few? Well, it's because we're using transfer learning as described earlier. The features in the neural network aren't starting from zero—they're already well trained. We just have to fine-tune them for our flowers, so we can do it quickly.

By the time we reach the end of Epoch 5, we can see that the accuracy is 0.9369, so this model is about 94% accurate *on the training set* at distinguishing between different types of flowers. If you were wondering what the [===] is before that, along with a number, such as 103/103, this is indicating that our data is being loaded into the model for training in *batches*. Instead of training the model one image at a time, TensorFlow can be more efficient by training it in batches of images. Remember that our dataset in this case had 3,670 images in it, and we used 90% of them for training? That would give us 3,303 images for training. Model Maker defaults to 32 images per batch, so we will get 103 batches of 32 during training. This is 3,296 images, so we will not use 7 images per epoch. Note that if batches are shuffled, each batch in each epoch will have a different set of images, so those seven will be used eventually! Training is typically faster if done in batches, hence this default.

Remember, we held back 10% of the data as a test set, so we can evaluate how the model does with that data like this:

```
loss, accuracy = model.evaluate(test_data)
```

And we'd see a result a bit like this:

```
12/12 [=========================] - 5s 123ms/step - loss: 0.5813 - accuracy: 0.9292
```

The accuracy here shows that on the test set—images that the network has *not* previously seen—we're at about 93% accuracy. We have a really good network that doesn't overfit to the training data! This is just a high-level look, and when you get into building models in more detail, you'll want to explore more detailed metrics—such as exploring how accurate the model is for each class of image (often called a "confusion matrix") so you can determine if you aren't overcompensating for some types. That's beyond the scope of this book, but check out other books from O'Reilly such as my *AI and Machine Learning for Coders* to learn more details about creating models.

Now all we need to do is export the trained model. At this point we have a *TensorFlow* model that executes in the Python environment. We want a TensorFlow *Lite* model that we can use on mobile devices. To that end, the Model Maker tools give us an export we can use:

```
model.export(export_dir='/mm_flowers/')
```

This will convert the model to the TFLite format, similar to what we saw in Chapter 8, but *also* encode metadata and label information into the model. This gives us a one-file solution that makes it easier to import the model into Android Studio for Android developers and have it generate the proper label details. We'll see that in

Chapter 10. Unfortunately, this is Android-specific, so iOS developers will need to also have the label file on hand. We'll explore that in Chapter 11.

If you're using Colab, you'll see the *model.tflite* file in the files explorer; otherwise, it will be written to the path you're using with your Python code. You'll use this in Chapters 10 and 11 for Android and iOS apps, respectively.

Before going there, though, let's look at some other options for creating models, starting with Cloud AutoML. This is an interesting scenario because, as its name suggests, it will automatically generate ML for you. But beyond not needing to write any code, it also takes some time to explore multiple model architectures to find the one that will work best for your data. So, creating models with it will be much slower, but you're going to get far more accurate and optimal ones. It also exports in a variety of formats, including TensorFlow Lite.

Creating a Model with Cloud AutoML

The goal behind AutoML is to give you a set of cloud-based tools that let you train custom machine learning models with as little coding effort and expertise as possible. There are tools for a number of scenarios:

- *AutoML Vision* gives you image classification or object detection, and you can run the inference in the cloud or output a model that can be used on devices.
- *AutoML Video Intelligence* gives you the ability to detect and track objects in video.
- *AutoML Natural Language* lets you understand the structure and sentiment of text.
- *AutoML Translation* lets you translate text between languages.
- *AutoML Tables* lets you build models using structured data.

For the most part, these tools are designed for models that run on a backend server. The one exception is AutoML Vision, and a specific subset called AutoML Vision Edge which lets you train image classification and labeling scenarios that can run on a device. We'll explore that next.

Using AutoML Vision Edge

AutoML Vision Edge uses the Google Cloud Platform (GCP), so in order to continue, you'll need a Google Cloud project with billing enabled. I won't cover the steps for that here, but you can find them on the GCP site (*https://oreil.ly/9GBFq*). There are a few steps you have to follow to use the tool. Go through these carefully.

Step 1: Enable the API

Once you have a project, open it in the Google Cloud Console. This is available at *console.cloud.google.com*. At the top lefthand side you can drop down a menu of options, and you'll see an entry for APIs and Services. See Figure 9-1.

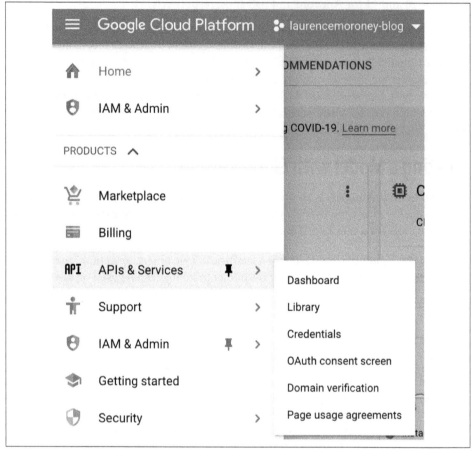

Figure 9-1. Selecting the APIs and Services option in the Cloud Console

From here, select Library to get the Cloud API Library screen. There'll be lots of tiles with a search bar at the top. Use this to search for "AutoML" and you'll find an entry for "Cloud AutoML API."

Select this, and you'll end up on the landing page for Cloud AutoML API. This gives you details about the model, including pricing. Click the Enable button to turn it on if you want to use it.

Step 2: Install the gcloud command-line tool

Depending on your developer workstation, there are a number of options for how you can install the Cloud SDK, which includes the gcloud command-line tool. I'm using a Mac for this chapter, so I'll go through installing it with that. (These instructions should also work on Linux.) For a full guide, check out the Google Cloud docs (*https://oreil.ly/nDKra*).

To use the "interactive" installer, which gives you options about your environment, do the following. From within a terminal enter the following command:

```
curl https://sdk.cloud.google.com | bash
```

You'll be asked for your directory. You'll usually use your home directory, which should be the default, so you can just say "yes" to continue when asked. You'll also be asked if you want to add the SDK command-line tools to your PATH environment. If so, make sure you say "yes." After the install is complete, restart your terminal/shell.

Once that's done, you should issue the following command in your terminal:

```
gcloud init
```

You'll be taken through a workflow to sign in to your project: a link is generated, and when you click on that your browser will open asking you to sign into your Google account. After this you'll be asked to give permissions to the API. To use it, you'll need to give these permissions.

You'll be asked also to provide the region that the Compute Engine resources will run in. You *must* pick a us-central-1 instance for these APIs to work, so be sure to do so. Note that this may change in the future, but at the time of writing, this is the only region that supports these APIs. Check out the Edge device model quickstart guide (*https://oreil.ly/Sn0ip*) before you select any others.

If you have more than one GCP project, you'll also be asked to select the appropriate one. Once all that's done, you'll be ready to use the command-line tool with AutoML!

Step 3: Set up a service account

Cloud supports a number of authentication types, but AutoML Edge *only* supports service-account-based authentication. So next up you'll have to create one and get the key file for it. You can do this using the Cloud Console. Open the IAM & Admin section in the menu (you can see it in Figure 9-1) and select Service Accounts.

At the top of the screen, there'll be an option to "Add a service" account. Select it, and you'll be asked to fill out details for the service account.

Give it a name in step 1, and in step 2 you'll be asked to grant this service account access to the project. Make sure you select the role AutoML Editor here. You can drop down the box and search for this role. See Figure 9-2.

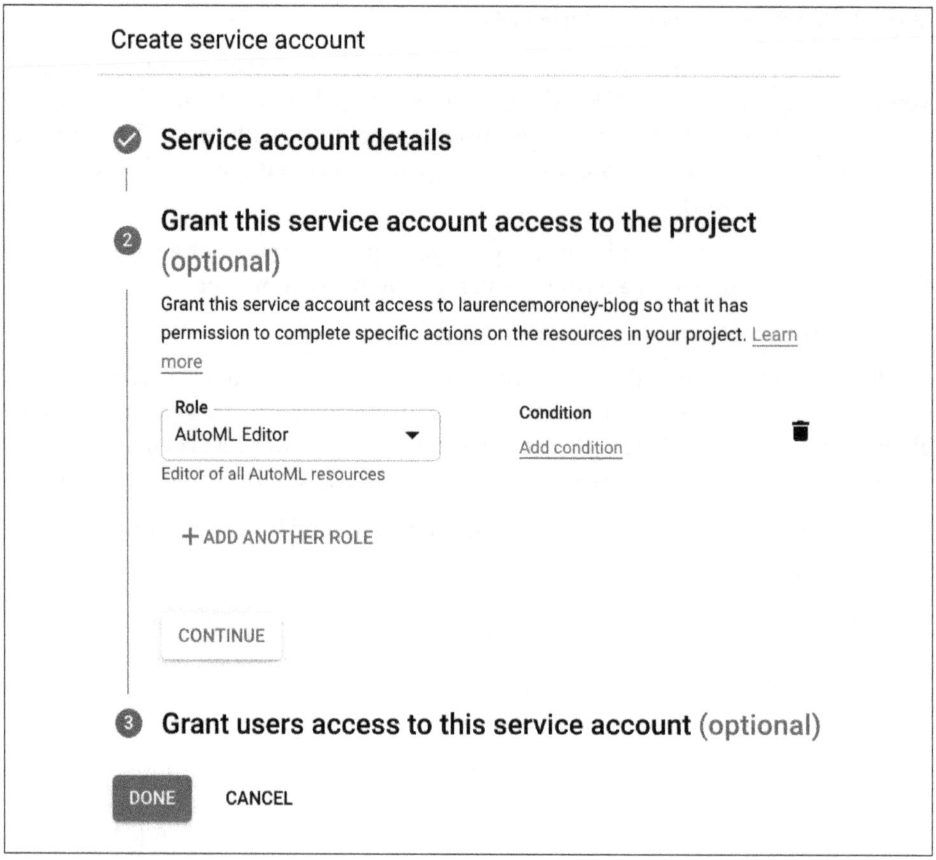

Figure 9-2. Service account details

In step 3, you'll be asked to enter service account users and service account admin roles. You can enter email addresses here, and if you're just doing this for the first time to learn about it, enter your email address for both.

When you're done, the account will be created and you'll be returned to a screen containing a number of service accounts. You may only have one if you're doing this for the first time. Either way, select the one you just created (you'll find it based on its name), and you'll be taken to the service account details page.

At the bottom of the screen, there's an Add Key button. Select this, and you'll be given a number of options for the key type. Select JSON, and a JSON file containing your key will download to your machine.

Return to your terminal and set up these credentials:

```
export GOOGLE_APPLICATION_CREDENTIALS=[[Path to JSON file]]
```

While you're there, here's a handy shortcut to set up your PROJECT_ID environment variable:

```
export PROJECT_ID=[[whatever your project id is ]]
```

Step 4: Set up a Cloud Storage bucket and store training data in it

When training a model with AutoML, the data also has to be stored where the cloud services can access it. You'll do this with a Cloud Storage bucket. You can create this with the mb command (for make bucket) in the gsutil. Earlier you set up the PROJECT_ID environment variable to point at your project, so this code will work. Note that you'll call the bucket by the same name as your project, but with -vcm appended using ${PROJECT_ID}-vcm:

```
gsutil mb -p ${PROJECT_ID}
           -c regional -l us-central1
           gs://${PROJECT_ID}-vcm/
```

You can then export an environment variable to point at this bucket:

```
export BUCKET=${PROJECT_ID}-vcm
```

The flower photos dataset we've been using in this chapter is available in a public cloud bucket at *cloud-ml-data/img/flower_photos*, so you can copy them to *your* bucket with this command:

```
gsutil -m cp
           -R gs://cloud-ml-data/img/flower_photos/
           gs://${BUCKET}/img/
```

Note that if you have been a heavy user of cloud services and have used the same service account in many roles, you may have conflicting permissions, and some people have reported not being able to write to their Cloud Storage bucket. If this is the case for you, try to ensure that your service account has storage.admin, storage.objec tAdmin, and storage.objectCreator roles.

When we used Model Maker or Keras earlier in this chapter, there were tools that organized the labeling of images based on their directories, but when dealing with AutoML like this it's a little more raw. The dataset provides a CSV file with the locations and labels, but it's pointing at the public bucket's URLs, so you'll need to update it to your own. This command will download it from the public bucket, edit it, and save it as a local file called *all_data.csv*:

```
gsutil cat gs://${BUCKET}/img/flower_photos/all_data.csv
| sed "s:cloud-ml-data:${BUCKET}:" > all_data.csv
```

And then this will upload that file to your Cloud Storage bucket:

```
gsutil cp all_data.csv gs://${BUCKET}/csv/
```

Step 5: Turn your images into a dataset and train the model

At this point you have a storage bucket with a lot of images in it. You'll next turn these into a dataset that can be used to train a model. To do this, visit the AutoML Vision dashboard at *https://console.cloud.google.com/vision/dashboard*.

You'll see cards to get started with AutoML Vision, Vision API, or Vision Product Search. Choose the AutoML Vision card and select Get Started. See Figure 9-3.

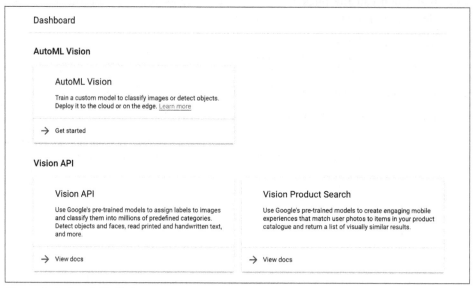

Figure 9-3. AutoML Vision options

You'll be taken to a list of datasets, which is probably empty if you haven't used GCP a lot, with a button at the top of the screen saying New Data Set. Click it and you'll get a dialog asking you to create a new dataset. There'll likely be at least three options: Single-Label Classification, Multi-Label Classification, or Object Detection. Choose Single-Label Classification and select Create Dataset. See Figure 9-4.

You'll be asked to select files to import. Earlier you created a CSV with the details of your dataset, so choose Select a CSV on Cloud Storage and in the dialog enter the URL of that. It should be something like *gs://project-name-vcm/csv/all_data.csv*. See Figure 9-5.

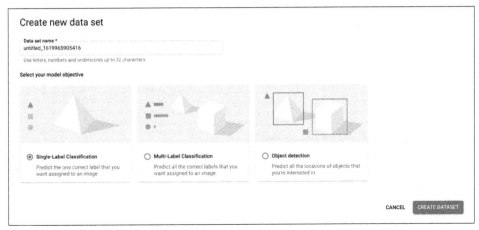

Figure 9-4. Creating a new dataset

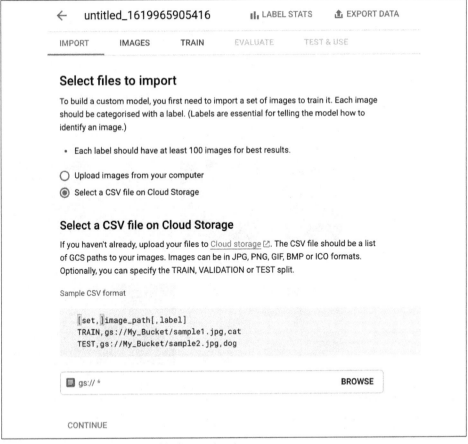

Figure 9-5. Importing a CSV file from Cloud Storage

You can click Browse to find it also. After doing this and selecting continue, your files will begin to import. You can return to the list of datasets to see this. See Figure 9-6.

Figure 9-6. Importing images to a dataset

This can take some time to complete, so keep an eye on the status on the left. With this dataset, when it's done, it will give you a warning, as in Figure 9-7.

Figure 9-7. When the data completes uploading

Once it's done, you can select it, and you'll be able to browse the dataset. See Figure 9-8.

Figure 9-8. Exploring the flowers dataset

Now that the data has been imported, training is as simple as selecting the Train tab and selecting Start Training. In the ensuing dialog, make sure you select Edge as the type of model you want to train, before selecting Continue. See Figure 9-9.

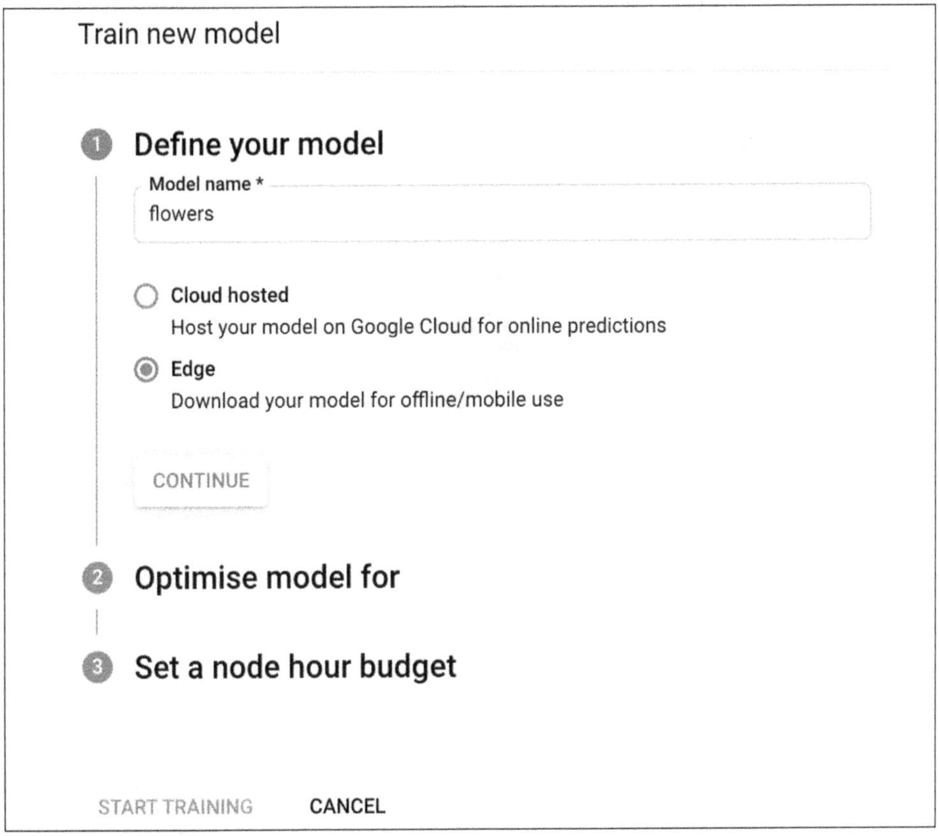

Figure 9-9. Defining the model

After selecting this, you're given the choice to optimize your model. This will give you the choice of a larger model that is more accurate, a smaller one that is faster, but maybe less accurate, or something in between. Next there'll be a choice for how many compute hours you want to use to train the model. The default is four node hours. Choose this and then select Start Training. It may take some time to train, and when it's done, AutoML will email you with the details of the training!

Step 6: Download the model

Once the training is complete, you'll get an email from Google Cloud Platform informing you that it's ready. When you return to the console using the link in the email, you'll see the results of the training. This training will have taken quite a while —as many as two to three hours—because it performed a neural architecture search to find the optimum architecture to classify these flowers, and you'll see that borne out in the results—the precision here is 99%. See Figure 9-10.

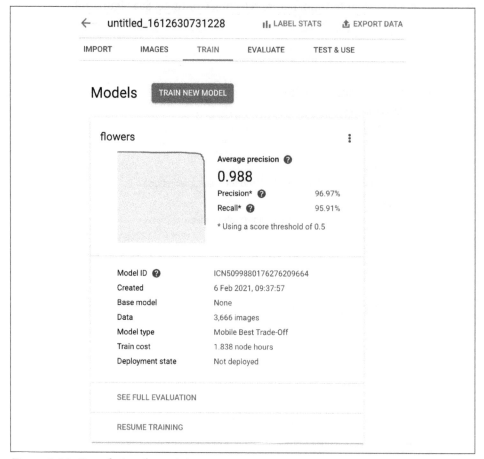

Figure 9-10. Completing the training

From here you can go to the Test and Use tab, where the model can be exported in a variety of formats, including TensorFlow Lite, TensorFlow.js and Core ML! Select the appropriate one (TensorFlow Lite mostly for this book, though we'll explore some Core ML in later chapters) and you can download it. See Figure 9-11.

Beyond these two methods of making models—Model Maker, and Cloud AutoML—which largely involve you avoiding writing code and having APIs handle the model training for you, there's a third method that's worth exploring where you'll have to do some coding, but the ML model is mostly created by others, and you take advantage of their architecture using transfer learning.

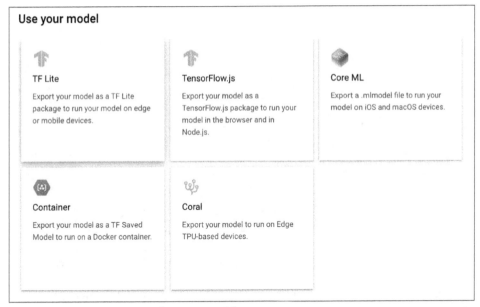

Figure 9-11. Export options for your model

Creating a Model with TensorFlow and Transfer Learning

As discussed earlier, the concept of transfer learning can underpin rapid development of machine learning models. The concept is to use parts of a neural network that were trained on a similar problem, and then override them for your own scenario. For example, the EfficientNet model architecture is designed for the ImageNet scenario where there are 1,000 classes of image; it is trained on millions of images. The resources to train a model like this for yourself would be incredibly expensive in time and money. When a model is trained on such a large dataset, it can be a very efficient feature selector.

What does that mean? Well, in short, a typical computer vision neural network uses what's called a convolutional neural network (CNN) architecture. A CNN consists of many filters where once the filter is applied to an image it will transform it. Over time, a CNN will learn the filters that will help distinguish images from each other. For example, Figure 9-12 shows an example of images from a cats versus dogs classifier that illustrates the areas of the image the CNN used to tell the difference between these types of animal. It was clear, in this case, that filters were learned that determined what a dog's eyes look like, and other filters were learned that determined what a cat's eyes look like. Of all the filters in the network, the decision of what was in a picture could be as simple as the results of those filters showing something.

Figure 9-12. Example of CNN filters activating different areas in different images

So, with an existing network, like EfficientNet, if the creators of the model expose the already-learned filters (usually called *feature vectors*), you can just use them with the logic being that if it has a set of filters that can be used to pick between 1,000 classes, the same set of filters will probably give you a decent classification for your datasets—in the case of flowers, the filters from EfficientNet can probably be used to pick between your five classes of flower. And thus, you don't need to train a whole new neural network; just add what's called a "classification head" to the existing one. This head can be as simple as a single layer with n neurons, where n is the number of classes you have in your data—in the case of flowers, this would be five.

Indeed, your entire neural network could look like this, and be defined with just three lines of code:

```
model = tf.keras.Sequential([
        feature_extractor,
        tf.keras.layers.Dense(5, activation='softmax')
])
```

Of course to do this you'll have to define the feature extractor and load it from an existing model like EfficientNet.

That's where TensorFlow Hub is your friend. It's a repository of models and parts of models, including feature extractors. You can find it at *tfhub.dev* (*https://tfhub.dev*). Using the filters on the left side of the screen, you can access the different model types —for example, if you want image feature vectors, you can use them to get a set of feature vectors (*https://oreil.ly/yWULK*).

When you have a model, it will have a URL—for example, the EfficientNet model, optimized for mobile and trained on ImageNet, can be found at *https://tfhub.dev/tensorflow/efficientnet/lite0/feature-vector/2.*

You can use this URL with the TensorFlow Hub Python libraries to download the feature vector as a layer in your neural network:

```
import tensorflow_hub as hub

url = "https://tfhub.dev/tensorflow/
            efficientnet/lite0/feature-vector/2"

feature_extractor =
    hub.KerasLayer(url, input_shape=(224, 224, 3))
```

And that's it—that's all you need to create your own model architecture that uses the learned features of EfficientNet!

With this approach, you can create models that use the foundations from state-of-the-art models to create your own! Exporting the model is as simple as converting it to TensorFlow Lite using the same techniques you saw in Chapter 8:

```
export_dir = 'saved_model/1'
tf.saved_model.save(model, export_dir)

converter =
    tf.lite.TFLiteConverter.from_saved_model(export_dir)

converter.optimizations = [tf.lite.Optimize.DEFAULT]

tflite_model = converter.convert()

import pathlib
tflite_model_file = pathlib.Path('model.tflite')
tflite_model_file.write_bytes(tflite_model)
```

We'll explore using these models in Chapters 10 and 11.

Transfer learning is a powerful technique, and what we cover here is merely a very light introduction. To learn more about it, check out books like *Hands-On Machine Learning with Scikit-Learn, Keras, and TensorFlow* by Aurelien Geron, or Andrew Ng's excellent tutorials such as the "Transfer Learning" video (*https://oreil.ly/MDOEu*).

Creating Language Models

In this chapter, you saw how to create models in a variety of ways, and how to convert them to TensorFlow Lite so that they can be deployed to mobile apps, which you'll see in the next chapter. An important nuance was that they were all image-based models, and with other model types there may be extra metadata that you'll need to deploy alongside the TFLite model so that your mobile app can use the model effectively. We won't go into detail on training natural language processing (NLP) models here—this is just a very high-level overview of the concepts that will impact creating them for mobile apps. For a more detailed walkthrough of creating and training a language model and of how NLP works, please check out my book *AI and Machine Learning for Coders*.

One such case is when you use language-based models. Building a classifier for text doesn't work on the text itself, but on *encoded* text, where you'll often create a dictionary of words, and build the classifier using them.

So, for example, say you have a sentence like "Today is a sunny day," and you want to use it in a model. An efficient way to do this would be to replace the words with numbers, a process called *tokenizing*. Then, if you were to also encode the sentence "Today is a rainy day," you could reuse some of the tokens, with a dictionary that might look like this:

```
{'today': 1, 'is': 2, 'a': 3, 'day': 4, 'sunny': 5, 'rainy': 6}
```

This would make your sentences look like this:

```
[1, 2, 3, 5, 4] and [1, 2, 3, 6, 4]
```

So when you train your model, you would train it with this data.

However, later, when you want to do inference in your mobile app, your app will need the same dictionary, or it won't be able to convert your user input to the sequences of numbers that the model is trained to understand (i.e., it will have no idea that "sunny" should use the token 5)

Additionally, when you train a model for language, in particular when you want to establish sentiment in language, the tokens for the words will be mapped to vectors, and the direction of those vectors will help determine sentiment.

Note that this technique isn't limited to sentiment. You can use these vectors to establish semantics, where words with similar meanings (such as cat and feline) can have similar vectors, but words with different ones (such as dog and canine) while similar to each other, will have a different "direction" than the cat/feline ones. But for the sake of simplicity, we'll explore words that map to labeled sentiments.

Consider these two sentences: "I am very happy today," which you label as having positive sentiment, and "I am very sad today," which has negative sentiment.

The words "I," "am," "very," and "today" are present in both sentences. The word "happy" is in the one labeled positive, and the word "sad" is in the one labeled negative. When a machine learning layer type called an "embedding" is used, all of your words will be translated into vectors. The initial direction of the vectors is determined by the sentiment; then over time, the directions of the vectors will be tweaked as new sentences are fed into the model. But just taking our very simple case where we only have these two sentences, these vectors might look like Figure 9-13.

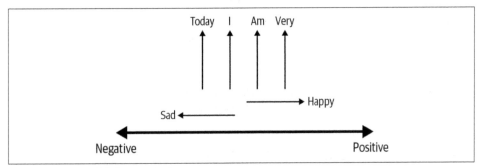

Figure 9-13. Establishing words as vectors

So, consider this space where the "direction" of the vectors determines the sentiment. A vector pointing to the right has positive sentiment. A vector pointing to the left has negative sentiment. Because the words "today," "I," "am," and "very" are in both sentences, their sentiment cancels out, so they don't point in either direction. Because "happy" is only present in the sentence labeled positive, it points in the positive direction, and similarly, "sad" points in the negative direction.

When a model is trained on many labeled sentences, vectors such as these are learned by an embedding, and are then ultimately used to classify the sentence.

Earlier in this chapter when we explored transfer learning for images, we were able to use feature extractors that were already learned from other models, with the logic being that they were trained on millions of images, with many labels, and as such became very good at learning features that you could reuse.

The same happens with language models, where vectors of words could have been prelearned, and you would simply use them for your scenario. This saves a lot of time and complexity in training your model!

In the next section, you'll explore how to use Model Maker to create a language-based model that can then be used in Android or iOS apps!

Create a Language Model with Model Maker

Model Maker makes it really simple to create language-based models with just a few lines of code. There's a full notebook in the download for this chapter, and we'll go through the highlights here. For this example, we'll use a data file I created that has emotional sentiment from tweets. I've abbreviated the URL in this code listing to make it fit, but the full URL is *https://storage.googleapis.com/laurencemoroney-blog.appspot.com/binary-emotion-withheaders.csv*:

```
# Download the data CSV
data_url= 'https://storage.googleapis.com/laurencemoroney-blog.appspot.com/
          binary-emotion-withheaders.csv'

data_file = tf.keras.utils.get_file(
                      fname='binary-emotion-withheaders.csv',
                      origin=data_url)
```

Next up you'll have Model Maker create the base model for you. It supports several model types, with more being added all the time, but the one we'll use is the simplest —it uses transfer learning from a preexisting set of word vectors:

```
spec = model_spec.get('average_word_vec')
```

The CSV file can be loaded into a training dataset using the `from_csv` method in the `TextClassifierDataLoader` (which is available in the Model Maker APIs), and you'll need to specify which column in the CSV contains the text and which contains the label. If you inspect the CSV file, you'll see there's a column called "label," which contains 0 for negative sentiment and 1 for positive. The tweet text is in the "tweet" column. You'll also need to define the model spec, so that Model Maker can start mapping the words in these tweets to the embedding vectors that the model uses. In the previous step, you specified that the model spec uses the average word vectors template:

```
# Load the CSV using DataLoader.from_csv to make the training_data
train_data = TextClassifierDataLoader.from_csv(
      filename=os.path.join(os.path.join(data_file)),
      text_column='tweet',
      label_column='label',
      model_spec=spec,
      delimiter=',',
      is_training=True)
```

Now building the model is as simple as calling *text_classifier.create*, passing it the data, the model spec, and a number of epochs to train for:

```
# Build the model
model = text_classifier.create(train_data, model_spec=spec, epochs=20)
```

Because your model doesn't need to learn the embeddings for each word, and instead uses existing ones, training is very fast—in Colab with GPU, I experienced it at about 5 seconds per epoch. After 20 epochs, it will show about 75% accuracy.

Once the model is done training, you can output the TFLite model simply with:

```
# Save the TFLite converted model
model.export(export_dir='/mm_sarcasm/')
```

For convenience for Android Studio users, this bundles the labels *and* the dictionary of words into the model file. You'll explore how to use this model, including that metadata, in the next chapter. For iOS developers, there's no add-in to Xcode to handle processing the built-in metadata, so you can export this separately, using:

```
model.export(export_dir='/mm_sarcasm/',
             export_format=[ExportFormat.LABEL, ExportFormat.VOCAB])
```

This will give you a file called *labels.txt* with the label specification, and another called *vocab* (no extension) containing the dictionary details.

If you want to inspect the model architecture used to created the model, you can see it by calling `model.summary()`:

```
Layer (type)                    Output Shape              Param #
=================================================================
embedding (Embedding)           (None, 256, 16)           160048

global_average_pooling1d (Gl    (None, 16)                0

dense (Dense)                   (None, 16)                272

dropout (Dropout)               (None, 16)                0

dense_1 (Dense)                 (None, 2)                 34
=================================================================
Total params: 160,354
Trainable params: 160,354
Non-trainable params: 0
```

The key thing to note is the embedding at the top, where the 256 denotes the length of the sentence that the model is designed for—it expects each sentence to be 256 words long. Thus, when passing strings to the model, you don't only encode them into the tokens for the words, but also need to pad them out to 256 tokens. So, if you want to use a 5 word sentence, you would have to create a list of 256 numbers, with the first 5 being the tokens for your 5 words, and the rest being 0.

The 16 is the number of dimensions for the sentiment of the words. Recall Figure 9-13 where we showed sentiment in two dimensions—in this case, in order to capture more nuanced meaning, the vectors will be in 16 dimensions!

Summary

In this chapter you looked at several tools that can be used to create models, including TensorFlow Lite Model Maker, Cloud AutoML Edge, and TensorFlow with transfer learning. You also explored some of the nuances when using language-based models, such as needing to have an associated dictionary so your mobile clients can understand how words are encoded in your model.

These hopefully gave you a taste for how models can be created. It's not the primary focus of this book to teach you how to create different model types, and you can check my other book, *AI and Machine Learning for Coders*, to explore how to do that. In Chapter 10, you'll take the models that you learned in this chapter and see how to implement them on Android, before going into using them in iOS in Chapter 11.

Using Custom Models in Android

In Chapter 9, you looked at various scenarios for creating custom models using TensorFlow Lite Model Maker, Cloud AutoML Vision Edge, and TensorFlow with transfer learning. In this chapter, you'll explore how you can use and integrate these into your Android app. Unfortunately, it's rarely as simple as dropping a model into an app, and as a result, it just "works." Often there are complications with handling data, as Android will represent things like images and strings differently from Tensor-Flow, and indeed, the output of the model will need to be parsed from the Tensor-based output to something more representative in Android. We'll explore this first, then go into some examples of how to use image and language models in Android.

Bridging Models to Android

When creating an app that uses a machine learning model, you'll have a binary blob with the extension *.tflite* that you'll incorporate into your app. This binary expects inputs as tensors (or some emulation of them) and will give you outputs as tensors. That'll be the first challenge. Additionally, the model only works well when there's associated metadata. So, for example, if you build a flower classifier, as in Chapter 9, the model will give you an output of five probabilities, and the idea is that each probability matches a particular flower type. However, the model doesn't output a flower type—such as rose. It simply gives you a set of numbers, so you need the associated metadata to know which output value matches which flower. Additionally, if you're using language models for text classification, you'll also need to understand the dictionary of words that the model was trained on. We'll also explore that in this chapter!

Consider the use of models in an Android app to look a little like Figure 10-1.

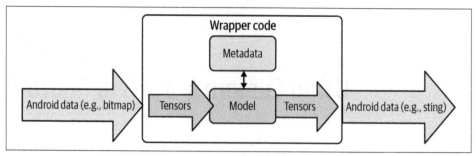

Figure 10-1. High-level architecture of using a model in an Android app

So, for example, let's consider the simple model we used in Chapter 8, where the model learned that the relationship between numbers was y = 2x − 1=2X-1, and explore the code.

First, let's look at the input to the model. It wasn't as simple as putting a number in and getting a number out. For the input, the model expected a NumPy array, but NumPy isn't available in Android. Thankfully you can use low-level basic primitive types in an array instead, and when using Kotlin, the `FloatArray` type can be parsed by the interpreter as a primitive array of floats. So, you could use this code, where `userVal` is the value to input to the model:

```
var inputVal: FloatArray = floatArrayOf(userVal)
```

Then, once the model provided an inference, it returned it as a stream of bytes. As the Android developer, you had to realize that these four bytes represented a float, and that you had to turn these into a float. Remember that the output of the model in its rawest form isn't a float; it's up to you to reinterpret the raw bytes as a float:

```
var outputVal: ByteBuffer = ByteBuffer.allocateDirect(4)
outputVal.order(ByteOrder.nativeOrder())
tflite.run(inputVal, outputVal)
outputVal.rewind()
var f:Float = outputVal.getFloat()
```

So, when using models in Android, you'll have to consider this, and of course with more complex input data, like images and strings, you'll have to handle low-level details like this. There's one exception and that's if you use TensorFlow Lite Model Maker with scenarios where it generates metadata; you can use this metadata when you import the model into Android Studio, and it will generate much of the wrapper code for you. We'll look into that first.

Building an Image Classification App from a Model Maker Output

In Chapter 9, you explored creating an image classifier for five different types of flowers using TensorFlow Lite Model Maker. Because you used this, it generated metadata for you—which in this case was quite simple—because it was just the associated labels for the five flowers. Make sure you download the model that you created using that Colab and have that available before continuing.

To see how to integrate this into an Android app, launch Android Studio and create a new app. Just use a simple single activity app.

Once you've created your app, you can add a new module by right-clicking on the *Java* folder (it will be called this even if you're using Kotlin) and selecting New → Other → TensorFlow Lite Model. See Figure 10-2.

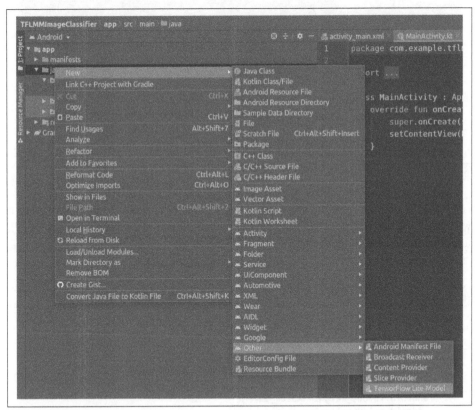

Figure 10-2. Adding a new module

This will give you the Import TensorFlow Lite Model dialog, where you'll specify the location of the model. Pick the one you downloaded, and keep everything else at

---

default, except the bottom checkbox about adding TensorFlow Lite GPU dependencies. Make sure that is checked. See Figure 10-3.

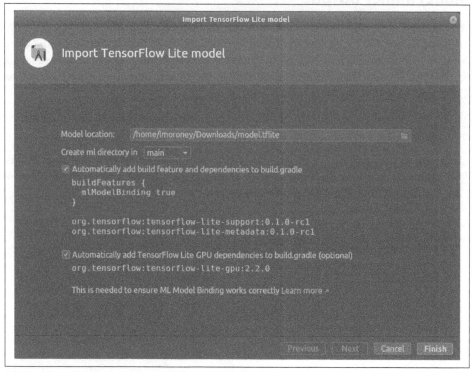

Figure 10-3. Importing a TensorFlow Lite model

Click Finish and the model will be imported, your Gradle file will be updated, and it will sync. When it's done, you'll see some sample code that was created for you. You'll use this a little later. This saves you a number of steps, such as editing the Gradle file, creating the assets folder, copying the model, and a lot more.

Next you can create a simple layout file that contains a number of images of flowers. I've put an example in the download that has six images loaded from resources. Here's a snippet:

```xml
<?xml version="1.0" encoding="utf-8"?>
<LinearLayout
    xmlns:android="http://schemas.android.com/apk/res/android"
    android:layout_width="match_parent"
    android:layout_height="match_parent"
    android:orientation="vertical"
    android:padding="8dp"
    android:background="#50FFFFFF"
    >
```

```
<LinearLayout android:orientation="horizontal"
    android:layout_width="match_parent"
    android:layout_height="0dp"
    android:gravity="center"
    android:layout_marginBottom="4dp"
    android:layout_weight="1">

    <ImageView
        android:id="@+id/iv_1"
        android:layout_width="0dp"
        android:layout_weight="1"
        android:scaleType="centerCrop"
        android:layout_height="match_parent"
        android:src="@drawable/daisy"
        android:layout_marginEnd="4dp"
        />

    ...
</LinearLayout>

</LinearLayout>
```

The ImageView controls are called iv_1 through iv_6. Note the source of the images are @drawable/<*something*>, for example @drawable/daisy. The UI will load the image with that name from the *drawable* directory. The GitHub for this book contains the full sample app, including several images. You can see them in the *drawable* folder in Figure 10-4.

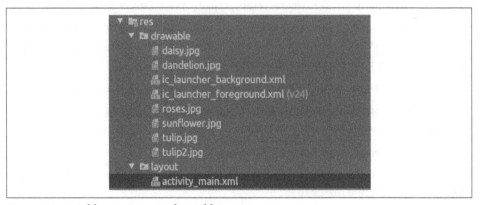

Figure 10-4. Adding images as drawables

Now in your code you can initialize the ImageView controls and set an on-click listener for each of them. The same method can be used for each:

```
override fun onCreate(savedInstanceState: Bundle?) {
    super.onCreate(savedInstanceState)
    setContentView(R.layout.activity_main)
    initViews()
```

```
    }

    private fun initViews() {
        findViewById<ImageView>(R.id.iv_1).setOnClickListener(this)
        findViewById<ImageView>(R.id.iv_2).setOnClickListener(this)
        findViewById<ImageView>(R.id.iv_3).setOnClickListener(this)
        findViewById<ImageView>(R.id.iv_4).setOnClickListener(this)
        findViewById<ImageView>(R.id.iv_5).setOnClickListener(this)
        findViewById<ImageView>(R.id.iv_6).setOnClickListener(this)
    }
```

This method can then implement a modified version of the code that you were provided when you input the model. Here's the entire method, and we'll then look at it piece by piece:

```
override fun onClick(view: View?) {
    val bitmap = ((view as ImageView).drawable as BitmapDrawable).bitmap
    val model = Model.newInstance(this)

    val image = TensorImage.fromBitmap(bitmap)

    val outputs = model.process(image)
    val probability = outputs.probabilityAsCategoryList
    val bestMatch = probability.maxByOrNull { it -> it.score }
    val label = bestMatch?.label

    model.close()

    runOnUiThread { Toast.makeText(this, label, Toast.LENGTH_SHORT).show() }
```

First, notice that the onClick method takes a view as a parameter. This will be a reference to the ImageView control that the user touched on. It will then create a bitmap variable containing the contents of the selected view with this:

```
val bitmap = ((view as ImageView).drawable as BitmapDrawable).bitmap
```

The process of converting the bitmap to a tensor is encapsulated in the helper APIs with the TensorImage class—all you have to do is this:

```
val image = TensorImage.fromBitmap(bitmap)
```

Now that we have the image loaded into a tensor, it's as simple as instantiating a model, and passing the image to it:

```
val model = Model.newInstance(this)
val outputs = model.process(image)
```

Recall that the model will return five outputs—these are the probabilities that the image contains a flower of each particular type. It's in alphabetical order, so the first value will be the probability that the image contains a daisy. In order to get the classification, you have to find the neuron with the highest value, and then use its respective label.

The model had the labels encoded into it by Model Maker, so you can take the outputs of the model as a list of probabilities, sort that list with the maximum value at the top, and then take the label of the top value with this code:

```
val probability = outputs.probabilityAsCategoryList
val bestMatch = probability.maxByOrNull { it -> it.score }
val label = bestMatch?.label
```

You now have the label, so displaying it is as easy as using a Toast like this:

```
runOnUiThread { Toast.makeText(this, label, Toast.LENGTH_SHORT).show()
```

And it's really as easy as that. I strongly recommend using Model Maker for image-based apps like this where possible due to the fact that it makes your apps much easier to code up!

Note that this approach using Android Studio's input will *only* work with image-based models built using TensorFlow Lite Model Maker. If you want to use other models, such as text-based ones, you'll use the TensorFlow Lite Task Libraries instead. We'll explore these later.

Using a Model Maker Output with ML Kit

In Chapter 4, you saw how to use ML Kit's image labeling API as an easy solution for computer vision. It gave you a general image classifier, so that if you showed it a picture of a flower, it would give you some details about that image. See Figure 10-5.

As you can see, this told us that we're looking at a petal, a flower, a plant, and the sky! While all accurate, it would be nice if we had a drop-in solution for the custom model we just created that recognizes specific flowers and would tag this as a daisy!

Thankfully, it's not too difficult, and we can update that app with just a few lines of code. You can get it from this book's GitHub page.

First, you'll need to add the ML Kit custom labeling API. So, in addition to the image-labeling libraries being added via build.gradle, simply add the image-labeling-custom libraries:

```
// You should have this already
implementation 'com.google.mlkit:image-labeling:17.0.1'
// Just add this
implementation 'com.google.mlkit:image-labeling-custom:16.3.1'
```

Figure 10-5. Running the general image classifier

Your app will have an assets directory where some of the sample images you were using in Chapter 4 were added. Add the *model.tflite* file that you created using TensorFlow Lite Model Maker there. You can also add some pictures of flowers. (The app is also in the Chapter 10 directory of this book's GitHub page (*https://oreil.ly/iXFmG*).)

Next, in your activity's onCreate function, you'll use LocalModel.Builder() to create a local model that you'll use instead of the default ML Kit one:

```
val localModel = LocalModel.Builder()
    .setAssetFilePath("model.tflite")
    .build()

val customImageLabelerOptions =
    CustomImageLabelerOptions.Builder(localModel)
        .setConfidenceThreshold(0.5f)
        .setMaxResultCount(5)
        .build()
```

The final change to the code is to use ImageLabeling.getClient() with the options you just created. This was done in btn.setOnClickListener in the original app, so you can just update it to this:

```
val labeler = ImageLabeling.getClient(customImageLabelerOptions)
```

Then everything is the same as the original app—you'll call `labeler.process` on the image and capture the output in its `onSuccessListener`:

```
btn.setOnClickListener {
  val labeler = ImageLabeling.getClient(customImageLabelerOptions)
  val image = InputImage.fromBitmap(bitmap!!, 0)
  var outputText = ""
  labeler.process(image)
    .addOnSuccessListener { labels ->
      // Task completed successfully
      for (label in labels) {
        val text = label.text
        val confidence = label.confidence
        outputText += "$text : $confidence\n"
      }
      txtOutput.text = outputText
}
```

Now when you run the app with the same daisy image, you'll see in Figure 10-6 that it classifies the image as a daisy with a high level of probability—almost 97%.

Figure 10-6. Classifying a daisy with the custom model

Using Language Models

When building models that use language, the pattern is very similar to what you saw in Figure 10-1; this is shown in Figure 10-7.

One major difference is that your app using an natural language processing (NLP)-based model needs the same dictionary of words that the underlying model was trained on. Recall from Chapter 9 that sentences are broken into lists of words, and words are given numeric tokens. Vectors are learned for these tokens that establish the sentiment for that word. For example, the word "dog" might be given the token 4, and a multidimensional vector like [0, 1, 0, 1] could be learned for token 4. The dictionary can then be used to map the word "dog" to 4 in your app. The model is also trained on fixed-length sentences, and your app will also need to know that data.

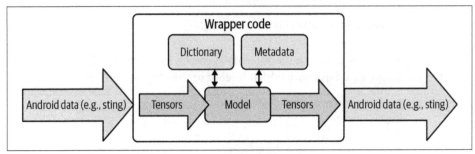

Figure 10-7. Using a model in an app for NLP

If you built your model using TensorFlow Lite Model Maker, the metadata and dictionary are actually compiled into the *.tflite* file to make your life a little easier.

For the rest of this section, I'm assuming you have an NLP model, trained using Model Maker, like the emotion classifier that was demonstrated in Chapter 9. You can also find one in the repo for this chapter, where the full app, including the model, has been implemented for you.

Creating an Android App for Language Classification

Create a new Android app using Android Studio. Just make it a simple one with an empty activity. When you're done, edit the build.gradle file to include TensorFlow Lite as well as the TensorFlow Lite Task Libraries for handling text:

```
implementation 'org.tensorflow:tensorflow-lite-task-text:0.1.0'
implementation 'org.tensorflow:tensorflow-lite:2.2.0'
implementation 'org.tensorflow:tensorflow-lite-metadata:0.1.0-rc1'
implementation 'org.tensorflow:tensorflow-lite-support:0.1.0-rc1'
implementation 'org.tensorflow:tensorflow-lite-gpu:2.2.0'
```

After a Gradle sync, you can then import the model. Use the same technique shown in Figure 10-2 by right-clicking on your package name in the project explorer and selecting New → Other → TensorFlow Lite Model. Accept all the default options and if needed do another Gradle sync when you're done.

Create a layout file

The app will have a super simple user interface—an EditText with text for the user to enter, a button that will trigger the inference, and a TextView to display the results of the inference. Here's the code:

```xml
<?xml version="1.0" encoding="utf-8"?>
<androidx.constraintlayout.widget.ConstraintLayout
    xmlns:android="http://schemas.android.com/apk/res/android"
    xmlns:app="http://schemas.android.com/apk/res-auto"
    xmlns:tools="http://schemas.android.com/tools"
    android:layout_width="match_parent"
    android:layout_height="match_parent"
    tools:context=".MainActivity">
    <ScrollView
        android:id="@+id/scroll_view"
        android:layout_width="match_parent"
        android:layout_height="0dp"
        app:layout_constraintTop_toTopOf="parent"
        app:layout_constraintBottom_toTopOf="@+id/input_text">

        <TextView
            android:id="@+id/result_text_view"
            android:layout_width="match_parent"
            android:layout_height="wrap_content" />
    </ScrollView>
    <EditText
        android:id="@+id/input_text"
        android:layout_width="0dp"
        android:layout_height="wrap_content"
        android:hint="Enter Text Here"
        android:inputType="textNoSuggestions"
        app:layout_constraintBaseline_toBaselineOf="@+id/ok_button"
        app:layout_constraintEnd_toStartOf="@+id/ok_button"
        app:layout_constraintStart_toStartOf="parent"
        app:layout_constraintBottom_toBottomOf="parent" />
    <Button
        android:id="@+id/ok_button"
        android:layout_width="wrap_content"
        android:layout_height="wrap_content"
        android:text="OK"
        app:layout_constraintBottom_toBottomOf="parent"
        app:layout_constraintEnd_toEndOf="parent"
        app:layout_constraintStart_toEndOf="@+id/input_text"
        />
</androidx.constraintlayout.widget.ConstraintLayout>
```

Note the names of the three controls—the output is called `result_text_view`, the input is called `input_text`, and the button is `ok_button`.

Code the activity

In your main activity, writing the code is pretty straightforward. Start by adding variables for the controls, the classifier, and the model:

```
lateinit var outputText: TextView
lateinit var inputText: EditText
lateinit var btnOK: Button
lateinit var classifier: NLClassifier
var MODEL_NAME:String = "emotion-model.tflite"
```

Then, within your `onCreate`, you will initialize the variables that were set up as `lateinit`:

```
outputText = findViewById(R.id.result_text_view)
inputText = findViewById(R.id.input_text)
btnOK = findViewById(R.id.ok_button)
classifier = NLClassifier.createFromFile(applicationContext, MODEL_NAME);
```

When the user clicks the button, you want to read the input text and pass it to the classifier. Note there is no dictionary management being done, as it's all built into the model. You simply get a string, and pass it to `classifier.classify()`:

```
btnOK.setOnClickListener{
    val toClassify:String = inputText.text.toString()
    val results:List<Category> = classifier.classify(toClassify)
    showResult(toClassify, results)
}
```

The model will return a `List` of `Category` objects. These objects contain data about the classification, such as the score and the label. In this case 0 is the label for negative sentiment, and 1 for positive sentiment. These will be mapped to a `Category` object in the label property, and the likelihood of each is in the score property. As there are two labels, there are two outputs, so you can inspect the likelihood of each.

So, to display the results, we can iterate through the list and print them out. This is in the `showResult` method:

```
private fun showResult(toClassify: String, results: List<Category>) {
    // Run on UI thread as we'll updating our app UI
    runOnUiThread {
        var textToShow = "Input: $toClassify\nOutput:\n"
        for (i in results.indices) {
            val result = results[i]
            textToShow += java.lang.String.format(
                "    %s: %s\n",
                result.label,
                result.score
```

```
            )
        }
        textToShow += "---------\n"

        outputText.text = textToShow
    }
}
```

And it's really as simple as that. By using Model Maker, you have the dictionary embedded within the model, and by using the Android APIs for Model Maker (included in your build.gradle file), the complexity of managing the conversion to and from tensors is also handled for you, so you can focus on simple code for your Android app.

To see it in action, see Figure 10-8, where I entered the text, "Today was a wonderful day, I had a great time, and I feel happy!"

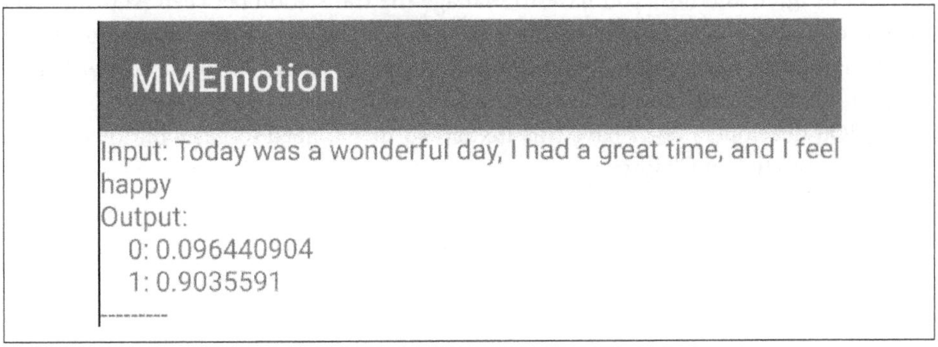

Figure 10-8. Text input with positive sentiment

As you can see, the sentence was positive, and the value for neuron 0 (negative) was very low, while the output from neuron 1 (positive) scored very highly. If you were to enter negative text, such as, "Today was an awful day, I had a terrible time, and I feel sad," then the output would be inverted. See Figure 10-9.

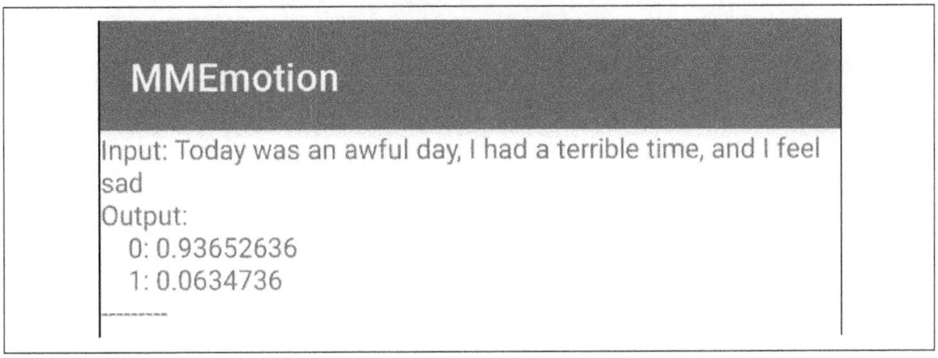

Figure 10-9. Output with negative sentiment

Admittedly, this is a very simple example, but it demonstrates the power of what's possible with Model Maker and language models, and how it can make them much easier to use in Android.

If you were to use a BERT-based spec when training your model with Model Maker, the code will work with very little modification—simply use the `BERTNLClassifier` class in place of `NLClassifier` in your Android code! BERT will give you much better text classification, where it could, for example, have fewer false positives and false negatives. But it will be at the cost of having a much larger model.

Summary

In this chapter you looked at the considerations for using custom models in your Android apps. You saw how it's not quite as simple as just dropping a model into your app and using it, and how you have to manage the translation between Android data structures and the tensors used within a model. For the common scenarios of image and NLP models, the recommendation for Android developers is to use Model Maker to create your models, and its associated APIs to handle data conversion. Unfortunately, iOS developers don't have this luxury, so they'll need to get a bit lower level. We'll look into this in Chapter 11.

Using Custom Models in iOS

In Chapter 9, you looked at various scenarios for creating custom models using TensorFlow Lite Model Maker, Cloud AutoML Vision Edge, and TensorFlow using transfer learning. In this chapter, you'll take a look at how to integrate these into an iOS app. We'll focus on two scenarios: image recognition and text classification. If you've landed here after reading Chapter 10, our discussions will be very similar, because it's not always as easy as just dropping a model into your app and it just works. With Android, models created with TensorFlow Lite Model Maker shipped with metadata and a task library that made integration much easier. With iOS, you don't have the same level of support, and passing data into a model and parsing the results back will involve you getting very low level in dealing with converting your internal datatypes into the underlying tensors the model understands. After you're done with this chapter, you'll understand the basics on how to do that, but your scenarios may differ greatly, depending on your data! One exception to this will be if you are using a custom model type that is supported by ML Kit; we'll explore how to use the ML Kit APIs in iOS to handle a custom model.

Bridging Models to iOS

When you train a model and convert it into TensorFlow Lite's TFLite format, you'll have a binary blob that you add to your app as an asset. Your app will load this into the TensorFlow Lite interpreter, and you'll have to code for input and output tensors at a binary level. So, for example, if your model accepts a float, you'll use a `Data` type that has the four bytes of that float. To make it easier, I've created some Swift extensions that are available in the code for this book. The pattern will look like Figure 11-1.

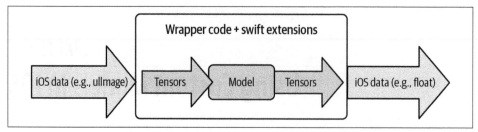

Figure 11-1. Using a model in an iOS app

So, for example, if you consider the simple model that we used in Chapter 8, where the model learned that the relationship between numbers was $y = 2x - 1$, you pass it a single float, and it will infer a result. So, for example, if you pass it the value 10, it will return the value 18.98 or close to it. The value going in will be a float, but you'll actually need to load the four bytes of the float into a buffer that is passed into the model. So, for example, if your input is in the variable data, you'll use code like this to turn it into a buffer:

```
let buffer: UnsafeMutableBufferPointer<Float> =
        UnsafeMutableBufferPointer(start: &data, count: 1)
```

This will create a pointer to the memory where the data is stored, and given that the generic `<Float>` was used and that you said the count was 1, the buffer will be the four bytes from the address of the data onwards. See what I mean about getting low level into bytes in memory!

You copy that buffer to the interpreter as a `Data` type to the first input tensor like this:

```
try interpreter.copy(Data(buffer: buffer), toInputAt: 0)
```

The inference will happen when you invoke the interpreter:

```
try interpreter.invoke()
```

And, if you want to get the results, you'll have to look at the output tensor:

```
let outputTensor = try interpreter.output(at: 0)
```

You know that the `outputTensor` contains a `Float32` as the result, so you'll have to cast the data in the `outputTensor` into a `Float32`:

```
let results: [Float32] =
    [Float32](unsafeData: outputTensor.data) ?? []
```

And now you can access the results. It's a single value in this case, which is easy. Later you'll see what it looks like for multiple neuron outputs, such as with an image classifier.

While this sample is really simple, it is the same pattern that you'll use for more complex scenarios, so keep it in mind as you go through this chapter.

You'll convert your input data into a buffer of the underlying data. You'll copy this buffer to the input tensor of the interpreter. You'll invoke the interpreter. You'll then read the data as a memory stream out of the output tensor, which you'll have to convert into a usable datatype. If you want to explore a mini app that uses the y = 2x − 1 model from Chapter 8, you can find it in the repo for this book. Next we'll look at a more sophisticated example—using images. And while that scenario is more complex than the single float input you just discussed, much of the pattern is the same because the data in an image is still quite structured, and the conversion to read the underlying memory isn't too difficult. The last pattern you'll explore will be towards the end of this chapter when you create an app that uses a model trained on natural language processing (NLP). In that case the input data to the model—a string—is vastly different from the tensor that the model recognizes—a list of tokenized words—so you'll explore the methodology of data conversion in more detail there. But first, let's look at an image classifier that recognizes images based on a custom model.

A Custom Model Image Classifier

Earlier in this book (Chapter 6), you saw how to build an image classifier on iOS using ML Kit. This had a base model that was pretrained to recognize hundreds of classes of image, and it worked really well to show you that there might be a cat in an image, or, as in the case of the image we used of a dog, the model recognized it as both a cat and a dog! But for most cases you probably don't want the ability to recognize generic images; you need to get more specific. You want to build an app that recognizes different types of crop disease on a leaf. You want one that can take a picture of a bird and tell you what type of bird it is, etc.

So, in Chapter 8, you saw how to use TensorFlow Lite Model Maker in Python to quickly train a model that recognizes five different species of flower from a photo. We'll use that as a template for any kind of app that will recognize a custom model.

As this is an image-based model, there's an easy solution to building an app with it using ML Kit's custom image loading capabilities, but before we get to that, I think it's good to see how you will need to use models in iOS and Swift where ML Kit isn't available. You're going to get low level over the next few steps, so let's buckle up!

Step 1: Create the App and Add the TensorFlow Lite Pod

Using Xcode, create a simple app using the usual flow. If you're starting the book at this chapter, take a look back to Chapter 3 for the process. When you're done creating the app, close Xcode, and in the folder where you created it, add a text file called *podfile* (no extension) that contains this content:

```
target 'Chapter11Flowers' do
  # Comment the next line if you're not using Swift and don't want to use dynamic
  # frameworks
```

```
    use_frameworks!

    # Pods for Chapter11Flowers
      pod 'TensorFlowLiteSwift'

  end
```

In this case my app was called *Chapter11Flowers*, and as you can see we're adding a pod to that called *TensorFlowLiteSwift*. Run **pod install** to have CocoaPods install the dependencies for you. When it's done, you can reopen Xcode and load the *.xcworkspace* file that was created for you (not the *.xcproject*!).

Step 2: Create the UI and Image Assets

You can see how custom image classification works in an app with a really simple UI. In Figure 11-2, we have a snippet of a screenshot of the app while it's running.

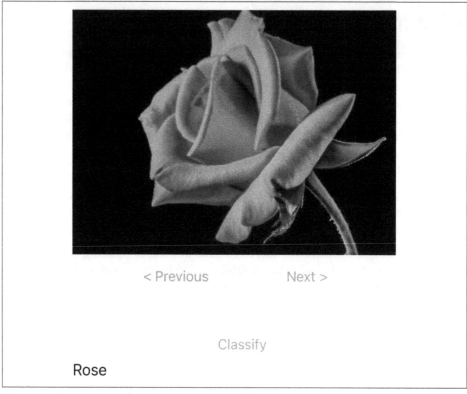

Figure 11-2. An app with a custom image model

The app comes preloaded with a few different types of flower, and by pressing the Previous and Next buttons you can navigate between them. Press the Classify button and it will tell you what type of flower the model inferred from the image. It should be a pretty easy update to this to get it to read the camera or a photo from your collection, but to keep the app simple, I just preloaded it with a few images of flowers. To design this, you can open *Main.storyboard* and design the storyboard to look like Figure 11-3.

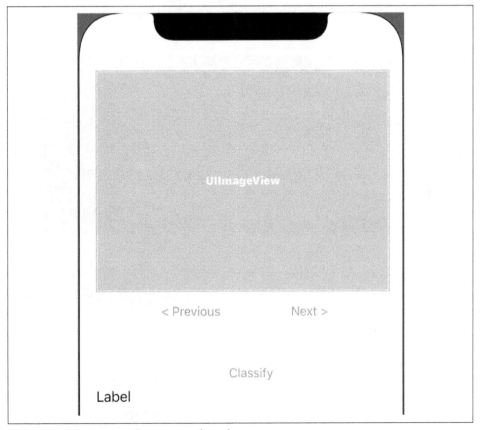

Figure 11-3. Designing the app storyboard

Using Ctrl+drag, you can drag the controls onto *ViewController.swift* to create outlets and actions.

For the three buttons, create actions called prevButton, nextButton, and classify Button.

You should create an outlet for the UIImageView that you call imageView. You should create an outlet for the UILabel that you call lblOutput.

The custom model is designed to recognize five types of flower—daisy, dandelion, rose, sunflower, or tulip. So you can download any images of these flowers to embed within your app. To make the coding easier, make sure you rename the images to

1.jpg, 2.jpg, etc., before putting them in the app. You can also use the images I provide in the GitHub repo.

To add an image to your app, open the *Assets.xcassets* folder, and drag the image to the asset navigator. So, for example, take a look at Figure 11-4. To add an image as an asset, simply drag it to the area beneath where it currently says AppIcon, and Xcode will do the rest.

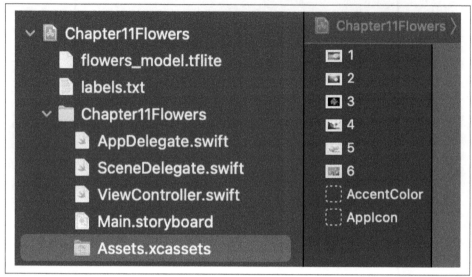

Figure 11-4. Adding assets to your app

You can see where I had six images that I named *1.jpg, 2.jpg*, etc., and after adding them they became named assets 1, 2, etc. You're now ready to begin coding.

Step 3: Load and Navigate Through the Image Assets

As the image assets are numbered, it now becomes easy to load and navigate through them with the Previous and Next buttons. With a class-level variable called `current Image` that is changed by the previous and next buttons, and a function called `load Image` that is also called from `viewDidLoad`, you can navigate between the images in your assets and render them:

```
var currentImage = 1
// The previous button changes the value of the current image.
// If it's <=0, set it to 6 (we have 6 images)
@IBAction func prevButton(_ sender: Any) {
    currentImage = currentImage - 1
    if currentImage<=0 {
        currentImage = 6
    }
    loadImage()
```

```
    }
// The next button changes the value of the current image.
// If it's >=7, set it to 1 (we have 6 images)
@IBAction func nextButton(_ sender: Any) {
    currentImage = currentImage + 1
    if currentImage>=7 {
        currentImage = 1
    }
    loadImage()
}

override func viewDidLoad() {
    super.viewDidLoad()
    // Do any additional setup after loading the view.
    loadImage()
}
```

The `loadImage` function will then just load the image asset that has the same name as `currentImage`:

```
// The load image function takes the image from the bundle.
// The name within the bundle is just "1", "2" etc.
// so all you need to do is UIImage(named: "1") etc. --
// so String(currentImage) will do the trick
func loadImage(){
    imageView.image = UIImage(named: String(currentImage))
}
```

Step 4: Load the Model

At this point, you need a model. You can create one yourself by following the steps in Chapter 8 to build a flowers model, or if you prefer, just use the one I created for you, which you can find in the repo. It'll be in the folder for this app, which I called *Chapter11Flowers*.

To load a model, you'll first need to tell the interpreter where it can find it. The model should be included in your app bundle, so you can use code like this to specify it:

```
let modelPath = Bundle.main.path(forResource: "flowers_model",
                                 ofType: "tflite")
```

The TensorFlow Lite interpreter was part of the pods you installed earlier, and you'll need to import its libraries to use it:

```
import TensorFlowLite
```

Then, to instantiate an interpreter and have it load the model you specified earlier, you can use code like this:

```
var interpreter: Interpreter
do{
    interpreter = try Interpreter(modelPath: modelPath!)
```

```
    } catch _{
        print("Error loading model!")
        return
    }
```

You now have an interpreter loaded into memory and ready to go. So the next thing you need to do is provide an image it can interpret for you!

Step 5: Convert an Image to an Input Tensor

This step is pretty complex, so before diving into the code, let's explore the concepts visually. Refer back to Figure 11-1, and you'll notice that iOS can store an image as a UIImage, which is very different from the tensors that a model will be trained to recognize. So first, let's understand how an image is typically stored in memory.

Every pixel in the image is represented by 32 bits, or 4 bytes. These bytes are the intensities of red, green, blue and alpha. See Figure 11-5.

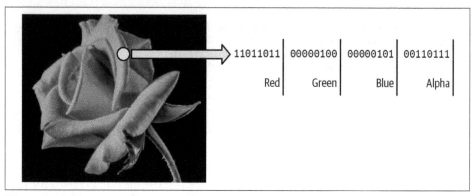

Figure 11-5. How an image is stored in memory

So, if your image is 1000 × 1000 pixels, for example, then the memory to store it will be one million concurrent sets of 4 bytes. The first set of 4 bytes in this block will be the upper left pixel, the next pixel will be the next set of bytes, and so on.

When you train a model (in Python with TensorFlow) to recognize images, you train a model using tensors that represent the image. These tensors typically only contain the red, green, and blue channels, and not the alpha. Additionally, these red, green, and blue channels are *not* the byte contents, but *normalized* byte contents. So, for example, in Figure 11-4, the red channel for the highlighted pixel is 11011011, which is 219. There are many ways that this could be normalized, but we'll choose the easiest, which is just to divide it by 255, as the range of values in a byte is between 0 to 255, so if we want to map that to a range between 0 and 1, we simply divide by 255. So the red channel in this pixel would be represented by a float with the value of 219/255. Similarly, the green and blue ones would be represented by 4/255 and 5/255, respectively. (Take a look at Figure 11-4, and you'll see that the green channel is 100 and the blue channel is 101, which are binary for 4 and 5)

But iOS doesn't let us structure data into tensors like TensorFlow, so instead we have to write the values of the tensors into raw memory and map them using a `Data` value type (*https://oreil.ly/BOO2S*). So, for an image, you would have to go through it pixel by pixel, extract the red/green/blue channels as bytes, and create three concurrent floats that contain the values of these bytes divided by 255. You'd do this for each pixel in the image, and pass the resulting `Data` blob to the interpreter, which it will then slice into the appropriate tensors! One other thing that you'll likely have to do before this is to make sure that the image is the correct size for the model. So, for our hypothetical 1000 × 1000 image, we'd need to resize it to the size the model recognizes. For mobile models, this is often 224 × 224.

Let's now get back to the code! First, you can create a `UIImage` from the `currentImage` variable:

```
let image = UIImage(named: String(currentImage))
```

The `UIImage` type exposes a `CVPixelBuffer` property that will let you do things like cropping the image, which you can get like this:

```
var pixelBuffer:CVPixelBuffer
pixelBuffer = image!.pixelBuffer()!
```

There are lots of ways you could change your current image into 224 × 224, including scaling it, but to keep things simple, I'm going to use the `centerThumbnail` property of the pixel buffer, which will find the biggest square at the center of the image, and then rescale that to 224 × 224:

```
// Crops the image to the biggest square in the center and
// scales it down to model dimensions.
let scaledSize = CGSize(width: 224, height: 224)
let thumbnailPixelBuffer =
        pixelBuffer.centerThumbnail(ofSize: scaledSize)
```

At this point we have a 224 × 224 image, but it's still 32 bits per pixel. We want to split that out into the red, green, and blue channels and load them into a data buffer. The size of this buffer will be 224 × 224 × 3 bytes, so in the next step you'll create a helper function called `rgbDataFromBuffer` that takes in the pixel buffer and slices the channels out, laying them out as a series of bytes. You'll call that function and have it return a `Data` like this:

```
let rgbData = rgbDataFromBuffer(
    thumbnailPixelBuffer!, byteCount: 1 * 224 * 224 * 3)
```

Here's where we're going to get really low level, so buckle up! The signature of the helper function that takes in a `CVPixelBuffer` and returns a Data should look like this:

```
private func rgbDataFromBuffer(
    _ buffer: CVPixelBuffer, byteCount: Int) -> Data? {
}
```

It returns a `Data?`, because that's what the interpreter will expect us to send it. You'll see that a little later.

First, you'll need to get a pointer (in this case called `mutableRawPointer`) to the address in memory where the buffer is kept. Remember from earlier that this buffer is the 224 × 224 cropping of the image that you created:

```
CVPixelBufferLockBaseAddress(buffer, .readOnly)
defer { CVPixelBufferUnlockBaseAddress(buffer, .readOnly) }
guard let mutableRawPointer =
            CVPixelBufferGetBaseAddress(buffer)
        else {
            return nil
        }
```

You'll also need the size of the buffer, which we will call `count`. It might seem odd to call it `count` instead of `size` or something like that, but as you'll see in the next line of code, when you create a `Data` object, it expects a parameter called `count`, which is the count of bytes! Anyway, to get the size of the buffer you can use `CVPixelBufferGetDa taSize` like this:

```
let count = CVPixelBufferGetDataSize(buffer)
```

Now that you have a pointer to the location of the pixel buffer, and the size of it, you can create a `Data` object like this:

```
let bufferData = Data(bytesNoCopy: mutableRawPointer,
                    count: count, deallocator: .none)
```

Each of the 8-bit channels will need to be extracted from this, converted into a float, and then divided by 255 to normalize it. So, for our `rgbData`, let's first create an array of `Float`s of the same size as the number of bytes in the image (recall that it was 224 × 244 × 3 and this is stored in the `byteCount` parameter):

```
var rgbBytes = [Float](repeating: 0, count: byteCount)
```

So now you can go through the buffer data byte by byte. Every fourth one will be the alpha channel component, so you can ignore it. Otherwise, you can read the byte, divide its value by 255 to normalize it, and then store the normalized value in `rgbBytes` at the current index:

```
var index = 0
for component in bufferData.enumerated() {
  let offset = component.offset
  let isAlphaComponent = (offset % 4) == 3
  guard !isAlphaComponent else { continue }
  rgbBytes[index] = Float(component.element) / 255.0
```

```
    index += 1
  }
```

Now that you have your sequence of normalized bytes that, to the interpreter will look like a tensor containing the image, you can return it as a `Data` like this:

```
return rgbBytes.withUnsafeBufferPointer(Data.init)
```

The next step will be to pass this `Data` object to the interpreter and get an inference back.

Step 6: Get Inference for the Tensor

At this point we have formatted our data from our image into a `Data` that contains the red, green, and blue channels as `Floats` containing the normalized data for each channel for each pixel. When the interpreter reads this `Data`, it will recognize it as an input tensor and read it float by float. To start, let's initialize the interpreter and allocate memory for the input and output tensors. You'll find this code in the `getLabel ForData` function within the app:

```
// Allocate memory for the model's input tensors.
try interpreter.allocateTensors()
```

The interpreter will read the raw data, so we have to copy the data to the memory location that the interpreter has allocated to its input tensor:

```
// Copy the RGB data to the input tensor.
try interpreter.copy(data, toInputAt: 0)
```

Note that we're just dealing with single image input and single inference output here, which is why we have it at input 0. It's possible to do batch inference, where you load in a bunch of images at once to get inference on them all, so you'd change the 0 here to *n* for the *n*th image.

Now if we invoke the interpreter, it will load the data, classify it, and write the result to its output tensor:

```
// Run inference by invoking the `Interpreter`.
try interpreter.invoke()
```

We can access the interpreter's output tensor using its `.output` property. Similar to the input, in this case we're doing one image at a time, so its output is at index 0. If we were batching images in, then the inference for image *n* will be at index *n*.

```
// Get the output tensor to process the inference results.
outputTensor = try interpreter.output(at: 0)
```

Recall that this model was trained on five different types of flower, so the output of the model will be five values, with each being the probability that the image contains a particular flower. The order is alphabetical, so as our recognized flowers are daisy, dandelion, rose, sunflower, and tulip, the five values will correspond to those. So, for example, the first output value will be the likelihood the image contains a daisy, and so on.

These values are *probabilities*, so they will be between 0 and 1, and as such are represented as a float. You can read the output tensor and convert it to an array like this:

```
let resultsArray =
    outputTensor.data.toArray(type: Float32.self)
```

Now if you want to determine the most likely flower that is contained in the image, you can get back into pure Swift, getting the maximum value, finding the index of that value, and looking up the label that corresponds to that index!

```
// Pick the biggest value in the array
let maxVal = resultsArray.max()
// Get the index of the biggest value
let resultsIndex = resultsArray.firstIndex(of: maxVal!)
// Set the result to be the label at that index
let outputString = labels[resultsIndex!]
```

You can then render the output string in the user interface to show the inference like I did back in Figure 11-2.

And that's it! That was a lot of messing around in low-level memory with pointers and buffers, but it was a good exercise in understanding the complexities in converting data between native types and tensors.

If you don't want to go so low, but are still using images, there's another alternative, and that is to use ML Kit and have it use your custom model instead of its standard one. It's pretty easy to do, too! You'll see that next.

Use a Custom Model in ML Kit

In Chapter 6, you saw how to build a simple app that used MLvKit's image labeling APIs to build an app that could recognize a few hundred classes of image, but, as in the preceding example, couldn't handle more specific things like types of a flower. For that you'd need a custom model. ML Kit can support this, and with just a few minor adjustments you can have it load your custom model and run inference with that, instead of using its base model. The repo for this book has the original app (in the Chapter 6 folder) as well as one that is updated for a custom model (in the Chapter 11 folder).

First of all, update your Podfile to use *GoogleMLKit/ImageLabelingCustom* instead of *GoogleMLKit/ImageLabeling*:

```
platform :ios, '10.0'
# Comment the next line if you're not using Swift and don't want to use dynamic
# frameworks
use_frameworks!
```

```
target 'MLKitImageClassifier' do
        pod 'GoogleMLKit/ImageLabelingCustom'
end
```

After running **pod install**, your app will now use the ImageLabelingCustom libraries instead of the generic ImageLabeling ones. To use these, you'll need to import them, so at the top of your view controller you can add:

```
// Import the MLKit Vision and Image Labeling libraries
import MLKit
import MLKitVision
// Update this to MLKitImageLabelingCustom if you are adapting the base model
// sample
import MLKitImageLabelingCommon
import MLKitImageLabelingCustom
```

For a custom model, you can use MLKit's LocalModel type. You'll load this from the bundle with your custom model (*flowers_model.tflite* as in the previous walkthrough) with this code:

```
// Add this code to use a custom model
let localModelFilePath = Bundle.main.path(
        forResource: "flowers_model", ofType: "tflite")
let localModel = LocalModel(path: localModelFilePath!)
```

With the base model, you had an ImageLabelerOptions object that you set up. For a custom model, you'll have to use CustomImageLabelOptions instead:

```
// Create Image Labeler options, and set the threshold to 0.4
// to ignore all classes with a probability of 0.4 or less
let options = CustomImageLabelerOptions(
                        localModel: localModel)
options.confidenceThreshold = 0.4
```

Now you'll create the ImageLabeler object with custom options, which in turn load the local model:

```
// Initialize the labeler with these options
let labeler = ImageLabeler.imageLabeler(options: options)
```

Everything else will work as before! You are using a lot less code than in the previous example where you had to hand-convert the raw image into a Data to represent it as tensors, and you had to read the output memory that you recast into an array to get the results. So if you are building an image classifier, I highly recommend using ML Kit if you can to prevent this. If you can't, I hope that presenting both methods is useful to you!

You can see a screenshot from the updated app in Figure 11-6. Here I used a picture of a daisy, and ML Kit's engine, using my custom model, reported back an inference of a 0.96 probability that the image is a daisy!

8:48

Do Inference

daisy : 0.9604372

Figure 11-6. The ML Kit-based app with a custom flowers model

It's always a useful exercise to understand the underlying data structures when building ML-based models that run on mobile. We'll explore one more scenario for an app that uses natural language processing, so you can dig a little deeper into using models in Swift. We'll again go with the raw data approach like we used for the image example, but this time we'll explore a model that is designed to recognize text and sentiment in text!

Building an App for Natural Language Processing in Swift

Before looking at building the app, it's good to understand the fundamentals of how natural language processing models work, so you can see how the data interchange between the on-device string for your text and the in-model tensors will work.

First of all, when you train a model on a set of text, called a corpus, you will limit the vocabulary that the model understands to *at most* the words that are in that corpus. So, for example, the model that you'll use in this app was trained back in Chapter 8 using text from several thousand tweets. Only the words used in that set of tweets will be recognized by the model. So for example, if you want to classify a sentence using the word "antidisestablishmentarianism" in your app, that word doesn't exist in the corpus, so your model will ignore it. The first thing you will need is the vocabulary that the model was trained with—i.e., the set of words that it *does* recognize. The notebook in Chapter 8 had code in it to export that vocabulary so it could be downloaded and used in your app. Also, I said *at most* it would be this set of words, because, if you think about it, there'll be many words used in the corpus only once or twice. You can typically tweak your model to be smaller, better, and faster by ignoring those words. That's a little beyond the scope of what we're doing here, so assume in this case that the vocabulary will be the entire set of words in the corpus, which, of course should be a small subset of all the words in existence!

Second, a model isn't trained on *words* but on *tokens that represent those words.* These tokens are numbers, because neural networks work on numbers! They are indexed in the vocabulary, and TensorFlow will sort the vocabulary into the frequency order of a word. So, for example, in the Twitter corpus, the word "today" is the 42nd most popular. It will be represented by the number 44, because tokens 0 through 2 are reserved for padding and out-of-vocabulary tokens. Thus, when you are trying to classify a string that your user enters, you will have to convert each word in the string into its relevant token. Again, for this you'll need the dictionary.

Third, as your words will be represented by tokens, you won't pass a string of words to the model, but a list of tokens, often called a *sequence.* Your model is trained on a fixed sequence length, so if your sentence is shorter than that, you'll have to pad it to fit. Or if your sentence is longer, you'll have to truncate it to fit.

And all this is before you convert the sequence of tokens into an underlying tensor! There's a lot of steps here, so we'll explore them bit by bit as we build the app.

Figure 11-7 shows what the app will look like in practice. There's an edit text field where the user can type in text like "Today was a really fun day! I'm feeling great! :)," and when the user touches the Classify button, the model will parse the text for sentiment. The results are rendered—in this case you can see the probability of negative sentiment is around 7%, where positive sentiment is around 93%.

Let's look at what's necessary to build an app like this! I'll assume you've created an app, added the TensorFlow Lite pod as shown earlier, and created a storyboard with a UITextView for the input (with an outlet called txtInput), a UILabel for the output (with an outlet called txtOutput), and an action on the button called classifySentence. The full app is in this book's repo, so I'm just going to go over the NLP-specific coding you'll need to do.

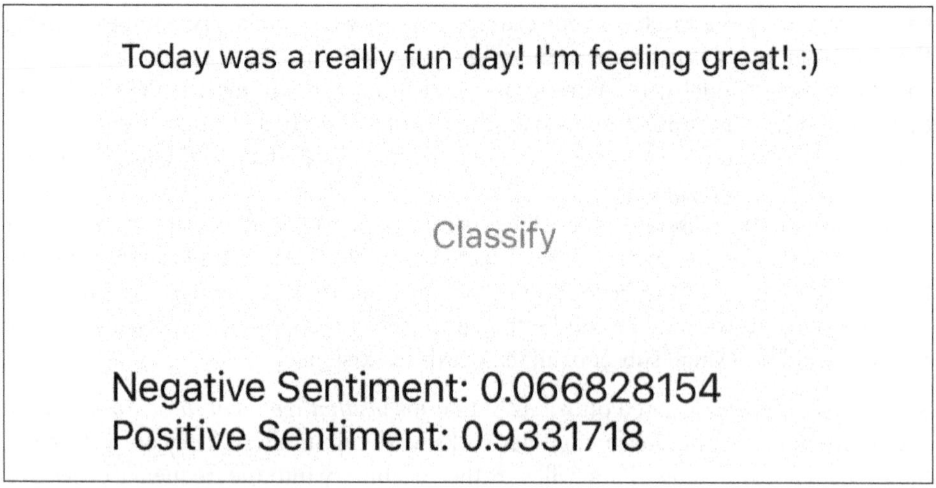

Today was a really fun day! I'm feeling great! :)

Classify

Negative Sentiment: 0.066828154
Positive Sentiment: 0.9331718

Figure 11-7. Parsing sentiment

Step 1: Load the Vocab

When you created the model using Model Maker (refer back to Chapter 8), you were able to download the model as well as a vocab file from the Colab environment. The vocab file was just called *vocab* with no extension, so rename it to *vocab.txt* and add it to your app. Make sure it's included in the bundle, or your app won't be able to read it at runtime.

Then, to use the vocab, you'll need a dictionary which is a set of key-value pairs. The key is a string (containing the word) and the value is an `int` (containing the index of the word) like this:

```
var words_dictionary = [String : Int]()
```

Then to load the dictionary, you can write a helper function called `loadVocab()`. Let's explore what it does. First, specify *vocab.txt* as the file you want to load by defining a `filePath`:

```
if let filePath = Bundle.main.path( forResource: "vocab",
                                    ofType: "txt") {}
```

If it is found, then the code within the braces will execute, so you can load the entire file into a `String`:

```
let dictionary_contents = try String(contentsOfFile: filePath)
```

You can then split this by new line constants into a set of lines:

```
let lines = dictionary_contents.split(
                              whereSeparator: \.isNewline)
```

You can iterate through this to split each line by a space. Within the file you'll see that the vocab has a word followed by its token, separated by a space, on each line. This can give you your key and value, so you can load `words_dictionary` with them:

```
for line in lines{
    let tokens = line.components(separatedBy: " ")
    let key = String(tokens[0])
    let value = Int(tokens[1])
    words_dictionary[key] = value
}
```

For convenience, here's the full function:

```
func loadVocab(){
// This func will take the file at vocab.txt and load it
// into a hash table called words_dictionary. This will
// be used to tokenize the words before passing them
// to the model trained by TensorFlow Lite Model Maker
    if let filePath = Bundle.main.path(
                        forResource: "vocab",
                        ofType: "txt") {
        do {
            let dictionary_contents =
                try String(contentsOfFile: filePath)
            let lines =
                dictionary_contents.split(
                        whereSeparator: \.isNewline)
            for line in lines{
                let tokens = line.components(separatedBy: " ")
                let key = String(tokens[0])
                let value = Int(tokens[1])
                words_dictionary[key] = value
            }
        } catch {
            print("Error vocab could not be loaded")
        }
    } else {
        print("Error -- vocab file not found")
    }
}
```

Now that the dictionary is loaded into memory, the next step will be to convert the user's input string into a sequence of tokens. You'll see that next.

The next few steps will use some sophisticated Swift extensions for handling low-level memory with unsafe data buffers. It's beyond the scope of this book to go into detail about how these extensions work, and in general they are code that you can reuse in your own apps with little or no modification.

Step 2: Convert the Sentence to a Sequence

As discussed earlier, when creating a language model, you train it on a sequence of tokens. This sequence is fixed length, so if your sentence is longer, you'll trim it to that length. If it's shorter, you'll pad it to that length.

The input tensors to the language model will be a sequence of 4-byte integers, so to begin creating it, you'll initialize your sequence to be Int32s, all of which are 0, where in the vocab, 0 is a not-found word indicated by <Pad> in the dictionary (for padding!). (Note: you'll see this code in the convert_sentence function in the app if you cloned it from the repo.)

```
var sequence = [Int32](repeating: 0, count: SEQUENCE_LENGTH)
```

Here is some Swift code to split a string into words, while removing punctuation and multiple spaces:

```
sentence.enumerateSubstrings(
    in: sentence.startIndex..<sentence.endIndex,
    options: .byWords) {(substring, _, _, _) -> ()
                        in words.append(substring!) }
```

This will give you a list of words in a data structure called words. It's pretty easy to loop through this, and if the word exists as a key in words_dictionary, you can add its value to the sequence. Note that you add it as an Int32:

```
var thisWord = 0
for word in words{
    if (thisWord>=SEQUENCE_LENGTH){
        break
    }
    let seekword = word.lowercased()
    if let val = words_dictionary[seekword]{
        sequence[thisWord]=Int32(val)
        thisWord = thisWord + 1
    }
}
```

Once you're done here, sequence will contain your words encoded as a sequence of Int32s.

Step 3: Extend Array to Handle Unsafe Data

Your sequence is an array of Int32s, but Swift will have some structure around this. For TensorFlow Lite to read it, it needs to read the raw bytes in sequence, and the easiest way for you to do this is to extend the Array type to handle the unsafe data. It's one of the nice features of Swift that you can extend types. Here's the full code:

```
extension Array {
```

```
init?(unsafeData: Data) {
    guard unsafeData.count % MemoryLayout<Element>.stride == 0 else
        { return nil }
    #if swift(>=5.0)
    self = unsafeData.withUnsafeBytes
        { .init($0.bindMemory(to: Element.self)) }
    #else
    self = unsafeData.withUnsafeBytes {
        .init(UnsafeBufferPointer<Element>(
            start: $0,
            count: unsafeData.count / MemoryLayout<Element>.stride
        ))
    }
    #endif  // swift(>=5.0)
  }
}
```

I won't go into detail on what this function does, but ultimately the idea is that it will use the `init` functionality of Swift to initialize a new array with the `unsafeBytes` within the `Data` constructor. In Swift 5.0+, you can use `bindMemory` to copy the underlying memory to the new array; otherwise, you'll use `unsafeData.withUnsafeBytes` to copy from the start of the original buffer with a count of the amount of `unsafeData`.

To create an input tensor using this from the sequence you created earlier, you can just use:

```
let tSequence = Array(sequence)
```

This will be used to create the `Data` type that's passed to the interpreter. You'll see that in the next step.

Step 4: Copy the Array to a Data Buffer

You now have an array of `Int32`s using just the underlying bytes of the `Int32`s; it's called `tSequence`. This needs to be copied to a `Data` for TensorFlow to be able to parse it. The easiest way to do this is to extend `Data` to handle a buffer you'll copy from. Here's the extension:

```
extension Data {
  init<T>(copyingBufferOf array: [T]) {
    self = array.withUnsafeBufferPointer(Data.init)
  }
}
```

This will just initialize the `Data` by copying the unsafe buffer data from the input array (called `array`). To use this to create a new `Data`, you can use code like this:

```
let myData =
    Data(copyingBufferOf: tSequence.map { Int32($0) })
```

As you can see, this will create myData by mapping tSequence, using the Int32 type. You now have data that TensorFlow Lite can interpret!

Step 5: Run Inference on the Data and Process the Results

After step 4, you have myData, which is a raw data buffer containing the Int32s for the tokens that make up the sequence that represents your sentence. So you can now initialize your interpreter by allocating tensors and then copying myData to the first input tensor. You'll find this code in the classify function if you use the code from the book's repo:

```
try interpreter.allocateTensors()
try interpreter.copy(myData, toInputAt: 0)
```

You'll then invoke the interpreter, and get the outputTensor:

```
try interpreter.invoke()
outputTensor = try interpreter.output(at: 0)
```

The tensor will output an array of two values, one for the negative sentiment, and one for the positive sentiment. These are values between 0 and 1, so you'll need to cast the array to Float32 to access them:

```
let resultsArray = outputTensor.data
let results: [Float32] =
    [Float32](unsafeData: resultsArray) ?? []
```

Now it's relatively easy (finally!) to access the values, simply by reading the first two entries in the array:

```
let negativeSentimentValue = results[0]
let positiveSentimentValue = results[1]
```

These values can then be processed, or simply output, like I did in this app; you can see that in Figure 11-7.

Summary

Using machine learning models from TensorFlow on iOS with Swift requires you to get pretty low level and manage the memory in and memory out when it comes to loading your data into a model to get an inference and then parse it. In this chapter, you explored that with respect to images, where you had to slice the channel bytes for red, green, and blue from the underlying image, normalize them, and write them out as float values using unsafe Data buffers loaded into the TensorFlow Lite Interpreter. You also saw how to parse the output from the model—and why it's vital to understand the model architecture, which in this case had five output neurons containing the probabilities that the image was one of five different flowers. In comparison, you saw that ML Kit made this scenario a lot easier by using its higher level APIs for a custom model, and I'd strongly recommend that if you are building models that are covered by ML Kit scenarios this would be the way to go, instead of dealing with the raw bits and bytes yourself! For another exercise in data management, you also saw a simple NLP app, where you want to classify a string, and how you would first token-ize that string, then turn it into a sequence, and then map the types of that sequence into a raw buffer that you'd pass to the engine. This scenario isn't supported in ML Kit, or any other high-level APIs, so it's important to get hands-on and explore how to do it! I hope that these two walkthroughs, and the extensions created to make them possible, will make your life easier as you create apps yourself. In the next chapter, we'll switch gears away from TensorFlow Lite towards the iOS-specific APIs of Core ML and Create ML.

## CHAPTER 12

Productizing Your App Using Firebase

So far in this book, you've explored using machine learning to create models, and you've looked into how to integrate them into Android or iOS apps using a variety of technologies. You could go low level with TensorFlow Lite, using the model directly, and dealing with the process of data conversion to and from the model. Or, for a number of common scenarios, you could take advantage of ML Kit to use a high-level API with an asynchronous programming methodology to make responsive applications easier to build. In all of these cases, though, you just built a very simple app that did inference in a single activity or view.

When it comes to productizing an app, you, of course, have to go much further, and Firebase is designed to be a cross-platform solution that intends to help you build, grow, and earn from your app.

And while a full discussion of Firebase is beyond the scope of this book, there is an important feature in Firebase that's available in the free (aka Spark) tier that you can really take advantage of: custom model hosting.

Why Use Firebase Custom Model Hosting?

As you've seen throughout this book, creating an ML model to solve a problem for your users doesn't have to be difficult. It's relatively straightforward, thanks to tools like TensorFlow or TensorFlow Lite Model Maker that quickly train a model based on your data. What's hard to do is to create the *right* model, on the obvious assumption that to be able to do this, you need to continually test and update your model with your users, validating how it performs, not just from a speed or accuracy perspective, but also how it impacts their use of your app. Does the right model lead to better engagement? Does the wrong model mean that users drop out of your app? Does it lead to more interaction with adverts or in-app purchases?

The goal of Firebase is to help you answer all of those questions through things like analytics, A/B testing, remote configuration, and more.

But when using ML models, of course, in order to be able to *ask* these questions effectively, you need a way to get multiple models deployed and have your audience segmented according to these models. You've created v1 of a model, and it's working well. You've learned a lot from your users about it, and have gathered new data to create a new model. You want to deploy that to some of your users to test it and have a carefully monitored rollout.

How would you proceed with this?

Well, that's where custom model hosting can be the onramp to the rest of Firebase's services for you as a developer using ML models. We'll explore one scenario in this chapter, called "remote configuration," and from there, if you're interested, you'll be able to expand to the rest of the services available on the platform.

So, in order to begin, let's first create a scenario where we have multiple models, and for that, we'll return to TensorFlow Lite Model Maker.

 While playing with the Firebase Console, you may have noticed a number of tiles for different APIs. These are actually for ML Kit, which we covered in earlier chapters! It used to be a part of Firebase before it spun out on its own, and links to it are still available within the console.

Create Multiple Model Versions

For this scenario, you can create a simple test of multiple models using TensorFlow Lite Model Maker. Instead of working with different datasets to see how different models may behave, you can also create multiple models using different underlying specs. As Model Maker uses transfer learning under the hood, it's the perfect vehicle for creating different models, and you could theoretically deploy different versions to different users to see which architecture works best for your scenario.

If we return to the "flowers" example from earlier chapters, we can get our data, and split it into training and validation sets like this:

```
url = 'https://storage.googleapis.com/download.tensorflow.org/' + \
    'example_images/flower_photos.tgz'

image_path = tf.keras.utils.get_file('flower_photos.tgz', url,
                                      extract=True)
image_path = os.path.join(os.path.dirname(image_path),
                          'flower_photos')
data = DataLoader.from_folder(image_path)
train_data, validation_data = data.split(0.9)
```

Then, using TensorFlow Lite Model Maker, we can create an image classifier and export it like this:

```
model = image_classifier.create(train_data,
                                validation_data=validation_data)
model.export(export_dir='/mm_flowers1/')
```

In the *mm_flowers* directory you'll now have a TensorFlow Lite model and associated metadata, which you can download and use in your apps as explored in Chapter 9.

You'll notice that you simply called `image_classifier.create` without defining any kind of spec. This will create an image classifier model using the EfficientNet model as the default underlying model type. This model architecture was chosen because it is recognized as a state-of-the-art image classifier that works with very small models, and thus is effective for mobile. You can learn more about EfficientNet at *https:// tfhub.dev/google/collections/efficientnet/1*.

However, there's a family of model architectures called MobileNet, which, as its name suggests, is perfectly suited for mobile scenarios. So, what if you *also* create a model that uses MobileNet as the underlying architecture, and have this as a second model. You can deploy the EfficientNet-based model to some of your users, and the MobileNet-based one to others. You can then measure the efficacy of these models to help you decide which one to roll out to all users.

So, to create a MobileNet model in TensorFlow Lite Model Maker, you can use the spec parameter to override the default, like this:

```
spec=model_spec.get('mobilenet_v2')

model = image_classifier.create(train_data, model_spec=spec,
                                validation_data=validation_data)
model.export(export_dir='/mm_flowers2/')
```

After the model has trained, you'll now have *another* TFLite model, this one based on MobileNet, present in the *mm_flowers2* directory. Download that and keep it separate from the first. You'll upload both of these to Firebase in the next section.

Using Firebase Model Hosting

Firebase Model Hosting gives you the ability to host models in Google's infrastructure. These models can be downloaded and used by your app, so, if your users are connected, you can manage which models they use and how to download them. You'll explore that in this section, but first, you'll need to create a project.

Step 1: Create a Firebase Project

To use Firebase, you'll have to create a Firebase project using the Firebase Console. To get started with this, visit *http://firebase.google.com*. You'll be able to try a demo and watch a video about Firebase. When you're ready, click "Get started." See Figure 12-1.

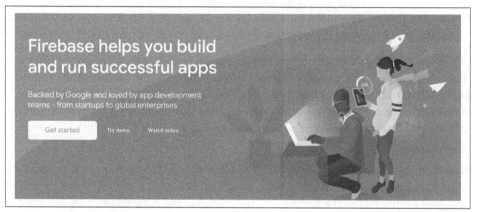

Figure 12-1. Getting started with Firebase

Once you click this button, you'll be taken to the console page with a list of your existing projects. If it's your first time, you'll just see the "Add project" button as shown in Figure 12-2.

Figure 12-2. The Firebase Console

Note that these screenshots were taken using the US version of the Firebase Console; your experience may vary slightly, but the broad concepts will be the same.

Click the "Add project" button and you'll be taken to a wizard that will guide you step by step through creating a project. You'll start with the project name. See Figure 12-3.

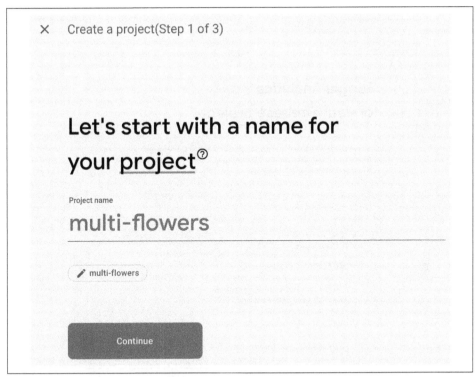

Figure 12-3. Naming your project

As you can see here, I named mine "multi-flowers," but you can choose whatever name you like! Press Continue and it will ask if you want to enable Google Analytics for your project. I'd recommend keeping this as the default, which is to enable them. You can see a full list of these analytics features in Figure 12-4.

The next step is to create or use a Google Analytics account as depicted in Figure 12-5.

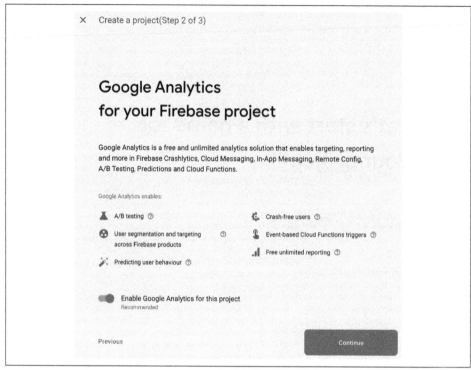

Figure 12-4. Adding Google Analytics

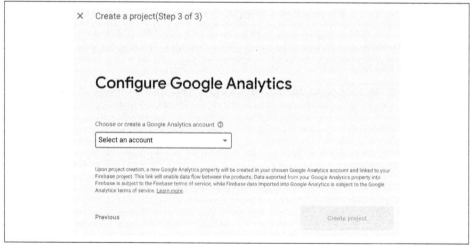

Figure 12-5. Configuring Google Analytics

If you don't have an account already, clicking on the Select an Account dropdown gives you the option to "Create a new account." See Figure 12-6.

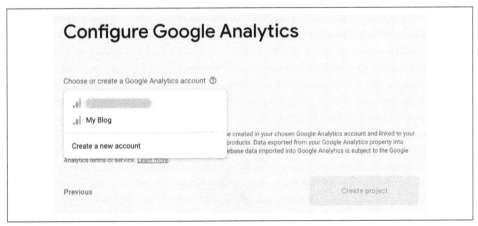

Figure 12-6. Creating a new Google Analytics account

Once you've done this, you can then check your settings for analytics, and after accepting the terms, you can create the project. See Figure 12-7.

Figure 12-7. Google Analytics configuration options

It may take a few moments, but once Firebase has done its thing and created your project, you'll see something like Figure 12-8, but with your project name instead of "multi-flowers."

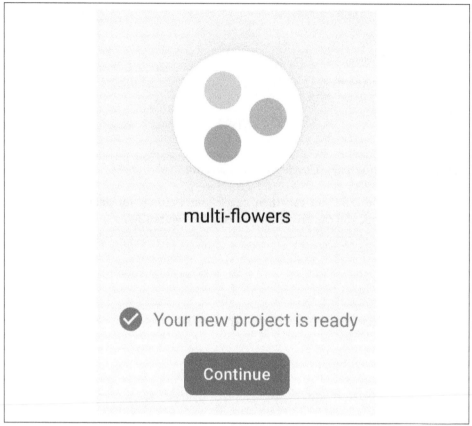

Figure 12-8. Firebase finishes creating your project

You are now ready to use Firebase with this project! In the next step, you'll configure model hosting!

Step 2: Use Custom Model Hosting

In the previous section, you went through the steps to create a new Firebase project that you can use to host multiple models. To do this, first, find the Machine Learning section in the Firebase Console. You should see a black toolbar on the righthand side of the screen containing all of the Firebase tools. One of them will look like a little robot head. See Figure 12-9.

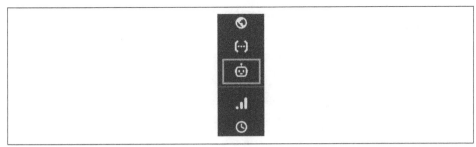

Figure 12-9. Finding the Machine Learning entry in the Firebase Console

Select this, and you'll see an option to "Get Started." This will take you to the Machine Learning page in the Firebase Console. At the top of the screen, you'll see three tabs: APIs, Custom, and AutoML. Select Custom to see the TensorFlow Lite model hosting screen. See Figure 12-10.

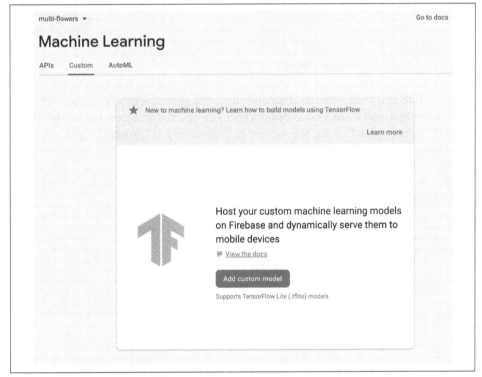

Figure 12-10. Custom model hosting

In the center of the screen, you'll see a big blue button to add a custom model. Click it and you'll get taken through a set of steps to host your models. Make sure you have the two models from earlier on and go through these steps.

So, for example, if you have your EfficientNet-based model, you can start uploading this by calling it "flowers1." See Figure 12-11.

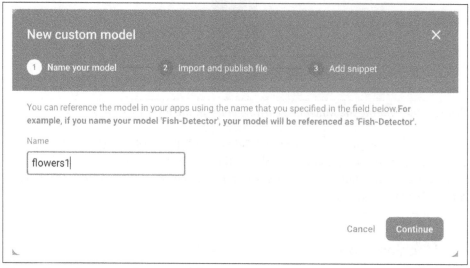

Figure 12-11. Starting to host a model

Hit Continue and then you can drag and drop the first model you created onto the form. After this, you'll see a code snippet that you can use to access the model. You'll use that later. Repeat this for the second model, calling it "flowers2," and you'll see something like Figure 12-12.

Figure 12-12. Hosting multiple models

Now that you have the models, you can start using them in your apps. In the next step, you'll see how to integrate Firebase into an Android app, so you can see how to use flowers1 in your app. After that, you'll extend with remote configuration so that some users get flowers1 and others get flowers2.

Step 3: Create a Basic Android App

In this step, you'll create a simple Android app that will use the hosted model to do a basic model inference on flowers. First, use Android Studio to create a new app with the empty activity template. Call it "multi-flowers." I'm not going to share all of the code for the app in this chapter, but you can access the full app in the repo if you need the code.

To complete the following example and present six different flower images, here's the file you'll need to edit (note that it's the same as the flowers sample (*https://oreil.ly/ KqJrM*) from Chapter 10).

Here's a snippet, cut for brevity:

```xml
<?xml version="1.0" encoding="utf-8"?>
<LinearLayout
    xmlns:android="http://schemas.android.com/apk/res/android"
    android:layout_width="match_parent"
    android:layout_height="match_parent"
    android:orientation="vertical"
    android:padding="8dp"
    android:background="#50FFFFFF"
    >

    <LinearLayout android:orientation="horizontal"
        android:layout_width="match_parent"
        android:layout_height="0dp"
        android:gravity="center"
        android:layout_marginBottom="4dp"
        android:layout_weight="1">

        <ImageView
            android:id="@+id/iv_1"
            android:layout_width="0dp"
            android:layout_weight="1"
            android:scaleType="centerCrop"
            android:layout_height="match_parent"
            android:src="@drawable/daisy"
            android:layout_marginEnd="4dp"
            />

        <ImageView android:layout_width="0dp"
            android:id="@+id/iv_2"
            android:layout_weight="1"
            android:layout_height="match_parent"
            android:scaleType="centerCrop"
            android:layout_marginStart="4dp"
            android:src="@drawable/dandelion"/>
```

```
    </LinearLayout>

    ...

    </LinearLayout>
```

You may notice that these ImageView controls refer to images such as dandelion and daisy. You should add these images to your app in the layout directory. You can get the images from the repo (*https://oreil.ly/8oqnb*).

If you launch the app now, it won't do much other than display the flowers. Before continuing, let's now explore how to add Firebase to it!

Step 4: Add Firebase to the App

Android Studio includes Firebase integration that makes it easy for you to use Firebase features in an Android app. You can find it on the Tools menu. See Figure 12-13.

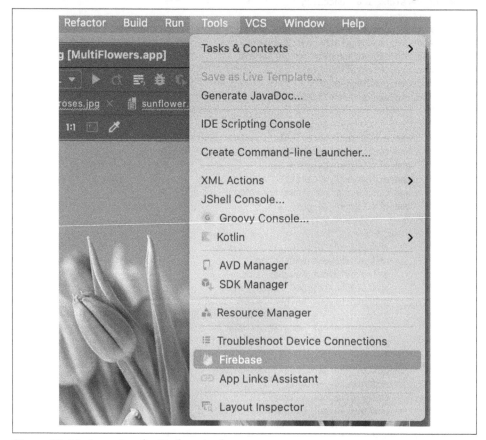

Figure 12-13. Accessing the Firebase tools

Select this and you'll be taken to the Firebase assistant pane on the righthand side of the screen. You'll use this to add Firebase, as well as Firebase remote configuration, to your app. Using the assistant, find Remote Config. Select "Set up Firebase Remote Config" as shown in Figure 12-14.

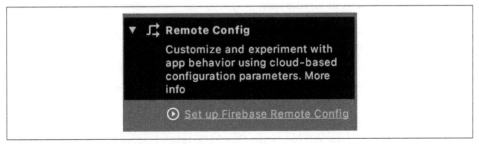

Figure 12-14. Using Remote Config

The pane will change to a number of steps to follow, the first of which is to Connect to Firebase. Press this button. Your browser will open and navigate to the Firebase Console. From there, you should select the project that you created earlier in this chapter. You should see a screen like Figure 12-15, where your Firebase Android app is connected to Firebase.

Figure 12-15. Connecting your app to Firebase

Press the Connect button, and when it's ready, go back to Android Studio and you'll see that your app is connected. The second option in the assistant is to "Add Remote Config to your app." Press the button. A dialog will pop up telling you the changes that are necessary to include Remote Config. It will add entries to your build.gradle and then synchronize your Gradle files.

Before continuing, also add TensorFlow Lite, the Vision Task Libraries, and other Firebase libraries to your app-level build.gradle:

```
implementation platform('com.google.firebase:firebase-bom:28.0.1')
implementation 'com.google.firebase:firebase-ml-modeldownloader-ktx'


implementation 'org.tensorflow:tensorflow-lite:2.3.0'
implementation 'org.tensorflow:tensorflow-lite-task-vision:0.1.0'
```

It's as easy as that to get Firebase connected to your app!

Step 5: Get the Model from Firebase Model Hosting

Earlier you uploaded the model to Firebase Model Hosting, with flowers1 being the name given to the EfficientNet-based model, and flowers2 the name for the MobileNet-based one.

The full code for this app is available at *https://github.com/lmoroney/odmlbook/tree/main/BookSource/Chapter12/MultiFlowers*.

Create a function for loading the model from Firebase Model Hosting. Within this you should set up a CustomModelDownloadConditions object, like this:

```
val conditions = CustomModelDownloadConditions.Builder()
    .requireWifi()
    .build()
```

This function is called loadModel in the sample app at the GitHub repo.

Once you've done that, you can get the model using FirebaseModelDownloader. This exposes a getModel method that allows you to pass in the name of the string representing the model (i.e., "flowers1" or "flowers2") and how to download the model, based on the conditions you created earlier. It exposes an addOnSuccessListener, which will get called when the model downloads successfully:

```
FirebaseModelDownloader.getInstance()
    .getModel(modelName,
            DownloadType.LOCAL_MODEL_UPDATE_IN_BACKGROUND,
```

```
                 conditions)
      .addOnSuccessListener { model: CustomModel ->
                 }
```

Within the onSuccessListener callback, you can then instantiate an ImageClassi
fier using the model (ImageClassifier comes from the TensorFlow Lite Task
Library that you included in your *build.gradle*):

```
val modelFile: File? = model.file
if (modelFile != null) {

    val options: ImageClassifier.ImageClassifierOptions = ImageClassifier.
    ImageClassifierOptions.builder().setMaxResults(1).build()

    imageClassifier = ImageClassifier.createFromFileAndOptions(modelFile, options)

    modelReady = true

    runOnUiThread { Toast.makeText(this, "Model is now ready!",
                Toast.LENGTH_SHORT).show() }
}
```

The callback returns an instance of CustomModel, called model, which can be passed
to the ImageClassifier's createFromFileAndOptions to instantiate the model. To
make later coding easier, we use the options to return only one result. Once this is
done, the model is ready to go and we can make inferences using it.

Inference using the task APIs is pretty straightforward. We convert the image to a
TensorImage, and pass this to the classify method of the imageClassifier. It will
return a set of results, the first entry of which will contain our answer, and we can
pull the label and score from that:

```
override fun onClick(view: View?) {
  var outp:String = ""
  if(modelReady){
    val bitmap = ((view as ImageView).drawable as
                             BitmapDrawable).bitmap
    val image = TensorImage.fromBitmap(bitmap)
    val results:List<Classifications> =
              imageClassifier.classify(image)

    val label = results[0].categories[0].label
    val score = results[0].categories[0].score
    outp = "I see $label with confidence $score"
  } else {
    outp = "Model not yet ready, please wait or restart the app."
  }

  runOnUiThread {
      Toast.makeText(this, outp, Toast.LENGTH_SHORT).show() }
}
```

Now, when you run the app, you'll see an inference result pop up in the `Toast` when the user selects a flower. The next step is to set up remote configuration so that different users get different models.

Step 6: Use Remote Configuration

One of the (many) services in Firebase you can use to improve apps that use machine learning is remote configuration. Let's now explore how to set it up so that some of your users will get the flowers1 model, and others will get the flowers2 one.

Start by finding the Remote Configuration section in Firebase Console. It will look like two diverging arrows as depicted in Figure 12-16.

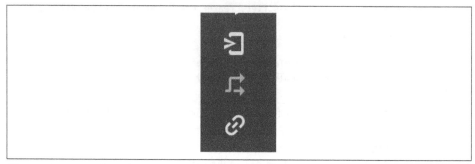

Figure 12-16. Finding the Remote Configuration section in Firebase Console

Once you've done this, you'll see the ability to "Add parameter," where you specify a parameter key and a default value. So, for example, you could use "model_name" and "flowers1" respectively as in Figure 12-17.

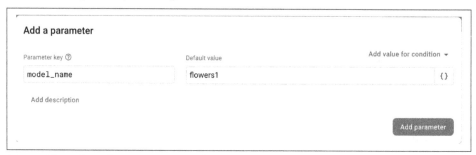

Figure 12-17. Initializing remote configuration

So now, instead of hardcoding "flowers1" as your model name, you could read it from remote configuration if you wanted. But that's not really very useful. Where remote configuration really begins to show its power is when you select "Add value for condition" on the top right.

Select this, and you'll be given a button to "Define new Condition." Select that, and you'll get a dialog for the condition. See Figure 12-18.

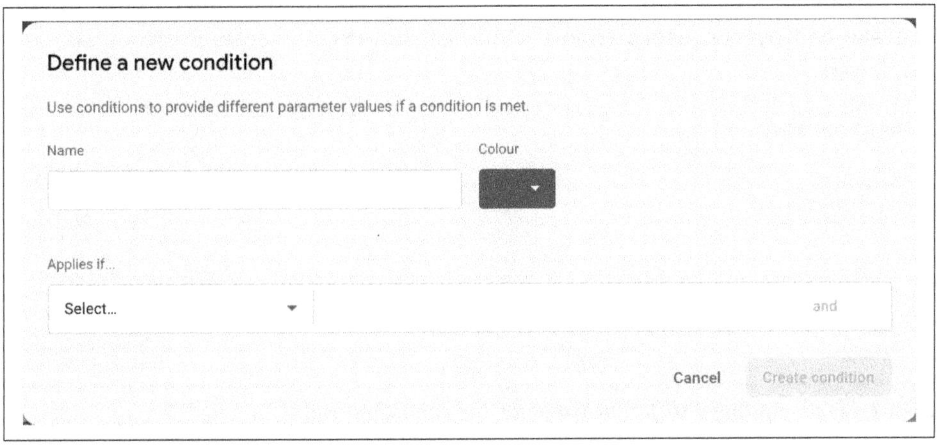

Figure 12-18. Defining a new condition

Once you've given the condition a name, you can then select the dropdown under "Applies if…" to specify the condition. For example, if you want users in particular countries to get a different value, you can select Country/Region in the "Applied if…" dialog, and select the countries you want. In Figure 12-19, you can see that I selected two countries (Ireland and Cyprus) and named the condition accordingly.

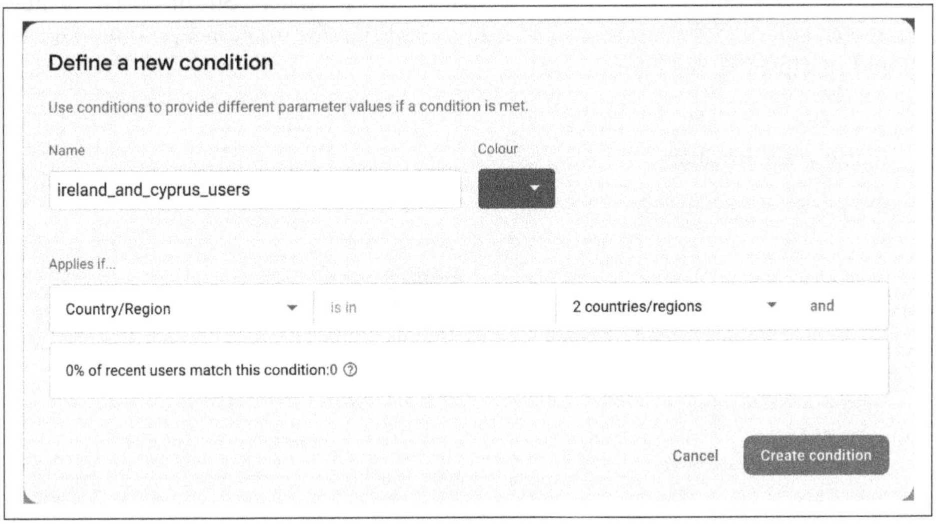

Figure 12-19. Setting up a condition by country

After clicking "Create condition," you'll be returned to the "Add a parameter" dialog, where you can specify the value for the users that match that condition. So, for example, see Figure 12-20, where I specified that the users in the `ireland_and_cyprus_users` cohort would get flowers2, whereas everyone else will get flowers.

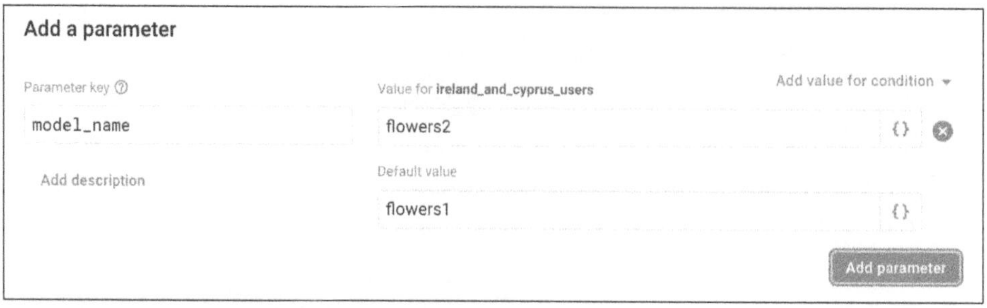

Add a parameter

Parameter key ⑦	Value for **ireland_and_cyprus_users**	Add value for condition ▾
model_name	flowers2	{} ✕
Add description	Default value	
	flowers1	{}

Add parameter

Figure 12-20. Adding a different value for the condition users

This is a bit of a silly example for testing like this, as I don't have *any* users, much less some in Ireland or Cyprus. So let's change it up a little. Delete the ireland_and_cyprus_users cohort, by clicking the black "x" to the right of the condition as shown in Figure 12-20. Then click to add a new parameter. You may be asked to "publish the changes" and if so, go ahead and do so.

After publishing, the dialog for configuring remote configuration will look a little different, but that's OK, it still works. Use the "Add parameter" button to add a new parameter, and call it "random_users." Add a condition for users in a random percentile and specify 50%. See Figure 12-21.

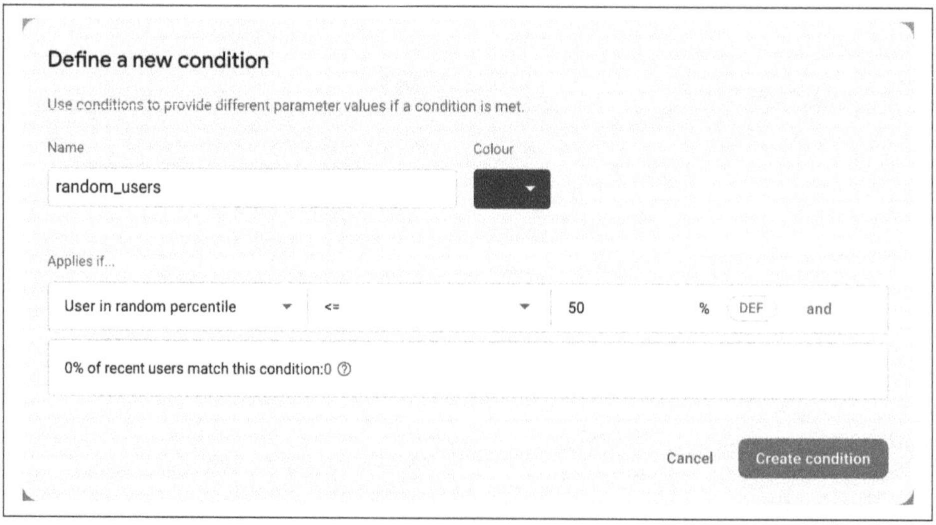

Define a new condition

Use conditions to provide different parameter values if a condition is met.

Name

random_users

Colour

Applies if...

| User in random percentile ▾ | <= ▾ | 50 | % | DEF | and |

0% of recent users match this condition:0 ⑦

Cancel   Create condition

Figure 12-21. Adding random users in the 50% percentile

For these users, ensure that their value is flowers2, and the rest are flowers1. Your dialog should look like Figure 12-22.

Figure 12-22. Giving half your users flowers2

Make sure that the configuration is published, and then you're ready to go to the next step.

Step 7: Read Remote Configuration in Your App

Return to your app and add the following method, which will get an instance of remote configuration, read it, and then get the value of the model name from it.

This will first set up a configuration object for remote configuration, which is just set in this case to time out after an hour. It will then use these with the `fetchAndActivate` method to read a variable from remote configuration. Then, at runtime, Firebase will determine which cohort this user is in and give them either flowers1 or flowers2 as the value for the remote variable:

```
private fun initializeModelFromRemoteConfig(){
  mFirebaseRemoteConfig = FirebaseRemoteConfig.getInstance()
  val configSettings = FirebaseRemoteConfigSettings.Builder()
    .setMinimumFetchIntervalInSeconds(3600)
    .build()

  mFirebaseRemoteConfig.setConfigSettingsAsync(configSettings)
  mFirebaseRemoteConfig.fetchAndActivate()
    .addOnCompleteListener(this) { task ->
      if (task.isSuccessful) {
        val updated = task.result
        Log.d("Flowers", "Config params updated: $updated")
        Toast.makeText(this@MainActivity,
                  "Fetch and activate succeeded",
                  Toast.LENGTH_SHORT).show()

        modelName = mFirebaseRemoteConfig.getString("model_name")
```

```
        } else {
          Toast.makeText(this@MainActivity,
                      "Fetch failed - using default value",
                      Toast.LENGTH_SHORT).show()
          modelName = "flowers1"
        }
        loadModel()
        initViews()
      }
    }
```

Once that is done, the `loadModel()` and `initViews()` methods will be called. Recall earlier that you called these in the `onCreate` event, so delete them from that, and replace them with a call to this new method:

```
override fun onCreate(savedInstanceState: Bundle?) {
    super.onCreate(savedInstanceState)
    setContentView(R.layout.activity_main)
    initializeModelFromRemoteConfig()
}
```

Now when you launch your app, you'll randomly get either flowers1 or flowers2 as the model!

Next Steps

Given that half of your users are now going to get flowers1, and the other half are going to get flowers2, you could, for example, add analytics to see the performance of inference and log it. Which users are getting faster inference? Or, you could also, for example, check user activity to see which users drop out of your app, and trace if that's as a result of the model. Beyond analytics, you could also run A/B tests, use predictions based on behavior, and a whole lot more!

While the needs of every app are different, hopefully this will give you some inspiration for what's possible in growing an ML app when using Firebase. For some inspiration from apps that were able to use things like analytics, predictions, and remote configuration to grow, check out *https://firebase.google.com/use-cases*.

Summary

In this chapter, you saw how you can use Firebase Model Hosting with a TensorFlow Lite model, and then explored how you could use some of the rest of the Firebase infrastructure, starting with remote configuration. Using this combination of technologies, you'll be able to, for example, manage multiple model versions or types across different audiences, and explore the optimal way to get models into your users' hands. We just touched the surface of what's possible, and I'd encourage you to explore other options! And while we just explored Firebase in Android, the APIs work equally well across iOS and the web too.

Speaking of iOS, no book about on-device machine learning would be complete without a look at the iOS-specific technologies Core ML and Create ML, so you'll explore them in Chapter 13!

Create ML and Core ML for Simple iOS Apps

In this book so far, you've been looking at technologies that bring machine learning to *multiple* devices, so that you could use a single API to reach Android, iOS, embedded systems, microcontrollers, and more. This was made possible by the TensorFlow ecosystem, and in particular TensorFlow Lite, which underpins ML Kit, which you used as a higher level API. And while we didn't go into embedded systems and microcontrollers, the concepts are the same, other than hardware limitations the smaller you go. To learn more about that space, check out the great book *TinyML* by Pete Warden and Daniel Situnayake (O'Reilly).

But I would be remiss if I didn't at least cover the iOS-specific Create ML tool and Core ML libraries from Apple, which are designed to let you use ML models when creating apps for iOS, iPadOS or MacOS. Create ML in particular is a really nice visual tool that lets you create models without any prior ML programming experience.

We'll look at a few scenarios, starting with creating a model that recognizes flowers, similar to the ones we did earlier with TensorFlow and TensorFlow Lite.

A Core ML Image Classifier Built Using Create ML

We'll start with creating our model. We can do this codelessly using the Create ML tool. You can find this by right-clicking on Xcode in the doc, and then in the Open Developer Tool menu, you can find Create ML. See Figure 13-1.

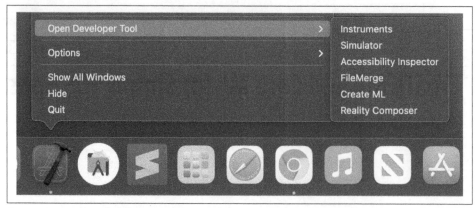

Figure 13-1. Launching Create ML

When the tool launches, you'll first be asked *where* you want to store the finished model. It's a little jarring if you aren't used to it, as you'd normally go through a template to select the type before you pick a location. It fooled me a couple of times where I thought this was a file dialog from another open app! From the dialog, select New Document at the bottom left (Figure 13-2).

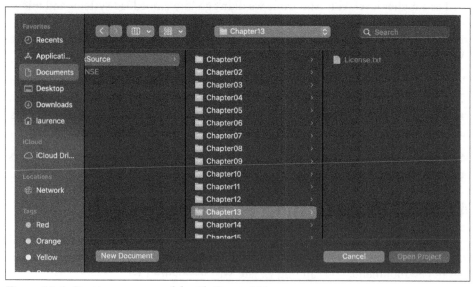

Figure 13-2. Starting a new model with Create ML

After selecting the location and clicking New Document, you'll be given a list of templates for the type of model you can create with Create ML. See Figure 13-3.

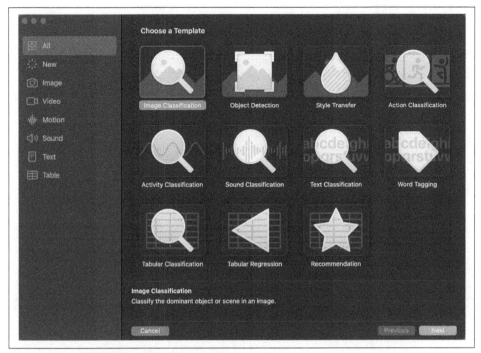

Figure 13-3. Choosing a Create ML template

In this scenario, we'll do an image classification model, so choose Image Classification and click Next. You'll be asked to give your project a name and other details like an Author, License, Description, etc. Fill these out and click Next.

You'll then be asked *again* where to store the model. You can create a new folder and put it in there, or just click Create. The model designer will open. You can see it in Figure 13-4.

To train a model with the model designer in Create ML, you'll need a set of images. You'll need to organize them into subfolders of each particular type of item you want to classify (i.e., the label), so, for example, if you consider the flowers dataset we've used throughout this book, your directory structure will probably look like Figure 13-5. If you download the flowers from the Google API directory and unzip, they'll already be in this structure. You can find the data at *https://oreil.ly/RuN2o*.

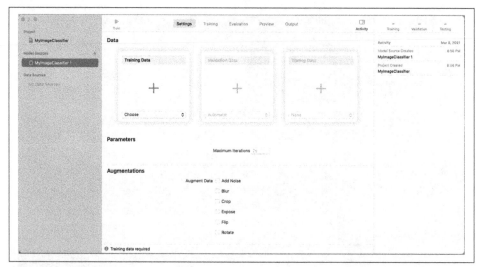

Figure 13-4. The model designer

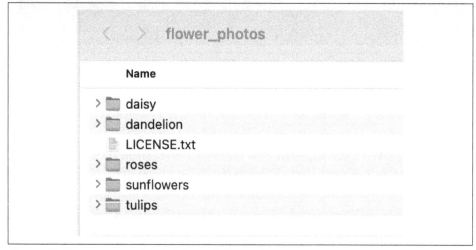

Figure 13-5. Images stored in labeled subdirectories

So, in this case, the folder called *daisy* contains images of daisies, *dandelion* contains images of dandelions, and so on. To train the dataset, drag this folder over the Training Data section in the model designer. When you're done it should look like Figure 13-6.

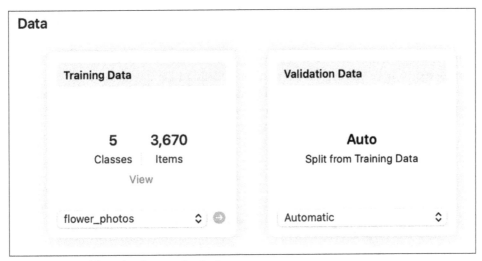

Figure 13-6. Adding the data to the designer

Note that there were five folders shown in Figure 13-5, and that correlates to the five classes you can see in Figure 13-6. Between these there are 3,670 images. Note also that the tool will automatically create a validation dataset from these by splitting from the training data. This saves you a lot of work! In this case, a percentage of your images will be held out of the training set so that on each epoch the model can be tested using images it hasn't previously seen. That way you can get a better estimate for its accuracy.

Note that at the bottom of the screen, you can choose Augmentations. This allows you to artificially extend the scope of your dataset by amending it on the fly as you are training. So, for example, pictures of flowers are *usually* taken with the stem at the bottom and the petals at the top. If your training data is oriented this way, then it will only be accurate with pictures taken the same way. If you give it an image that has a flower lying on its side, it might not accurately classify it. So, instead of taking the expensive action of taking lots more pictures of flowers in other orientations to get effective training coverage, you can use augmentation. So, for example, if you check the Rotate box, then some of the images will be randomly rotated while training, in order to simulate the effect of you taking new flower pictures. If your models overfit to your training data—they get really good at recognizing data that looks like the training data, but not so good for other images—it's worth investigating different augmentation settings. But for now you don't need them.

When ready, press the Train button at the top left of the screen. Create ML will process the features in the images, and after a couple of minutes will present you with a trained model. Note that it's using *transfer learning* here, instead of training from scratch, similar to Model Maker, and as such, the training can be both accurate *and* fast.

When a model is stable in its accuracy metrics for a number of epochs, it's generally considered to have *converged*, where it's not likely to get any better with continued training, so it will be stopped early. The default number of epochs that Create ML uses for training a model is 25, but the flowers model will likely converge at around 10, and you'll see its accuracy metrics appearing to look a bit like Figure 13-7.

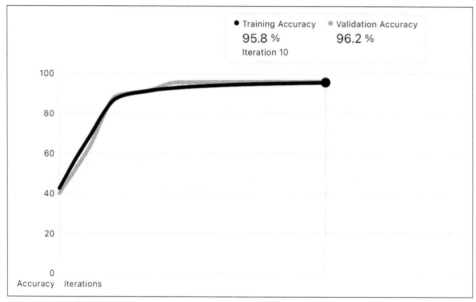

Figure 13-7. The model converges

You can click the Evaluation tab to explore how well the model did on each different class. On the lefthand side you can choose the Training Set, Validation Set, or Testing Set. As I didn't create a testing set in this instance, I just have the first two, and you can see the results of the training in Figure 13-8.

In this case you can see that 594 of the daisy images were used for training, and 39 for validation. Similar splits can be seen in the other flowers. There are two columns, precision and recall, where precision is the percentage of instances where the classifier classified an image correctly, i.e., of the 594 daisies, the classifier correctly identified it as a daisy 95% of the time. The recall value in this case should be very close to the accuracy value and is generally only one you should pay attention to if there are *other* elements in the picture other than the particular flower. As this dataset is a simple one, i.e., a daisy picture *only* contains a daisy, or a rose picture *only* contains a rose, then it's safe not to pay attention to it. You can learn more about precision and recall on *Wikipedia (https://oreil.ly/4dscv)*.

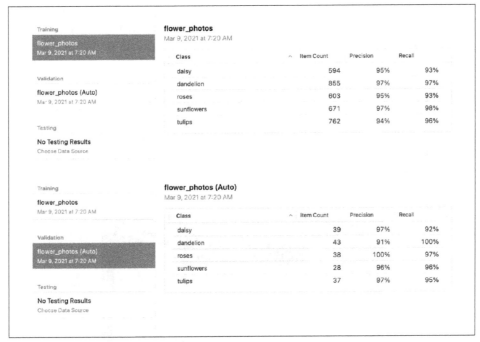

Class	Item Count	Precision	Recall
daisy	594	95%	93%
dandelion	855	97%	97%
roses	603	95%	93%
sunflowers	671	97%	98%
tulips	762	94%	96%

Class	Item Count	Precision	Recall
daisy	39	97%	92%
dandelion	43	91%	100%
roses	38	100%	97%
sunflowers	28	96%	96%
tulips	37	97%	95%

Figure 13-8. Exploring the training accuracy

You can go to the Preview tab and drag/drop images onto it to try out the model. So, for example, in Figure 13-9, I dropped images that are neither in the training set nor the validation set onto Create ML and checked out the classifications. As you can see, it correctly identified these tulips with 99% confidence.

Figure 13-9. Using the Preview to test my model

Finally on the output tab you can export the model. You'll see a button called Get at the top left. Click that, and you'll be given the option to save an MLModel file. Save it as something simple, like *flowers.mlmodel*, and you'll use it in an iOS app in the next step.

Making a Core ML App That Uses a Create ML Model

Let's now explore how this will look in an app. You can get the full app in the repo for this book, so I won't go into the specifics of how to set up the user interface. It will have six images stored as assets named "1" through "6," with buttons to allow the user to cycle through these, and a classify button to perform the inference. You can see the storyboard for this in Figure 13-10.

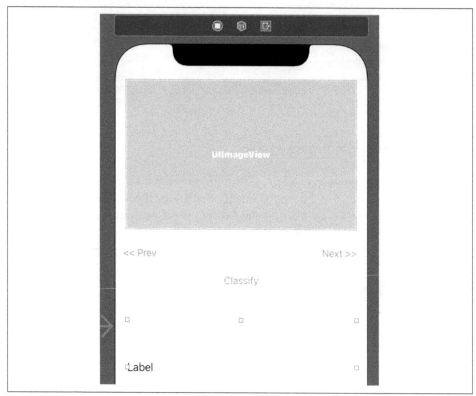

Figure 13-10. Storyboard for flowers classifier

Add the MLModel File

To add the MLModel file that you created with Create ML, simply drag and drop it onto the project window in Xcode. Xcode will import the model *and* create a Swift wrapper class for it. If you select the model within Xcode you should see lots of details for it, including the list of labels, version, author, and more. See Figure 13-11.

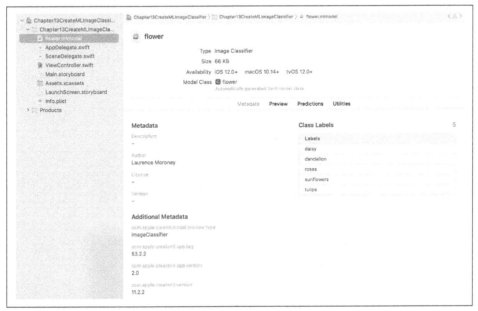

Figure 13-11. Browsing the model

You can even test out the model in a Preview tab just like in Create ML! With the Utilities tab you can also encrypt your model and prepare it for cloud deployment. That's beyond the scope of this book; you can find out details on the Apple developer site (*https://oreil.ly/NZdPM*).

Finally, before going further, in the Model Class section at the top center of the screen, you can see the automatically generated Swift model class, in this case called "flower." You can click on it to see the autogenerated code. The important thing to note is the name—which in this case is "flower," as you'll need that later.

Run the Inference

When the user presses the button, we want to load the current image, and pass it to Core ML to invoke our model and get an inference. Before getting into the code for this, it might be good to review the coding pattern used, as it is a little complex.

The Core ML inference pattern

You can use this model in an app that uses Core ML. This API has been designed to make it easy to use ML models in an iOS app, but until you understand the overall pattern of building using ML with Core ML, it may seem a little convoluted.

The idea with Core ML is to ensure asynchronous performance wherever possible, and model inference can be a bottleneck. As Core ML is designed as a mobile API, it uses patterns to ensure that the user experience doesn't pause or break while model inference is going on. Thus, to use an image model like this in a Core ML app, you'll see a number of asynchronous steps. You can see this in Figure 13-12.

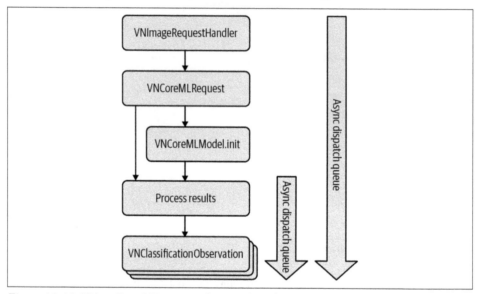

Figure 13-12. Using Core ML to asynchronously infer images and update the UI

The pattern will be to create a handler within a dispatch queue to ensure asynchronicity. This is represented by the larger of the two downward arrows in Figure 13-12. This handler will be a `VNImageRequestHandler` as we are doing an image classification (VN for "VisioN"). This handler will perform a classification request.

The classification request (of type `VNCoreMLRequest`) will initialize the model, and specify a request to the model, with a callback function to process the results. This callback will happen upon a successful `VNCoreMLRequest`.

The callback will generally be asynchronous, as it updates the UI, and will read the classification results (as `VNClassificationObservations`), and write them out to the UI. This is represented by the smaller dispatch queue arrow in Figure 13-12.

Writing the code

Let's now explore the code for this. When the user takes the action of pressing the button, you'll call a function called `interpretImage` to kick off the inference workflow, and it looks like this:

```
func interpretImage(){
    let theImage: UIImage = UIImage(named: String(currentImage))!
    getClassification(for: theImage)
}
```

This simply creates a UIImage from the currently selected image and passes it to a function called `getClassification`. This function will implement the pattern from Figure 13-10, so let's explore it. I've abbreviated the output strings to make the printed code here more readable:

```
func getClassification(for image: UIImage) {

    let orientation = CGImagePropertyOrientation(
        rawValue: UInt32(image.imageOrientation.rawValue))!
    guard let ciImage = CIImage(image: image)
      else { fatalError("...") }

    DispatchQueue.global(qos: .userInitiated).async {
        let handler = VNImageRequestHandler(
            ciImage: ciImage, orientation: orientation)
        do {
            try handler.perform([self.classificationRequest])
        } catch {
            print("...")
        }
    }
}
```

The code will first get our UIImage, and turn it into a CIImage. Core ML is built using Core Image, which requires the image to be represented in that format. So we'll need to start with that.

Then, we'll invoke our first DispatchQueue, which is the larger, outer one in Figure 13-10. Within it, we'll create our handler, and have it call its perform method on a `classificationRequest`. We haven't created that yet, so let's explore it now:

```
lazy var classificationRequest: VNCoreMLRequest = {
    do {
        let model = try VNCoreMLModel.init(for: flower().model)
        let request = VNCoreMLRequest(model: model,
          completionHandler: { [weak self] request, error in
            self?.processResults(for: request, error: error)
        })
        request.imageCropAndScaleOption = .centerCrop
        return request
    } catch {
```

```
        fatalError("...")
    }
}()
```

The `classificationRequest` is a `VNCoreMLRequest`, which works for a model that it
initializes internally. Note that the `init` method takes a `flower()` type, and reads the
`model` property from it. This is the class that was autocreated when you imported the
MLModel. Refer back to Figure 13-11 and you'll see the autogenerated code discussed
there. You noted the name of your class—in my case it was flower—and that's what
you'll use here.

Once you have a model, you can create the `VNCoreMLRequest`, specifying the model
and the completion handler function, which in this case is `processResults`. You've
now constructed the `VNCoreMLRequest` that the `getClassification` function
required. If you look back to that function, you'll see that it called the `perform`
method; this code implements that for you. If that runs successfully, the `processRe
sults` callback will be called, so let's look at that next:

```
func processResults(for request: VNRequest, error: Error?) {
    DispatchQueue.main.async {
        guard let results = request.results else {
            self.txtOutput.text = "..."
            return
        }

        let classifications = results as! [VNClassificationObservation]

        if classifications.isEmpty {
            self.txtOutput.text = "Nothing recognized."
        } else {
            let topClassifications =
                classifications.prefix(self.NUM_CLASSES)
            let descriptions = topClassifications.map
            { classification in

                return String(format: "  (%.2f) %@",
                              classification.confidence,
                              classification.identifier) }
            self.txtOutput.text = "Classification:\n" +
                              descriptions.joined(separator: "\n")
        }
    }
}
```

This function begins with another `DispatchQueue`, as it will update the user interface.
It receives results from the initial request, and if they are valid, it can cast them into a
set of `VNClassificationObservation` objects. Then it's simply a matter of iterating
through these and getting the confidence and identifier for each classification and
outputting these. This code will also sort them into the top classifications, giving you

the probability output for each class. NUM_CLASSES is a constant for the number of classes, and in the case of the flowers model I, set it to 5.

And that's pretty much it. Using Create ML simplified the process of making the model, and the Xcode integration, including class file generation, made it relatively straightforward to do the inference. The complexity is necessarily added by the need to keep the process as asynchronous as possible to avoid breaking the user experience when running inference on the model!

You can see the app, with its inferences for a rose picture, in Figure 13-13.

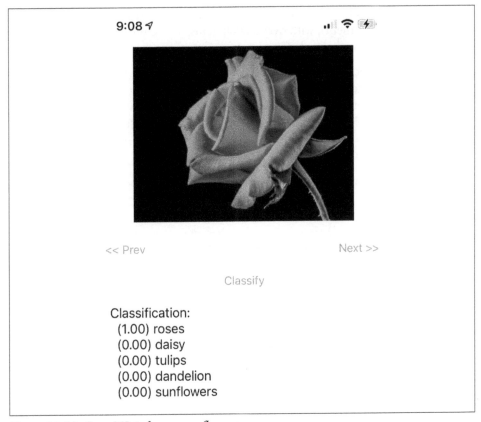

Figure 13-13. Core ML inference on flowers

Next we'll explore a natural language processing (NLP) example, beginning with creating a model using Create ML.

Using Create ML to Build a Text Classifier

Create ML allows you to import CSV files for classification, but your text must be in a column called "text," so if you've been following this book and using the emotion sentiment dataset, you'll need to amend it slightly, or use the one I provide in the repo for this chapter. The only amendment is to name the first column (containing the text) "text."

At that point you can create a new Create ML document using the steps outlined earlier, but in this case, choose a Text Classifier template. As before you can drop your data onto the data field, and you'll see that there are two classes (in this case for positive and negative sentiment), with over 35,000 items. You should split your validation data from your training data as before.

In the Parameters section, there are a number of options for the algorithm. I have found I can get excellent results by choosing Transfer Learning, and then for the feature extractor choosing Dynamic Embedding. This will be slow, as all of the embeddings will be learned from scratch, but can give very good results. Training with these settings will be slow—for me, on an M1 Mac Mini, it took about an hour, but when it was done, it hit a training accuracy of 89.2% after 75 iterations.

The Preview tab allows you to type in a sentence, and it will be automatically classified! See Figure 13-14 where I typed in what is obviously a negative sentence, and we can see it hit label 0 with 98% confidence!

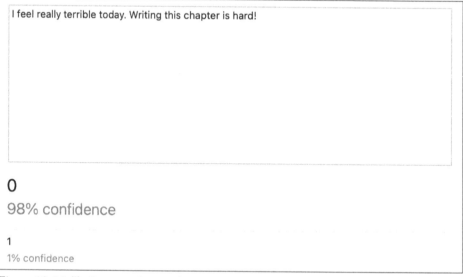

Figure 13-14. Testing negative sentiment

But of course, that's not true. I'm having a wonderful time writing this chapter and playing with this technology, so let me see what will happen if I change the text to suit! See Figure 13-15.

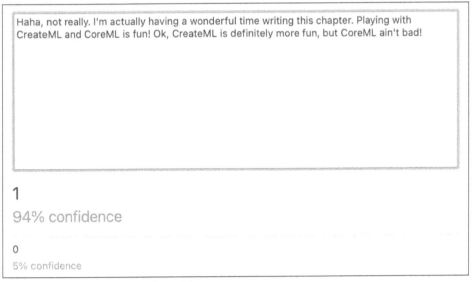

Figure 13-15. A sentence with positive sentiment

As you can see in that case, label 1 scored with 94% confidence. What's really cool is that the classification updates on the fly as you type!

Anyway, enough playing. Let's get back to work. To build an app that uses this, you'll first need to export your model. You can do that on the Output tab. Use the Get button to save it and give it an easy-to-remember name. In my case, I called it *emotion.mlmodel*.

Use the Model in an App

Language models like this one are super simple to use in an app. Create a new app and add a UITextView with an outlet called txtInput, a UILabel with an outlet called txtOutput, and a button with an action called classifyText. Your storyboard should look like Figure 13-16.

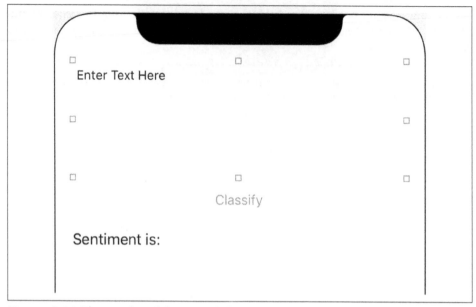

Figure 13-16. The storyboard for a simple language app

Within the `classifyText` action, add a call to `doInference()`. This function doesn't exist yet; you'll add it shortly. The code at the top of your class should look like this:

```
@IBOutlet weak var txtInput: UITextView!
@IBOutlet weak var txtOutput: UILabel!
@IBAction func classifyText(_ sender: Any) {
    doInference()
}
```

To use Core ML with natural language processing, you should also be sure to import both these libraries using:

```
import NaturalLanguage
import CoreML
```

Now you can do your inference. Drag and drop the model that you created earlier into Xcode, and it will generate a class for you that has the same name as the saved model. In my case I called it "emotion," so I'll have a class of that name.

You'll start by creating an `mlModel` type using `emotion`, like this:

```
let mlModel = try emotion(
              Configuration: MLModelConfiguration()).model
```

Once you have this, you can use it in turn to create an `NLModel` (NL stands for natural language):

```
let sentimentPredictor = try NLModel(mlModel: mlModel)
```

You can read the input string from the `txtInput` and pass that to the `sentimentPredictor` to get the label for it:

```
let inputText = txtInput.text
let label = sentimentPredictor.predictedLabel(for: inputText!)
```

This label will be a string representing the classes. As you saw in the data for this model, they were "0" and "1". So, you can output the predictions simply like this:

```
if (label=="0"){
    txtOutput.text = "Sentiment: Negative"
} else {
    txtOutput.text = "Sentiment: Positive"
}
```

And that's it! As you can see the natural language libraries make this really easy! You don't have to deal with tokenizing or embedding; just give it a string and you're done!

You can see the app in action in Figure 13-17.

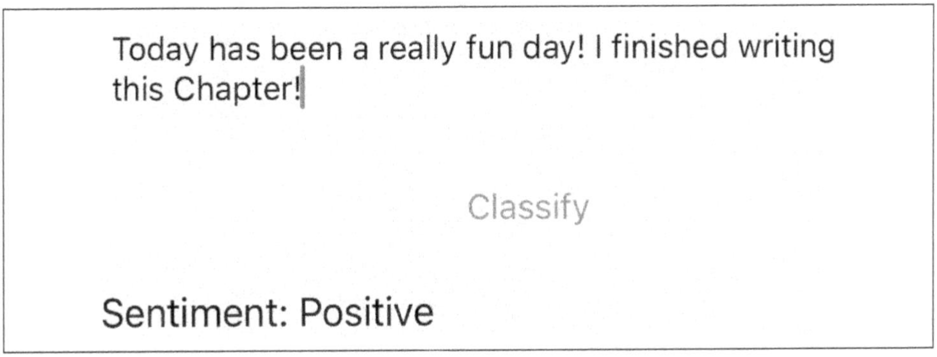

Figure 13-17. Using the emotion classifier

This is very much a barebones app, but you can see how you might use it to create new functionality into your apps; you could, for example, detect if the app was being used to send spam or toxic messages, and deter the user from sending them. This could be used in conjunction with backend security to ensure the best possible user experience.

Summary

This chapter introduced you to two of the templates in Create ML—image classification and text sentiment analysis—and guided you through training models with no ML experience, before using them in simple apps. You saw how Create ML gave you a tool that trains models for you, typically using transfer learning, very quickly, and how its output can be dropped into Xcode to take advantage of code generation to encapsulate the complexity of the ML model and let you focus on your user interface. You stepped through a complex interaction when doing an image classification, where you ensure that your user experience isn't broken when you try to do the inference. That being said, it was still pretty easy for you to write something that manages the inference; in particular, you don't have to worry about the image format and stripping the image down into tensors in order to pass it to the inference engine. As such, if you are only writing for iOS and not thinking about other platforms, Create ML and Core ML are a great option, and they are definitely worth looking into.

## CHAPTER 14

Accessing Cloud-Based Models from Mobile Apps

Throughout this book you've been creating models and converting them to the TensorFlow Lite format so they could be used within your mobile apps. This works very well for models that you want to use on mobile for the reasons discussed in Chapter 1, such as latency and privacy. However, there may be times when you don't want to deploy the model to a mobile device—maybe it's too large or complex for mobile, maybe you want to update it frequently, or maybe you don't want to risk it being reverse-engineered and have your IP used by others.

In those cases you'll want to deploy your model to a server, perform the inference there, and then have some form of server manage the requests from your clients, invoke the model for inference, and respond with the results. A high-level view of this is shown in Figure 14-1.

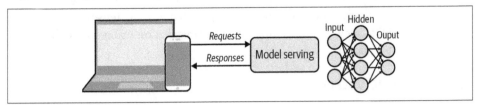

Figure 14-1. A high-level look at a server architecture for models

Another benefit of this architecture is in managing model drift. When you deploy a model to devices, you can end up in a situation with multiple models in the wild if people don't or can't update their app to get the latest model. Consider then the scenario where you *want* model drift; perhaps people with more premium hardware can have a bigger and more accurate version of your model, whereas others can get a smaller and slightly less accurate version. Managing that can be difficult! But if the model is hosted on a server, you don't have to worry about this because you control the hardware platform on which the model runs. Another advantage of server-side model inference is that you can easily test different model versions with different audiences. See Figure 14-2.

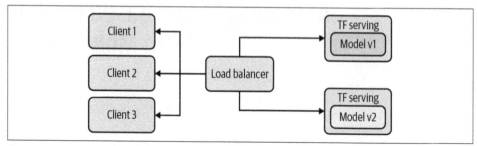

Figure 14-2. Managing different models using hosted inference

Here you can see that I have two different versions of the model (called Model v1 and Model v2), which are deployed to different clients using a load balancer. In the diagram I show that these are managed by something called TensorFlow Serving, and we'll explore how to install and use that next, including training and deploying a simple model to it.

Installing TensorFlow Serving

TensorFlow Serving can be installed with two different server architectures. The first, `tensorflow-model-server`, is a fully optimized server that uses platform-specific compiler options for various architectures. In general it's the preferred option, unless your server machine doesn't have those architectures. The alternative, `tensorflow-model-server-universal`, is compiled with basic optimizations that should work on all machines, and provides a nice backup if `tensorflow-model-server` does not work. There are several methods by which you can install TensorFlow Serving, including using Docker as well as a direct package installation using `apt`. We'll look at both of those options next.

Installing Using Docker

Docker (*https://docker.com*) is a tool that lets you encapsulate an operating system plus software dependencies into a single, simple-to-use image. Using Docker is perhaps the easiest way to get up and running quickly. To get started, use `docker pull` to get the TensorFlow Serving package:

```
docker pull tensorflow/serving
```

Once you've done this, clone the TensorFlow Serving code from GitHub:

```
git clone https://github.com/tensorflow/serving
```

This includes some sample models, including one called Half Plus Two that, given a value, will return half that value, plus two. To do this, first set up a variable called TESTDATA that contains the path of the sample models:

```
TESTDATA="$(pwd)/serving/tensorflow_serving/servables/tensorflow/testdata"
```

You can now run TensorFlow Serving from the Docker image:

```
docker run -t --rm -p 8501:8501 \
    -v "$TESTDATA/saved_model_half_plus_two_cpu:/models/half_plus_two" \
    -e MODEL_NAME=half_plus_two \
    tensorflow/serving &
```

This will instantiate a server on port 8501—you'll see how to do that in more detail later in this chapter—and execute the model on that server. You can then access the model at *http://localhost:8501/v1/models/half_plus_two:predict*.

To pass the data that you want to run inference on, you can POST a tensor containing the values to this URL. Here's an example using curl (run this in a separate terminal if you're running on your development machine):

```
curl -d '{"instances": [1.0, 2.0, 5.0]}' \
    -X POST http://localhost:8501/v1/models/half_plus_two:predict
```

You can see the results in Figure 14-3.

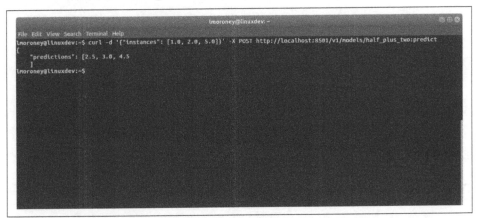

Figure 14-3. Results of running TensorFlow Serving

While the Docker image is certainly convenient, you might also want the full control of installing it directly on your machine. You'll explore how to do that next.

Installing Directly on Linux

Whether you are using `tensorflow-model-server` or `tensorflow-model-server-universal`, the package name is the same. So, it's a good idea to remove `tensorflow-model-server` before you start so you can ensure you get the right one. If you want to try this on your own hardware, I've provided a Colab notebook (*https://oreil.ly/CYiWc*) in the GitHub repo with the code:

```
apt-get remove tensorflow-model-server
```

Then add the TensorFlow package source (*https://oreil.ly/NDwab*) to your system:

```
echo "deb http://storage.googleapis.com/tensorflow-serving-apt stable
tensorflow-model-server tensorflow-model-server-universal" |
tee /etc/apt/sources.list.d/tensorflow-serving.list && \
curl https://storage.googleapis.com/tensorflow-serving-apt/tensorflow-
serving.release.pub.gpg | apt-key add -
```

If you need to use `sudo` on your local system, you can do so like this:

```
sudo echo "deb http://storage.googleapis.com/tensorflow-serving-apt stable
tensorflow-model-server tensorflow-model-server-universal" |
sudo tee /etc/apt/sources.list.d/tensorflow-serving.list && \
curl https://storage.googleapis.com/tensorflow-serving-apt/tensorflow-
serving.release.pub.gpg | sudo apt-key add -
```

You'll need to update `apt-get` next:

```
apt-get update
```

Once this has been done, you can install the model server with `apt`:

```
apt-get install tensorflow-model-server
```

And you can ensure you have the latest version by using:

```
apt-get upgrade tensorflow-model-server
```

The package should now be ready to use.

Building and Serving a Model

In this section we'll do a walkthrough of the complete process of creating a model, preparing it for serving, deploying it with TensorFlow Serving, and then running inference using it.

You'll use the simple "Hello World" model that we've been exploring throughout the book:

```
import numpy as np
import tensorflow as tf
xs = np.array([-1.0,  0.0, 1.0, 2.0, 3.0, 4.0], dtype=float)
ys = np.array([-3.0, -1.0, 1.0, 3.0, 5.0, 7.0], dtype=float)
```

```
model = tf.keras.Sequential([tf.keras.layers.Dense(units=1, input_shape=[1])])
model.compile(optimizer='sgd', loss='mean_squared_error')
history = model.fit(xs, ys, epochs=500, verbose=0)
print("Finished training the model")
print(model.predict([10.0]))
```

This should train very quickly and give you a result of 18.98 or so, when asked to predict y when x is 10.0. Next, the model needs to be saved. You'll need a temporary folder to save it in:

```
export_path = "/tmp/serving_model/1/"
model.save(export_path, save_format="tf")
print('\nexport_path = {}'.format(export_path))
```

You can export it to whatever directory you want, but I like to use a temp directory. Note that here I saved it in */tmp/serving_model/1/*, but later when we are serving we'll use */tmp/serving_model/* only—that's because TensorFlow Serving will look for model versions based on a number, and it will default to looking for version 1.

If there's anything in the directory you're saving the model to, it's a good idea to delete it before proceeding (avoiding this issue is one reason why I like using a temp directory!).

The TensorFlow Serving tools include a utility called saved_model_cli that can be used to inspect a model. You can call this with the show command, giving it the directory of the model in order to get the full model metadata:

```
$> saved_model_cli show --dir {export_path} --all
```

The output of this command will be very long, but will contain details like this:

```
signature_def['serving_default']:
  The given SavedModel SignatureDef contains the following input(s):
    inputs['dense_input'] tensor_info:
        dtype: DT_FLOAT
        shape: (-1, 1)
        name: serving_default_dense_input:0
  The given SavedModel SignatureDef contains the following output(s):
    outputs['dense'] tensor_info:
        dtype: DT_FLOAT
        shape: (-1, 1)
        name: StatefulPartitionedCall:0
```

Note the contents of the signature_def, which in this case is serving_default. You'll need them later.

Also note that the inputs and outputs have a defined shape and type. In this case, each is a float and has the shape (−1, 1). You can effectively ignore the −1, and just bear in mind that the input to the model is a float and the output is a float.

To run the TensorFlow model server with a command line, you need a number of parameters. First you need to specify a couple of parameters to the tensor flow_model_server command. rest_api_port is the port number you want to run the server on. Here it's set to 8501. You then give the model a name with the model_name switch—here I've called it helloworld. Finally, you then pass the server the path to the model you saved in the MODEL_DIR operating system environment variable with model_base_path. Here's the code:

```
$> tensorflow_model_server --rest_api_port=8501 --model_name="helloworld" --
model_base_path="/tmp/serving_model/" > server.log 2>&1
```

At the end of the script is code to output the results to *server.log*. Open this file and take a look at it—you should see that the server started successfully with a note showing that it is exporting the HTTP/REST API at *localhost:8501*:

```
2021-02-19 08:56:22.271662:
  I tensorflow_serving/core/loader_harness.cc:87] Successfully loaded
  servable version {name: helloworld version: 1}
2021-02-19 08:56:22.303904:
  I tensorflow_serving/model_servers/server.cc:371] Running gRPC ModelServer
  at 0.0.0.0:8500 ...
2021-02-19 08:56:22.315093:
  I tensorflow_serving/model_servers/server.cc:391] Exporting HTTP/REST API
  at:localhost:8501 ...
[evhttp_server.cc : 238] NET_LOG: Entering the event loop ...
```

If it fails, you should see a notification about the failure. Should that happen, you might need to reboot your system.

If you want to test the server, you can do so within Python:

```
import json
xs = np.array([[9.0], [10.0]])
data = json.dumps({"signature_name": "serving_default",
                   "instances": xs.tolist()})
print(data)
```

To send data to the server, you need to get it into JSON format. So with Python it's a case of creating a NumPy array of the values you want to send—in this case it's a list of two values, 9.0 and 10.0. Each of these is an array in itself, because as you saw earlier the input shape is (–1,1). Single values should be sent to the model, so if you want multiple ones it should be a list of lists, with the inner lists having single values only.

Use json.dumps in Python to create the payload, which is two name/value pairs. The first is the signature name to call on the model, which in this case is serving_default (as you'll recall from earlier, when you inspected the model). The second is instan ces, which is the list of values you want to pass to the model.

Do note that when passing values to a model using serving, your input data to the model should be in a list of values, even if there's only a single value. So, for example, if you want to use this model to get an inference for the value 9.0, you still have to put it in a list such as [9.0]. If you want two inferences for two values, you might expect it to look like [9.0, 10.0], but that would actually be wrong! Two separate inputs, expecting two separate inferences, should be two separate lists, so [9.0], [10.0]. However, you are passing these as a single *batch* to the model for inference, so the batch itself should be a list containing the lists that you pass to the model—thus [[9.0], [10.0]]. Keep this also in mind if you are only passing a single value for inference. It will be in a list, and that list will be within a list, like this: [[10.0]].

So, to get this model to run inference twice, and calculate the values for y where the values for x are 9.0 and 10.0, the desired payload should look like this:

```
{"signature_name": "serving_default", "instances": [[9.0], [10.0]]}
```

You can call the server using the requests library to do an HTTP POST. Note the URL structure. The model is called helloworld, and you want to run its prediction. The POST command requires data, which is the payload you just created, and a headers specification, where you're telling the server the content type is JSON:

```
import requests
headers = {"content-type": "application/json"}
json_response = requests.post(
    'http://localhost:8501/v1/models/helloworld:predict',
    data=data, headers=headers)

print(json_response.text)
```

The response will be a JSON payload containing the predictions:

```
{
    "predictions": [[16.9834747], [18.9806728]]
}
```

Note that the requests library in Python also provides a json property, which you can use to automatically decode the response into a JSON dict.

Accessing a Server Model from Android

Now that you have a server running and exposing the model over a REST interface, putting together code to use it on Android is really straightforward. We'll explore that here, after creating a simple app with just a single view (check back to Chapter 4 for several examples of this), containing an EditText that you can use to input a number, a label that will present the results, and a button that the user can press to trigger the inference:

```
<ScrollView
    android:id="@+id/scroll_view"
    android:layout_width="match_parent"
    android:layout_height="0dp"
    app:layout_constraintTop_toTopOf="parent"
    app:layout_constraintBottom_toTopOf="@+id/input_text">
    <TextView
```

```
            android:id="@+id/result_text_view"
            android:layout_width="match_parent"
            android:layout_height="wrap_content" />
    </ScrollView>

    <EditText
        android:id="@+id/input_text"
        android:layout_width="0dp"
        android:layout_height="wrap_content"
        android:hint="Enter Text Here"
        android:inputType="number"
        app:layout_constraintBaseline_toBaselineOf="@+id/ok_button"
        app:layout_constraintEnd_toStartOf="@+id/ok_button"
        app:layout_constraintStart_toStartOf="parent"
        app:layout_constraintBottom_toBottomOf="parent" />
    <Button
        android:id="@+id/ok_button"
        android:layout_width="wrap_content"
        android:layout_height="wrap_content"
        android:text="OK"
        app:layout_constraintBottom_toBottomOf="parent"
        app:layout_constraintEnd_toEndOf="parent"
        app:layout_constraintStart_toEndOf="@+id/input_text"
        />
```

The code will use an HTTP library called Volley that handles the request and response asynchronously to and from the server. To use this, add this code to your app's build.gradle file:

```
implementation 'com.android.volley:volley:1.1.1'
```

The code for this activity can then look like this—setting up the controls and creating an onClickListener for the button that will call the model hosted on TensorFlow Serving:

```
lateinit var outputText: TextView
lateinit var inputText: EditText
lateinit var btnOK: Button
override fun onCreate(savedInstanceState: Bundle?) {
    super.onCreate(savedInstanceState)
    setContentView(R.layout.activity_main)
    outputText = findViewById(R.id.result_text_view)
    inputText = findViewById(R.id.input_text)
    btnOK = findViewById(R.id.ok_button)
    btnOK.setOnClickListener {
        val inputValue:String = inputText.text.toString()
        val nInput = inputValue.toInt()
        doPost(nInput)

    }
}
```

Remember that the model hosting served it from *http://<server>:8501/v1/models/ helloworld:predict*—if you are using your developer box and running the Android code in the Android emulator, you can use the server bridge at 10.0.2.2 instead of localhost.

So, when pressing the button, the value of the input will be read, converted to an integer, and then passed to a function called doPost. Let's explore what that function should do.

First, you'll use Volley to set up an asynchronous request/response queue:

```
val requestQueue: RequestQueue = Volley.newRequestQueue(this)
```

Next, you'll need to set up the URL of the hosting service. I'm using the server bridge of 10.0.2.2 instead of localhost, or whatever the server name would be, as I'm running the server on my developer box, and running this Android app on the emulator:

```
val URL = "http://10.0.2.2:8501/v1/models/helloworld:predict"
```

Recall that if you want to pass values to the server via JSON, every set of input values for input to the model needs to be in a list, and then all of your lists need to be stored within another list, so passing a value such as 10 to it for inference will look like this: [[10.0]].

The JSON payload would then look like this:

```
{"signature_name": "serving_default", "instances": [[10.0]]}
```

I've called the list containing the value the *inner* list, and the list containing that list the *outer* list. These are both going to be treated as JSONArray types:

```
val jsonBody = JSONObject()
jsonBody.put("signature_name", "serving_default")
val innerarray = JSONArray()
val outerarray = JSONArray()
innerarray.put(inputValue)
outerarray.put(innerarray)
jsonBody.put("instances", outerarray)
val requestBody = jsonBody.toString()
```

Then, to have the requestQueue manage the communication, you'll create an instance of a StringRequest object. Within this you'll override the getBody() function to add the requestbody string you just created to add it to the request. You'll also set up a Response.listener to catch the asynchronous response. Within that response you can get the array of predictions, and your answer will be the first value in that list:

```
val stringRequest: StringRequest =
  object : StringRequest(Method.POST, URL,
  Response.Listener { response ->
    val str = response.toString()
```

```
        val predictions = JSONObject(str).getJSONArray("predictions")
                                     .getJSONArray(0)
        val prediction = predictions.getDouble(0)
        outputText.text = prediction.toString()
    },
    Response.ErrorListener { error ->
      Log.d("API", "error => $error")
    })
    {
        override fun getBody(): ByteArray {
          return requestBody.toByteArray((Charset.defaultCharset()))
        }
    }
}

    requestQueue.add(stringRequest)
```

Volley will then do the rest—posting the request to the server, and catching the asynchronous response; in this case the Response.Listener will parse the result, and output the values to the UI. You can see this in Figure 14-4.

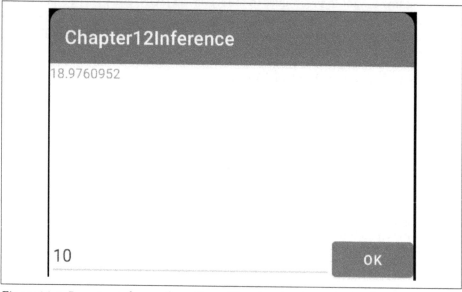

Figure 14-4. Running inference from TensorFlow Serving in an Android app

Note that in this case our response was very simple, so we just decoded a string out of it. For more complex data coming back in JSON, it would be best to use a JSON parsing library such as GSON (*https://oreil.ly/cm35R*).

While this is admittedly a very simple app, it provides a workflow for what you'd expect any Android app to use when running remote inference. The key things to keep in mind are the JSON payload design. Ensure that you have your data in JSON arrays, and that these arrays are hosted within another, so that even a single number

will be uploaded as [[10.0]]. Similarly the return values from the model will be encoded as a list of lists, even if it's just a single value!

Note that this example uses an unauthenticated server. There are various technologies
that could be used to add authentication on the backend and then use this on
Android. One such is Firebase Authentication (*https://oreil.ly/WTSaa*).

Accessing a Server Model from iOS

Earlier you created a model and hosted it on TensorFlow Serving, where it was available at *http://<server>:8501/v1/models/helloworld:predict*. For this example, my server
is at *192.168.86.26*, so I'll create a simple iOS app that can access the server, pass it
data, and get an inference back. To do this, and get inference for a single value, you'll
need a JSON payload posted to the server that looks like this:

```
{"signature_name": "serving_default", "instances": [[10.0]]}
```

And if this is successful, you'll get a payload back containing the inference:

```
{
    "predictions": [[18.9806728]]
}
```

So, we'll first need an app to pass the payload to the server, and parse what's returned.
Let's explore how to do this in Swift. You can find a full working app at the book's
repo (*https://oreil.ly/wPL4V*). In this section, I'll just explore how this app does the
remote inference:

First of all, in Swift, it's easiest to decode JSON values if you have the equivalent struct
set up. So, to decode the predictions, you can create a struct like this:

```
struct Results: Decodable {
  let predictions: [[Double]]
}
```

So now, if you have value stored as a double, you can create the payload to upload to
the server like this:

```
let json: [String: Any] =
    ["signature_name" : "serving_default", "instances" : [[value]]]

let jsonData = try? JSONSerialization.data(withJSONObject: json)
```

Next, you can post this payload to the URL. You'll do this by creating a request from
the URL, setting the request to be a POST request, and adding the JSON payload to
the request's body.

```
// create post request
let url = URL(string: "http://192.168.86.26:8501/v1/models/helloworld:predict")!

var request = URLRequest(url: url)
```

```
request.httpMethod = "POST"

// insert json data to the request
request.httpBody = jsonData
```

The request/response is asynchronous, so instead of locking up the thread while waiting for the response, you'll use a task:

```
let task = URLSession.shared.dataTask(with: request)
    { data, response, error in
```

The URLSession is created with the request from earlier, which is a POST to the URL with the JSON body containing the input data. This will give you back data with the response payload, the response itself, and any error information.

You can use the results to parse out the response. Recall earlier that you created a results struct that matched the format of the JSON payload. So here, you can decode, using the JSONDecoder() the response in the format of that struct, and load the predictions into results. As this contains an array of arrays, and the inner array has the inferred values, you can access them in results.predictions[0][0]. As this is on a task, and we're going to update a UI item, it has to be done within a DispatchQueue:

```
let results: Results =
    try! JSONDecoder().decode(Results.self, from: data)

            DispatchQueue.main.async{
                self.txtOutput.text = String(results.predictions[0][0])
            }
```

And that's it! It's super simple to do in Swift because of the struct for parsing the output, and inner and outer lists can be set up using the [String : Any] format. You can see what an app using this will look like in Figure 14-5.

As with accessing the model with TensorFlow Serving via Python, the most important thing is to get your input and output data correct. The easiest gotcha is forgetting that the payloads are lists of lists, so make sure you get that correct when using more complex data structures!

Figure 14-5. Accessing the 2x – 1 model from TensorFlow Serving on iOS

Summary

In this chapter you got an introduction to TensorFlow Serving and how it provides an environment that lets you give access to your models over an HTTP interface. You saw how to install and configure TensorFlow Serving, as well as how to deploy models to it. You then looked into performing remote inference using these models by building super simple Android and iOS apps that took user input, created a JSON payload from it, posted that to a TensorFlow Serving instance, and parsed the return values containing the model's inference on the original data. While the scenario was very basic, it provided the framework for any type of serving where you'll create POST requests with a JSON payload and parse the response.

## CHAPTER 15

Ethics, Fairness, and Privacy for Mobile Apps

While recent advances in machine learning and AI have brought the concepts of ethics and fairness into the spotlight, it's important to note that disparity and unfairness have always been topics of concern in computer systems. In my career, I have seen many examples where a system has been engineered for one scenario without considering the overall impact with regard to fairness and bias.

Consider this example: your company has a database of its customers and wants to target a marketing campaign to get more customers in a particular zip code where it has identified a growth opportunity. To do so, the company will send discount coupons to people in that zip code whom it has connected with, but who haven't yet purchased anything. You could write SQL like this to identify these potential customers:

```
SELECT * from Customers WHERE ZIP=target_zip AND PURCHASES=0
```

This might seem to be perfectly sensible code. But consider the demographics of that zip code. What if the majority of people who live there are of a particular race or age? Instead of growing your customer base evenly, you could be overtargeting one segment of the population, or worse, discriminating against another by offering discounts to people of one race but not another. Over time, continually targeting like this could result in a customer base that is skewed against the demographics of society, ultimately painting your company into a corner of primarily serving one segment. In this case, the variable—zip code—was explicit, but systems with proxy variables that aren't so explicit can still grow into biased ones without careful monitoring.

The promise of AI-based systems is that you will be able to deliver more powerful applications more quickly...but if you do so at the cost of not mitigating bias in your systems, then you could potentially *accelerate* disparity through the use of AI.

The process of understanding and eliminating this, where possible, is a huge field that would fill many books, so in this single chapter we'll just get a general overview of where you need to be aware of potential bias issues, and methodologies and tools that can help you fix them.

Ethics, Fairness, and Privacy with Responsible AI

Building an AI system with responsibility as part of your DNA means that responsible AI practices can be incorporated at every step in the ML workflow. While there are many patterns for this, I'm going to follow the very general one with the following steps:

1. Defining the problem: who is your ML system for
2. Constructing and preparing your data
3. Building and training your model
4. Evaluating your model
5. Deploying and monitoring your model's usage

Let's look at some tools that are available for you as you navigate through these steps.

Responsibly Defining Your Problem

When you are creating an app to solve a problem, it's good to consider issues that might arise from the very existence of the app. You might build something as innocent as a bird song detector, where you classify birds based on the sounds they make. But how might that impact your users? What if your data is limited to birds that are prevalent in a particular area, and what if that area is populated primarily by a single demographic. You would have, unconsciously, written an app that is only available to that demographic. Is that what you want? With an app like this, accessibility concerns can also arise. If your concept is that you hear a bird singing, and you want to identify it...you are assuming that the person *can* hear the birds, and as a result you are not being inclusive to people with reduced or no hearing. Now while this is a very trivial example, extend the concept to apps or services that can deeply impact someone's life. What if your rideshare app avoided certain neighborhoods, excluding people? What if your app is useful for healthcare, such as helping one manage their medication, but it fails for a certain demographic? It's easy to imagine where you could do *harm* with an app , even though those consequences were unintentional. Thus, it's very important to be mindful of all of your potential users and have tools that help guide you through this.

It's impossible to predict all scenarios where you could introduce a bias unintentionally, so, with that in mind, Google has prepared the *People + AI Guidebook* (*https://oreil.ly/enDYK*). The guidebook has six chapters, taking you from understanding user needs and defining success, all the way through data preparation, model building, gathering feedback fairly, and more. It's particularly useful in helping you understand *which* types of problems AI is uniquely positioned to solve. I strongly recommend referring to this before you start coding any app!

The people who created this book also have a set of AI Explorables (*https://oreil.ly/ldhCV*), which give you interactive workbooks that help you find issues such as hidden bias in your data. These will lead you through understanding core scenarios not just in your data, but in how your model behaves after being trained on that data. These can help you come up with a strategy for testing your models postdeployment.

Once you've defined and understood your problem, and eliminated potential sources of bias within it, the next step is to construct and prepare the data you'll use in your system. Again, this is a way that biases may be unintentionally introduced.

Often bias in AI is solely attributed to the data that was used to train the model. While data is often the primary suspect, it's not the sole one. Bias can creep in through feature engineering, transfer learning, and a myriad of other ways. You'll often be "sold" on fixing your data to fix the bias, but one cannot simply clean up their data and declare victory. Keep this in mind as you create your systems. We'll focus a lot on data in this chapter, as that's where generic tools are possible, but again, try to avoid the mindset that bias is only introduced via data!

Avoiding Bias in Your Data

Not all data biases are easy to spot. I once attended a student competition where the participants took on the challenge of image generation using generative adversarial networks (GANs) to predict what the lower half of a face looks like based on the upper half of the face. It was prior to the COVID-19 pandemic, but still flu season in Japan, and many people would wear face masks to protect themselves and others.

The idea was to see if one could predict the face below the mask. For this task they needed access to facial data, so they used the IMDb dataset of face images with age and gender labels (*https://oreil.ly/wR5Vl*). The problem? Given that the source is IMDb, the vast majority of the faces in this dataset are *not* Japanese. As such, their model did a great job of predicting *my* face, but not their own. In the rush to produce an ML solution when there wasn't adequate data coverage, the students produced a biased solution. This was just a show-and-tell competition, and their work was brilliant, but it was a great reminder that rushing to market with an ML product when one isn't necessarily needed, or when there isn't sufficient data to build a proper model, can lead you down the road of building biased models and incurring heavy future technical debt.

It won't always be as easy as that to spot potential biases, and there are many tools out there to help you avoid it. I'd like to look into a couple of freely available ones next.

The What-If Tool

One of my favorites is the What-If Tool from Google. Its aim is to let you inspect an ML model with minimal coding required. With this tool, you can inspect the data and the output of the model for that data together. It has a walkthrough (*https:// oreil.ly/dX7Qm*) that uses a model based on about 30,000 records from the 1994 US Census dataset that is trained to predict what a person's income might be. Imagine, for example, that this is used by a mortgage company to determine whether a person may be able to pay back a loan, and thus to determine whether or not to grant them the loan.

One part of the tool allows you to select an inference value and see the data points from the dataset that led to that inference. For example, consider Figure 15-1.

This model returns a probability of low income from 0 to 1, with values below 0.5 indicating high income and others low. This user had a score of 0.528, and in our hypothetical mortgage application scenario could be rejected as having too low an income. With the tool, you can actually change some of the user's data—for example, their age—and see what the effect on the inference would be. In the case of this person, changing their age from 42 to 48 gave them a score on the other side of the 0.5 threshold, and as a result changed them from being a "reject" on the loan application to an "accept." Note that nothing else about the user was changed—just their age. This gives a strong signal that there's a potential age bias in the model.

The What-If Tool allows you to experiment with various signals like this, including details like gender, race, and more. To prevent a one-off situation being the tail that wags the dog, causing you to change your entire model to prevent an issue that lies with one customer and not the model itself, the tool includes the ability to find the nearest counterfactuals—that is, it finds the closest set of data that results in a different inference so you can start to dive into your data (or model architecture) in order to find biases.

I'm just touching the surface of what the What-If Tool can do here, but I'd strongly recommend checking it out. There are lots of examples of what you can do with it on the site (*https://oreil.ly/kgZkZ*). At its core—as the name suggests—it gives you tools to test "what if" scenarios before you deploy. As such, I believe it can be an essential part of your ML toolbox.

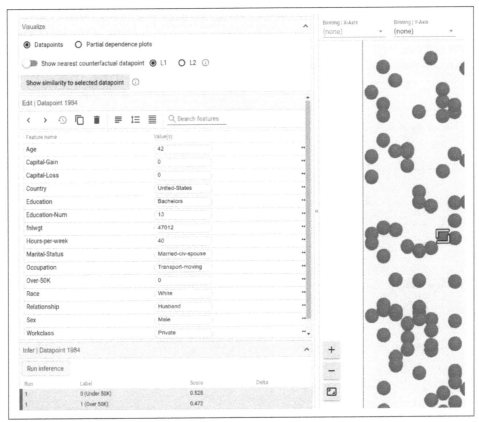

Figure 15-1. Using the What-If Tool

Facets

Facets (*https://oreil.ly/I1x6L*) is a tool that can work in complement to the What-If Tool to give you a deep dive into your data through visualizations. The goal of Facets is to help you understand the distribution of values across features in your dataset. It's particularly useful if your data is split into multiple subsets for training, testing, validation, or other uses. In such cases, you can easily end up in a situation where data in one split is skewed in favor of a particular feature, leading you to having a faulty model. This tool can help you determine whether you have sufficient coverage of each feature for each split.

For example, using the same US Census dataset as in the previous example with the What-If Tool, a little examination shows that the training/test splits are very good, but use of the capital gain and capital loss features might have a skewing effect on the training. Note in Figure 15-2, when inspecting quantiles, that the large crosses are very well balanced across all of the features except these two. This indicates that the majority of the data points for these values are zeros, but there are a few values in the dataset that are much higher. In the case of capital gain, you can see that 91.67% of the training set is zeros, with the other values being close to 100k. This might skew your training, and can be seen as a debugging signal. This could introduce a bias in favor of a very small part of your population.

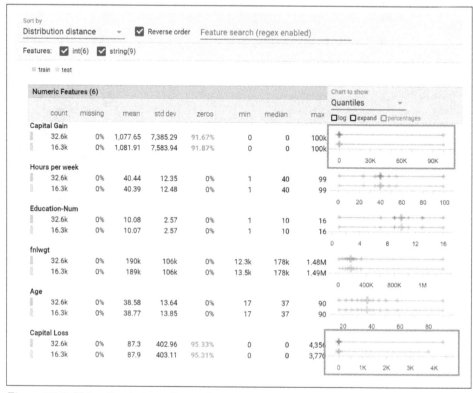

Figure 15-2. Using Facets to explore a dataset

Facets also includes a tool called Facets Dive that lets you visualize the contents of your dataset according to a number of axes. It can help identify errors in your dataset, or even preexisting biases that exist in it so you know how to handle them. For example, consider Figure 15-3, where I split the dataset by target, education level, and gender.

Red means "high income predicted," and left to right are levels of education. In almost every case the probability of a male having a high income is greater than a female, and in particular with higher levels of education the contrast becomes stark. Look for example at the 13–15 column (which is the equivalent of a bachelor's degree): the data shows a far higher percentage of men being high earners than women with the same education level. While there are many other factors in the model to determine earning level, having such a disparity for highly educated people is a likely indicator of bias in the model.

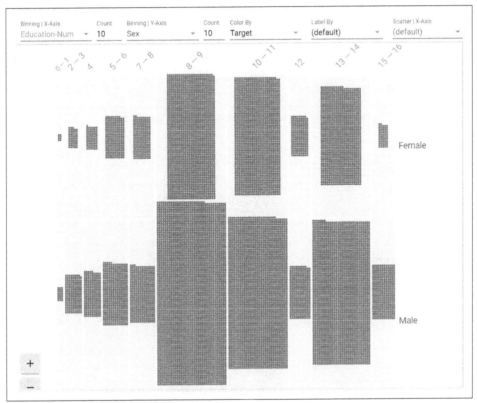

Figure 15-3. A deep dive with Facets

To help you identify features such as these, along with the What-If Tool, I strongly recommend using Facets to explore your data and your model's output.

TensorFlow Model Card Toolkit

If you intend to publish your models for other people to use, and want to be transparent about the data that was used to build the model, the TensorFlow Model Card Toolkit can help. The goal of this toolkit is to provide context and transparency into the metadata about your model. The toolkit is fully open-sourced, so you can explore how it works, and available at *https://github.com/tensorflow/model-card-toolkit*.

To explore a trivial example of a model card, you might be familiar with the famous cats versus dogs computer vision training example. A model card produced for this could look something like Figure 15-4, where transparency about the model is published. While this model is very simple, the cards show the data split as an example, and it's clear that there are more dogs in the dataset than cats, so a bias is introduced. Also, the folks that produced the model, who have expertise in it, were able to share other ethical considerations, such as the fact that it *assumes* the image will always contain either a cat or a dog, and as such might be harmful if passed an image that contains neither. It could, for example, be used to insult a human, by classifying them as a cat or a dog. For me, personally, this was a major "a-ha!" moment, because being too close to teaching ML, I never considered that eventuality, and now need to ensure that it stays part of my workflow!

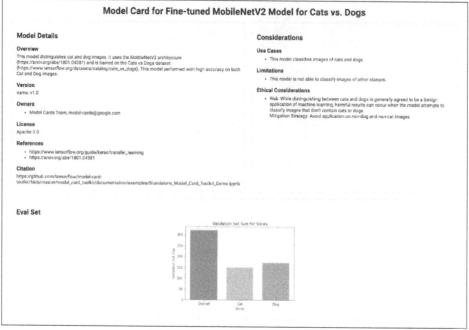

Figure 15-4. Model card for cats versus dogs

A more complex model card, demonstrating a model that was trained to predict income based on demographic features, can be found on GitHub (*https://oreil.ly/LiEkn*).

In it, you can see transparency around the demographics in both the training and evaluation sets, as well as quantitative analysis about the datasets. Thus, someone using this model is *prewarned* about biases that the model may introduce to their workflow and can mitigate accordingly.

TensorFlow data validation

If you use TensorFlow Extended (TFX), and have your data in a TFX pipeline, there are components within TFX to analyze and transform it. It can help you find things like missing data, such as features with empty labels, or with values outside the ranges you might expect and other anomalies. Going into TensorFlow Data Validation is beyond the scope of this book, but you can learn more by looking through the TFDV guide (*https://oreil.ly/7qydA*).

Building and Training Your Model

Beyond exploring your data, and any models you might be deriving from as outlined above, there are considerations you can take into account when building and training your model. Again, each of these are super-detailed, and not all of them may apply to you. I won't go into them in detail here, but I'll link you to resources where you can learn more.

Model remediation

When you create your model, you may introduce biases to outcomes that result from the use of that model. One source of this is that your model may underperform on certain slices of data. This can be massively harmful. For example, what if you build a model for disease diagnosis that performs extremely well for males and females, but not so well on people who don't express a gender or are nonbinary, due to lack of data for these classes. There are typically three methods to fix this—changing the input data, intervening on the model by updating the architecture, or postprocessing your results. A process called *MinDiff* can be used to equalize distributions of data, and balance error rates across slices of your data. Thus, *while training*, differences in distributions can be brought closer together, so that the outcome of a future prediction can be more equitable across the slices of data.

So, for example, consider Figure 15-5. On the left are the prediction scores for two different slices of data where the MinDiff algorithm was *not* applied during training. The result was that the predicted outcomes were vastly different. On the right the same prediction curves are overlaid, but they're much closer to each other.

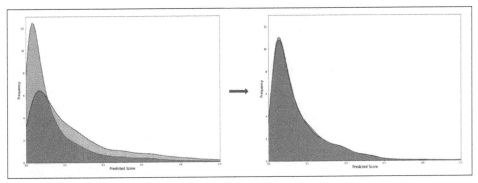

Figure 15-5. Using MinDiff

This technique is something worth exploring, and a detailed tutorial is available on the TensorFlow website (*https://oreil.ly/3LgAl*).

Model privacy

In some cases, a smart attacker can use your model to infer some of the data that the model was trained on. One method to prevent this is to train models using *differential privacy*. The idea behind differential privacy is to prevent an observer using the output from telling if a particular piece of information was used in the computation. For example, on a model that is trained to infer salary from demographics, if an attacker knows that a person is in the dataset, they may know the demographics for that person, enter it into the model, and given that their salary was in the training set, expect a very accurate value for their salary. Or, for example, if a model was created using health metrics, an attacker could potentially, knowing that their neighbor is in the training set, use a portion of the data to derive more data about their target.

With this in mind, TensorFlow Privacy (*https://oreil.ly/anZhq*) provides implementations of optimizers for training models using differential privacy.

Federated learning

Perhaps most of interest to mobile developers but not widely available yet, is federated learning. In this case you can continually update and improve your model based on how your users are using it. As such, users are sharing their personal data with you in order to help you improve your model. One such use is having their keyboard autopredict the word that they're typing. Everybody is different, so if I start typing "anti," I might be typing antibiotic, or I might be typing "antidisestablishmentarianism," and the keyboard should be smart enough to provide suggestions based on *my* previous usage. With that in mind, federated learning techniques have been created. The privacy implications here are obvious—you would want to be able to provide a way that your users can share very personal information—like the words they type—with you, in a way that cannot be misused.

As I mentioned, this is not yet available as an open API for you to use in your apps, but you can *simulate* how to do it with TensorFlow Federated.

TensorFlow Federated (*https://oreil.ly/GpiID*) (TFF) is an open source framework that gives you federated learning functionality in a simulated server environment. At the time of writing it's still experimental, but it's worth looking into. TFF is designed with two core APIs. The first is the Federated Learning API, which gives you a set of interfaces that add federated learning and evaluation capabilities to your existing models. It allows you to, for example, define distributed variables that are impacted by learned values from distributed clients. The second is the Federated Core API, which implements the federated communication operations within a functional programming environment. It's the foundation for existing deployed scenarios such as the Google keyboard, Gboard (*https://oreil.ly/csPTi*).

Evaluating Your Model

In addition to the tools mentioned above that can be used to evaluate your model during the training and deployment process, there are several others that are worth exploring.

Fairness Indicators

The Fairness Indicators tool suite is designed to enable computation and visualization of commonly identified fairness metrics in classification models—such as false positives and false negatives—with a view to comparing performance in these across different data slices. It's integrated into the What-If Tool as outlined earlier if you want to get started playing with it. You can also use it standalone by using the open source fairness-indicators package (*https://oreil.ly/I9A2f*).

So, for example, when using Fairness Indicators to explore the false negative rate in a model that was trained on human labeling of comments where the human attempted to label that the comment was written by male, female, transgender, or other creators, the lowest error was amongst males and the highest amongst "other gender." See Figure 15-6. Female and other gender also showed above the overall rate.

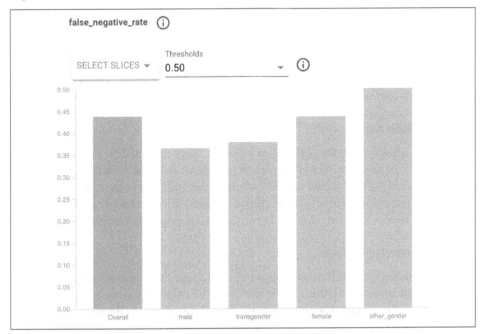

Figure 15-6. Fairness Indicators for gender inference from text model

When looking at false positives in the same model with the same data, in Figure 15-7, the results were flipped. The model is more likely to give a false positive about male or transgender.

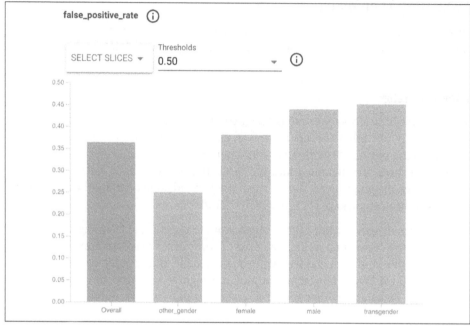

Figure 15-7. False positives presented by Fairness Indicators

With this tool, you can explore your model and tweak the architecture, learning, or data to try to balance it out. You can explore this example for yourself at *https://github.com/tensorflow/fairness-indicators*.

TensorFlow Model Analysis

TensorFlow Model Analysis (TFMA) is a library that's designed to evaluate Tensor-Flow models. At the time of writing, it's in prerelease stage, so it may change by the time you're reading this! Details about how to use it and how to get started are available on the TensorFlow website (*https://oreil.ly/oduzl*). It's particularly useful in letting you analyze slices of training data and how the model would perform on them.

Language Interpretability Toolkit

If you're building models that use language, the Language Interpretability Tool (LIT) will help you understand things like the types of examples your model performs poorly on, or the signals that drove a prediction helping you to determine undesirable training data or adversarial behavior. You can also test model consistency if you change things like the style of text, verb tenses, or pronouns. Details on how to set it up and use it are available at *https://pair-code.github.io/lit/tutorials/tour*.

Google's AI Principles

TensorFlow was created by Google's engineers as an outcropping of many existing projects built by the company for its products and internal systems. After it was open sourced, many new avenues for machine learning were discovered, and the pace of innovation in the fields of ML and AI is staggering. With this in mind, Google decided to put out a public statement (*https://oreil.ly/OAqyB*) outlining its principles with regard to how AI should be created and used. They're a great guideline for responsible adoption and worth exploring. In summary, the principles are:

Be socially beneficial

Advances in AI are transformative, and as that change happens the goal is to take into account all social and economic factors, proceeding only where the overall likely benefits outstrip the foreseeable risks and downsides.

Avoid creating or reinforcing unfair bias

As discussed in this chapter, bias can easily creep into any system. AI—particularly in cases where it transforms industry—presents an opportunity to *remove* existing biases, as well as to ensure that *new* biases don't arise. One should be mindful of this.

Be built and tested for safety

Google continues to develop strong safety and security practices to avoid unintended harm from AI. This includes developing AI technologies in constrained environments and continually monitoring their operation after deployment.

Be accountable to people

The goal is to build AI systems that are subject to appropriate human direction and control. This means that appropriate opportunities for feedback, appeal, and relevant explanations must always be provided. Tooling to enable this will be a vital part of the ecosystem.

Incorporate privacy design principles

AI systems must incorporate safeguards that ensure adequate privacy and inform users of how their data will be used. Opportunities for notice and consent should be obvious.

Uphold high standards of scientific excellence

Technological innovation is at its best when it is done with scientific rigor and a commitment to open enquiry and collaboration. If AI is to help unlock knowledge in critical scientific domains, it should aspire to the high standards of scientific excellence that are expected in those areas.

Be made available for uses that accord with these principles

> While this point might seem a little meta, it's important to reinforce that the principles don't stand alone, nor are they just for the people building systems. They're also intended to give guidelines for how the systems you build can be used. It's good to be mindful of how someone might use your systems in a way you didn't intend, and as such good to have a set of principles for your users too!

Summary

And that's where this waypoint on your journey to become an AI and ML engineer for mobile and web comes to an end, but your real journey of building solutions that can change the world may really begin. I hope this book was useful for you, and while we didn't go very deep into any particular topics, we were able to encapsulate and simplify some of the complexity of bridging the worlds of machine learning and mobile development.

It's my firm belief that if AI is to reach its full, positive potential, it will be through its use in low-powered, small models that are focused on solving common problems. While research has been going bigger and bigger, I think that the real growth potential that everyone can take advantage of is in models that are smaller and smaller, and this book gives you the platform where you can see how to take advantage of that!

I'm looking forward to seeing what you build, and I'd love it if you gave me the opportunity to share that with the world. Reach me on Twitter @lmoroney.

Index

transformedRect object, 53
transformMatrix function, 53, 109
turnkey solutions, 13
    (see also ML Kit)
typealias, 157

U

UIImage class, 53, 165, 218
UITextViewDelegate, 120
UIUtilities class, 114
unsafe data, extending Array to handle, 228
UnsafeMutableBufferPointer, 159
user interface, creating
    computer vision apps, 59, 105-106, 214-217
    face detector apps, 38-39, 48-51
    to host TFLite on iOS, 153-156, 162-164
    initializing to call entity extraction, 82-84
    language classification, 206-209

V

validation of data, TFX, 295
video, object detection in
    Android, 70-76
    iOS, 112-115
View Controller, 49

allowing for text entry, 120
    editing to use ML Kit, 100-102
viewDidLoad() function, 50, 100, 107, 120, 216
viewFinder, 73
Vision Edge, 179-188
VisionImage object, 53, 108
VNClassificationObservations, 264
VNCoreMLRequest, 264, 266
VNImageRequestHandler, 264
vocab, loading, 226-227
vocabulary for NLP, 226-227

W

Warden, Pete
    Tiny ML (O'Reilly), 255
What-If Tool (Google), 290-290

X

Xcode environment
    adding MLModel file with Create ML, 263
    face detector apps, 45-45
    image classifier app, 96
    TFLite model in, 151-167, 213-216
.xcworkspace versus xcproject files, 98

About the Author

Laurence Moroney leads AI Advocacy at Google. His goal is to educate the world of software developers in how to build AI systems with machine learning. He's a frequent contributor to the TensorFlow YouTube channel (*https://oreil.ly/LbAWw*), a recognized global keynote speaker, and author of more books than he can count—including several best-selling science fiction novels and a produced screenplay. He's based in Washington state, where he drinks way too much coffee. You can reach him on Twitter at @lmoroney, or on LinkedIn (*https://oreil.ly/BuVKJ*).

Colophon

The bird on the cover of *AI and Machine Learning On-Device Development* is a great bustard (*Otis tarda*). This bird can be found in grasslands across south and central Europe and temperate climates in east Asia, as well as in some parts of northern Morocco. The majority of the bird's population, however, is in Portugal and Spain.

This ground-nesting bird is extraordinarily sexually dimorphic. While female great bustards typically have a wingspan of 180 cm (5 ft 11 in) and weigh 3.1 to 8 kg (6.8 to 17.6 lb), the adult male great bustard is among the heaviest living flying animals, ranging in weight from 5.8 to 18 kg (or 13 to 40 lb) with a wingspan of 2.1 to 2.7 m (6 ft 11 in to 8 ft 10 in). They are normally quiet birds, though the adult male may produce booming, grunting, and raucous noises during the breeding season, and the female may utter guttural calls at the nest. Brooded young will make a soft, trilling call in communication with their mothers.

Great bustards are strong fliers and can reach speeds upwards of 98 kmh (60.8 mph) during migration. These migration patterns will vary depending on the home location of a given population. Because of a wide range of environmental impacts and habitat loss, the great bustard has been listed as "Vulnerable" on the IUCN Red List since 1996. Many of the animals on O'Reilly covers are endangered; all of them are important to the world.

The cover illustration is by Karen Montgomery, based on a black and white engraving from Routledge's *Picture Natural History*. The cover fonts are Gilroy Semibold and Guardian Sans. The text font is Adobe Minion Pro; the heading font is Adobe Myriad Condensed; and the code font is Dalton Maag's Ubuntu Mono.

9 781098 101749